The Dayton Experiment

Be Open to Discovery!

The Dayton Experiment

How a public school in rural Oregon reimagined education,
unleashed its students' creative potential,
and became a model for the nation

Thompson Morrison

with

Jami Fluke & Ward Cunningham

Prime Pattern Press

Prime Pattern Press
Portland, Oregon

The Oregon Edition

ISBN 978-0-578-63439-5

For information about special discounts for bulk purchases, please visit www.daytonexperiment.com.

Manifesto of Agile Learning

As we seek to reimagine education, we believe:

We all have creative genius.

Purpose is essential for passionate learning.

Students can learn faster than they can be taught.

The process of learning is more important than the product of learning.

Empowering students as makers and creators unleashes their potential.

Partnerships allow us to develop new learning opportunities.

Failure is essential for success.

We are all co-learners.

The future belongs to a very different kind of person with a very different kind of mind – creators and empathizers, pattern recognizers and meaning makers.

– Daniel Pink

How to Read this Book

The book you are holding looks like other books, but it's not meant to read that way. It began its life as a *hyperbook*, formed organically in a new hypertext writing platform created by Ward Cunningham. More about Ward and the genesis of this book in Thompson's foreword.

This volume is a reconstruction of that book in a traditional format. Obviously, we can't have hyperlinks in this version, so you will see bold typed words and phrases that are footnoted with the page number where you can flip to, if you like, as a surrogate for a hyperlink experience.

There are three main elements of this book: *The Story*, *The Garden* and *The Path*. *The Story* tells the tale of a journey, introducing different concepts along the way. These concepts can be further explored in *The Garden*. *The Path* provides a framework for your own journey of transformation.

You can read this book many different ways. One is to read *The Story* straight through, noting concepts you find intriguing. Then, at the end, you can head into *The Garden* to further explore these concepts. Another approach, for those less patient, is to dog-ear the page you are on and immediately follow your curiosity into *The Garden*, returning back to *The Story* when you are sated.

In other words, this book does not start in one place and end in another. It has many paths to travel however you see fit, exactly as you would navigate through a website. You will arrive not at the words The End, but – one hopes – a new understanding of what education needs to look like if we are to compete and thrive in this new world of ours.

Again, please read Thompson's foreword to learn why *The Dayton Experiment* is written in this fashion.

Contents

Jami's Foreword

Here is the story of a 5-year experiment that took place in Dayton, Oregon. As the principal of the school, I can honestly say that living in this experiment was the most difficult yet fulfilling work I have ever been engaged in. Being a pioneer of a new movement required me to be vulnerable in an experience that was challenging, inspiring, fast-paced, uncharted, and joyful. However, seeing that story in print, so publicly displayed, has taken me to a new level of vulnerability. What Thompson and I did was real. It changed people's lives – it made a difference. This story, and all the people who made it happen, hold a special place in my heart. Now it is time to share the story.

Reimagining education feels like an insurmountable challenge. It is hard work, but it is the right work. The time has come to empower our courageous changemakers that are ready to act. It starts with a deep belief that every child has brilliance. As courageous leaders, it is our responsibility to engage in transforming our system into one that not only allows that brilliance to be discovered, but to be a beacon of light, shining brightly for all to see.

There is no formula or program or package that will make this transformation happen. It is the people and their ideas that will drive real, lasting change. This book will give you context. It tells the story of what we did in Dayton and more importantly, what we learned along the way. You see, transforming a culture is no easy task. It is painful at times and the work is never done. However, we walked into the unknown with our hearts wide open, faced our fears head-on, and discovered moments of inspiration that were life-giving. We began to model new practices that we mirrored from industry and awakened the creative problem solvers in ourselves and those around us. We found a new purpose and meaning in our work, and more importantly, rediscovered joy for the educators and the students.

This reading experience will allow you to start where you are and follow your own path of curiosity. The first courageous act you can take is deciding to do something. My hope is that our story of discovery, connection, and meaning-making will ignite deeper learning and exploration for you.

You are about to embark on a journey where you will discover something you didn't know. Consider this book a living guide. The insights you gain will mean something more with each new experience. Be courageous. Record your experience and insights along the way. Share your learning with others, and above all find your joy.

Welcome to The Dayton Experiment.

Thompson's Foreword

The topic of this book is transforming the culture of education to unleash students' creativity at new and unprecedented levels. As you will read, the Dayton Experiment showed just how it could be done. The first step was understanding how students today think differently from those of the past. We then had to create a learning environment that worked for those students.

The final and most important step was to build a framework for replicating this cultural transformation in other school districts, to spread the impact of what we learned in Dayton.

My colleague Jami and I knew that cultural transformation would look different in every district. But might there be common elements in each journey that could help guide others?

A book was needed to explain our discoveries. But as it was about a different kind of learning, it had to be a different kind of book.

To create it I sought guidance from Ward Cunningham. Ward helped revolutionize the software industry by introducing a new mindset for software development that was to become Agile, a transformative approach to process management that underpins our new creative economy. I thought he might have insights into how we could build our framework.

Ward agreed to help. But then he continued, "Might you be interested in learning about my new wiki?"

At the time, I didn't realize the significance of this simple offer.

Ward created the original wiki to enable software developers to share new practices, called pattern languages, with each other. That platform went on to become the foundation for Wikipedia, the single largest repository of knowledge ever created. But Ward felt that his original wiki design didn't fulfill his intention. So he redesigned it, calling this new platform *federated wiki*. I soon discovered that he had developed a remarkably powerful hypertext writing environment, one that was potentially as revolutionary as his first wiki, if not more so.

Ward's instructions were simple: note insights, label them, and then find a time to reflect on them by writing a page in this new wiki.

And so I did, trying to better understand the meaning of what I had learned in these years of working with Jami. I would note insights as they appeared in my thoughts, and then find time to explore them and try to explain their essence as simply as I could.

Day after day. Page after page. Before long I had more than 450 pages of concepts. As I wrote, I began to notice how different concepts connected with each other, so I began to hyperlink these pages together. The result was a complex labyrinth of interconnected ideas.

Since I'd seen Ward use graphic tools to visualize pattern languages, I asked if he could graphically map these linked ideas, recognizing that some concepts were frequently referenced. These concepts were, in a sense, anchors that might allow decipherable patterns to form. And they did.

But they were still difficult to share, for it was too easy to get lost along all these paths. It was then I realized that to guide others into the meaning of what I had learned, I needed to employ the most traditional of methods: telling a story.

Through a story arc I could introduce concepts that might lead the reader into a garden of concepts that would appear in a subset of my original pages. In this garden one could follow different paths to meaning. In other words, I would tell the story through hypertext.

Hypertext was inspired by Jorge Borges' short story, *The Garden of Forking Paths*. My hope is that this unusual book structure might provide you, dear reader, with *the experience of hypertext* – an experience that allows you to create your own meaning, inspired by *your* curiosity. You can form this meaning spatially, just as hypertext enables spatial learning through an internet-enabled Web.

This book, then, is hypertext in a traditional book format.

All of this to help answer the question, "Why, as a digital native, did my daughter think differently from me?"

You can find the original wiki version of the book at daytonexperiment.com.

However you arrive at the meaning of the Dayton Experiment, I hope it inspires you as it has me, the educators I have shared it with, and the many students who are now unleashing their creative genius as never before.

Prologue

The Question

My world changed that day.

It was 1986 and the plane was on its final descent. I looked out the window and all I could see were rice paddies.

We were landing in Shanghai, China, and all I could think was, "What have we just done?"

We had left behind everything we knew, and all those who we loved. Sold everything. And now here we were, landing in a strange land without knowing a single word of Chinese and having no idea what we were doing.

But it was here we had set off to build a new life. We did not know for how long, but it was to be our new reality.

It was a cosmic slap.

We were soon tossed into a place that we profoundly did not understand. My wife was setting out to be one of the first western photographers living in China, and I was to open a sales office for foreign manufacturers seeking to enter the newly opened Chinese market. We were both totally in over our heads.

When we arrived, Shanghai, the economic powerhouse of China, had been frozen in time for the last forty years. It felt like a time machine had brought us back to 1949. But in less than ten years, the entire city, the entire country would be transformed. China would soon come to dominate the global economy, changing everything, everywhere.

And there we were, at the dawn of this new era, bearing witness to this transformation.

But it made no sense. My wife and I had been partners in a successful design and media company in Cleveland, Ohio. Our life had been comfortable, it was good; yet we had left it all.

It had started with a conversation in which we confessed to each other a quiet terror that was residing in each of our hearts. A terror that this was all there was.

For we could see into our future, our future home, our future family, our future in a place that was likely to be comfortable and secure. And it terrified us.

Was this all? Was there more to life?

So we threw it all away and, mustering all of our courage, flew to Shanghai – a place that forced us to become profoundly comfortable being uncomfortable.

I had won the challenge. My wife wanted to move to South America. I wanted to move to China. We agreed that we would go to the first place where one of us was able to land a job. I scored first.

China had always fascinated me, particularly after I had taken a course on Buddhism in college. It was in that class that I first had to face the limits of my ability to understand.

As I studied Chan Buddhism (which would become Zen Buddhism as it traveled to Japan), I realized that my intellectual tools, those that I had depended on to make sense of the world up to that point, were largely useless. To understand, truly understand, the deep wisdom of Buddhism and Taoism that had been woven together in China to form this new school of Buddhism, I would need to go beyond the thinking I knew.

Broadly speaking, my Western Mind could not parse the meaning of what we might call the Eastern Mind.

At its most fundamental level, while one mind held the self as the *source* of understanding the other mind held the self as the *barrier* to understanding – a seemingly irreconcilable conflict. But two minds, together, might hold a deeper understanding of the human experience. Or so I believed.

Going to China, then, was for me not just an exploration of culture, but an exploration of the self. Of who we are and who we could become.

It has been said that, as an expatriate, after seven years you can never go home.

Oh, of course, you can physically go back to the place of your birth. But, after that much time living in a different culture, something inside of you has permanently changed. You become, in some sense, a stranger in your own land.

We ended up living in Asia for almost twelve years. After a few years in China, we then moved down to Hong Kong. I also had a two-year stint in Taiwan. Most of those years, while I was working as a marketing consultant for the computer industry, my wife was working as a photographer covering the region for US and international publications.

During that time, we traveled extensively from Japan down to Australia and most of the countries in between.

Asia became our new home, with all of its rich cultural complexity. We were continually learning, tossing ourselves into new places, each with their own stories and own meaning. Our lives were continually being shaped by our curiosity.

But what was this America I was returning to? And who was I, landing back in this place which now felt, in some ways, a foreign land? Most importantly, what had I learned from this journey that would guide my path forward?

The discoveries were many. One, in particular, stood out. Having seen the economic explosion of Asia, I deeply appreciated the profound reshaping of the global economy that was underway. I was shocked by how many Americans were blithely unaware that the world had been transformed while they slept. America was quickly losing its competitive advantage not only in manufacturing but in all areas of innovation. Our country's economic future was fundamentally at risk.

I could not shake off this concern.

We returned home soon after Britain returned Hong Kong to China. By that act, Britain finally acknowledged the end of their colonial power in that region. China had risen and was now the new center of gravity for Asia.

Back in the US, I started a software company that developed a new kind of survey technology. We used that software to help companies more deeply understand the needs of their customers.

Soon after we launched, my business partner, who headed up the software development team, handed me a book. "Read it," he said. The book opened my eyes to a nascent new reality.

It was Eric Raymond's *The Cathedral and the Bazaar*. In this book, Raymond sought to explain how Linux, an open source operating system, came to be.

It made no sense. How was it that this operating system, the most complicated of all software code, could be written by a global collection of volunteers? And, in just five years, could threaten the core business of Microsoft, the largest software company in the world?

This story fundamentally challenged the theories of Adam Smith and David Ricardo upon which our entire economic system is based. Real economic value was being created, not by workers at the service of companies, but by volunteers following their creative passions. How could this be?

It was also during those years that I was introduced to **Agile**[1] and the practices of Extreme Programming (XP) that were being used by our software developers.

Their development speed never ceased to amaze me. We learned to dream together, and then to create together so fast that often I felt I had to rush to catch up with them, rather than the other way around.

I quickly learned that my job was to guide a creative process that required me to understand, support and then to align their passions toward a common goal. If I was able to do that, we could, together, move mountains.

I began to wonder: what is this thing we call passion?

I was also curious about this thing called Agile. How was it that it could not only transform my company but the entire software industry and beyond, unleashing and aligning passions to create in new ways?

I started to apply what I had I learned from Agile in different areas in my community. I led an initiative by the City of Portland to co-create an economic development strategy with the software industry, co-founded TaborSpace to reimagine a church as a community gathering place, and then co-founded a new community organization called the Rosewood Initiative to build a place that empowered a community. Each time I applied agile practices to unleash and align transformational passions.

But that larger question still nagged me: What does our future, our children's future, look like when new global competitive pressures threaten our wellbeing?

At the core of any economy is its people. And those people are shaped by their education. Empower people through education and a promising future unfolds. Shackle them and our worst fears will be realized.

1 Page **103** - **Agile** refers to a broad collection of experiences, mindsets and practices that have created a new paradigm for how we learn, how we create, and how we manage. As a paradigm, it underpins the new economy.

As many will agree, our current education system, designed for another era, is not only profoundly failing our students, it is *undermining our economy*.

So the table was set for the critical question: Might the mindsets and skillsets of Agile help us reimagine how we educate our students to unleash new passions, new potential, new prosperity? I didn't know, but I was committed to finding out.

Agile. Passion. Education. I felt a new truth was in there. Somewhere.

And further, I wondered, might that truth provide us insight into the deeper questions about our human experience?

This story is deeply personal. But it is also the story of our children, our country and our future. We need to open our eyes. We need to summon our courage. We need to step into the unknown and reimagine. We have no choice.

The Road to Dayton

The Dayton Experiment

It started as an experiment.

What might happen if you modeled the educational experience after the learning culture of fast-growing technology companies?

In 2015, under the banner of **Innovate Oregon**[1], we embarked on this adventure in Dayton Oregon, a rural community in Yamhill County. Dayton is a town of 2,500 people where more than two-thirds of its students live near the poverty line. In this culturally diverse community, about a third of its students are Hispanic.

We call this new culture Agile. It was birthed in 2001 as a movement and continues to transform how software is being developed and how companies are being managed. Could it also transform how we are preparing the next generation of students to be the makers in a new creative economy?

The experiment blossomed beyond anyone's expectations. In four years, Dayton's graduation rate increased 14% to 97%, one of the highest in the state – 18% above the state average. The town has a 10 Gig fiber internet network, the fastest on the entire west coast, built by a committed local partner. Dayton's teachers are working with industry partners to pioneer new programs for other schools.

And Dayton is becoming an inspirational model for other districts around the state and beyond. It's a story worth telling.

The Beginning

Other than the Big Bang, there is no one beginning of anything. But for this story, let's start in 2010.

Our economy was emerging from the 2008 crash, a growth that was being driven in large part by technology-based companies. I was on the board of the Technology Association of Oregon (TAO) and often found myself in board meetings discussing how hard it was for companies to hire the people they needed to support this growth.

Several initiatives were launched to attract new talent to our state. These initiatives

1 Page **160** - **Innovate Oregon** is a strategic initiative to reimagine how we prepare students to be the makers and creators in a new creative economy.

focused on telling our story to potential employees in major markets around the country.

The pitch was something like this: Come to Oregon. We have a great quality of life. And, if the job doesn't work out, don't worry, we have a vital industry here so there are a lot of other employment opportunities.

Techlandia – a place of new opportunity. We branded and hit the road. There was only one problem. Importing talent is only a short-term fix. You cannot build long-term economic competitiveness using imported talent.

This problem went beyond our industry since new production technologies were transforming every kind of Oregon company.

So we asked ourselves a simple question: How well are we preparing Oregon students for Oregon jobs?

Understanding the Problem

We quickly found that Oregon had a serious graduation problem. Back in 2010, we were ranked 45th in the country for graduation rates. Nine years later, we are ranked 49th. Most people are shocked when we share this reality with them. Oregon?

Yes. The sad joke is that we are called the Mississippi of the West, except that Mississippi has a higher graduation rate.

So we started researching how our current education system was preparing the next generation of makers and creators in this technology-enabled economy. We started by looking at computer science education in our K-12 system.

What we found astonished us. Our teaching capacity in this area was not only paltry but chaotic as well.

Based on the number of classes on offer, we could reach less than 5% of our students with an important skill needed for the new economy. On top of that, there was no consistency in what was being taught. It was all over the map – defined by the personal interest of an individual teacher.

We also discovered that the Portland School District, Oregon's largest with fifty thousand students, had only one computer science teacher.

While we had a talent crisis in industry, we discovered that the education system also had a crisis of capacity. We were in deep trouble.

The Switch

It happened when I was sitting at a table at Franklin High School in Portland, attending a site council meeting in the library.

Years before, my wife Mary Beth and I had cut a deal. If we were going to have our kids in the public school system, we had to be involved with their schools. The success of our kids was tied directly to the success of their schools.

Mary Beth committed to being involved in the annual auctions that raised money as a meager firewall against the financial cuts that the school system continually faced.

Me? I committed to being on their site councils.

Site councils are committees mandated in Oregon, comprised of administrators, teachers, parents, and students to oversee each school's culture and professional development programs. They help craft their school's yearly School Improvement Plan (SIP) that is submitted to the district.

In truth, many site councils are perfunctory and the principal often ends up writing most of the SIP. I was really there to build relationships in the school to help my kids navigate their school experience.

One of our concerns with having our kids in large public schools was that they might get lost. Developing relationships with the principal and key teachers could help us keep an eye on the support infrastructure that was around our kids while they were at school. Numerous times these relationships were helpful when things went sideways with our kids. Which, occasionally, they did.

The Franklin High School Site Council was the fourth site council I had sat on. By then I knew the ropes.

So there we were, sitting in the library, discussing that year's student survey that would help shape the writing of the SIP. At previous schools, I had helped run these surveys using my company's web-based survey technology. My company at that time was designing and running sophisticated multi-branching surveys for global brands, so this was an area I was very familiar with.

The council members wanted to do the same simple paper-based surveys with the students that they had done for many years. I asked if we might be able to do it online, so students could do it either on their own mobile devices or in the computer labs. This approach would also allow us to also have a more powerful data analysis.

The pushback was immediate. It couldn't be done. Too complicated and the computers in the lab were too old. No, the only way to do it was by paper with hand tabulation of the data. Welcome to 1955.

Really, for 1,500 students?

And then I asked a question: "As we can't use technology to better understand the needs and aspirations of our students, are we at least thinking about how we might introduce them to new technologies to prepare them for the creative economy?"

Oh, we have technology classes, I was told. Probing further, I found that they meant a couple of introductory classes teaching students how to use some software products. Word. PowerPoint. Excel.

The switch went off. I felt it in my whole body. Not outrage, exactly, but close.

I then asked them if they had any idea what I was doing when I wasn't sitting around this table with them in their library. They said no.

So I began to explain that I ran a software company and sat on the board of directors for the Technology Association of Oregon (TAO). That organization, representing technology-based companies throughout Oregon, was focused on helping to build a new creative economy in Oregon. But we didn't have the talent needed for this new economy and we were running scared.

And here, in Portland, at the heart of this new Oregon economy, at one of its largest high schools, we were teaching our kids how to use Word and PowerPoint and thinking that this was sufficient preparation for them to thrive in this new economy?

You have got to be kidding. I was indignant. We were failing our kids. We were failing our future.

But that was not all. I had a personal reason for this outrage: my daughter.

The Personal Reason

When it comes to our own kids, there is no room for compromise. We will lay down our lives for them. I have two children, a son, and a daughter who is younger by three years.

My son has always done well in a traditional education environment. He understands what it takes for others to see his success and works hard toward that goal. And his self-discipline has been rewarded many times over.

He was, like his dad, what is called a "compliant learner".

A compliant learner learns where the lines are and colors inside those lines. My son thrived throughout his academic journey. But not my daughter.

She had trouble not only understanding the lines but why she should even color within them. It started early. Why learn the alphabet? Why learn to read an analog clock?

By 4th grade my son could name every state capital in the country, asking us over and over again to have us challenge him on a map. At that same age, my daughter, when I asked what time it was on a clock, would look at me blankly and say a random number like 3320, hoping that this number might satisfy me. I would then ask again and receive another random number. She had no interest in the question, much less the answer.

I was worried. This worry continued through middle school and into high school. She was a puzzle to me.

But something interesting happened the summer before she entered high school. That summer, my wife Mary Beth wanted to sign her up for a camp. Perhaps she could raft down the Deschutes like her brother had done or go sailing up in the San Juans? What great adventure would she like to have?

The answer baffled her mother. After looking at the catalogs of different camp programs, she told Mary Beth that she wanted to learn how to program ATMs in C. Mary Beth didn't understand. So my daughter patiently explained that C was a language that could be used to program ATMs, which are, in essence, just personal computers. Despite multiple attempts to dissuade her, her mother finally relented and signed her up.

She loved it. Though she was the only girl in the class, something about the challenge of learning a computer language, and making something work with it, empowered her and gave her a sense of belonging. She felt a nascent superpower.

My daughter was a sophomore in high school at the time that I found myself in that site council meeting. A few weeks before, I had asked her if she was still interested in coding. She wasn't.

My heart sank. I asked why. She explained that none of her friends were interested in it, so she no longer was.

Social bonding is so important in high school. Clearly, she didn't want to be alone.

Wearing my industry hat, her words worried me. We desperately needed not only coders but female coders in particular. And here was my own daughter who was no longer interested in entering my world.

Wearing my dad hat, her comments were even more worrying. I had seen a spark of her curiosity and glimpses of her confidence that summer that I had never seen before. And now that delicate flame was being extinguished. Extinguished because she was in a traditional academic environment that had not changed in well over 100 years. An environment where no one was excited by the opportunity of being a maker in the new creative economy.

A learning environment designed for compliant learners was not for students like her – someone who, I began to understand, learns only when they need to know something to solve a problem that they care about.

A **Just-In-Time Learner**[1], perhaps?

But I soon realized that my daughter was not alone. Many of her fellow students were just showing up and going through the motions, not sure why they were there.

Might this lack of purpose and lack of engagement be related to the low graduation rates? Could there be another way of learning that mirrored how our best technology companies were innovating?

---

1 Page **167** - The concept of a **Just-in-Time Learner** is derived from a key concept from the Toyota Production System, just-in-time manufacturing, one that transformed industrial production. This concept recognizes that students today, given the ubiquitous access to the internet, are more engaged to learn information when they know why they need it they rather than "just-in-case" they might need it sometime in a vaguely defined future.

The First Experiment

At the next site council meeting, I asked if we could try an experiment with a group of students who might be interested in solving a problem. And, in this process, might we experiment with learning in a new way, one similar to how we learn in our agile-based companies?

Tech companies operate in hyper-competitive markets. The pressures to adapt and innovate are intense. In order to remain competitive, they must continually out-learn and out-innovate their competitors.

This market dynamic is very different from that faced by companies in an industrial economy. There, competitive advantage was based on improving the efficiency of the sourcing, production and distribution process, something called a value chain. Whoever manages that process most efficiently is able to drive costs down and gain market share.

Not in the tech world. The winners are defined by those who get new products to the market faster. Competitive advantage is defined by the rate of innovation. Tech companies don't focus on value chains but on **Value Networks**[1].

These market pressures force tech companies to explore how to learn faster – because the innovation is based on the speed with which they learn.

Tech companies understand that collaborative teams working with clear purpose and commitment are able to solve complex problems faster. This learning process is not structured and sequential, but asynchronous, using fast **Learning Cycles**[2].

A week later the teachers found the students for the experiment. I also found Gage, a software developer, who was interested in working with the students. We were ready to start. Now we had to find a problem.

---

1 Page **217** - In the new economy, the nature of competitive advantage has shifted from a focus on efficiency to one on innovation. As a result, companies look toward building **Value Networks**, not just Value Chains, developing organizations that are complex adaptive systems.

2 Page **174** - Companies have found that the key to solving complex problems is fast, iterative development cycles called sprints. Each sprint allows teams to define clear objectives and then to quickly learn from the experience. We can think of these sprints as **Learning Cycles**.

Finding the Problem

When my daughter heard who was on the team, she had no interest in being involved. They were the geeky boys who lived in a different social world than hers. Oh well...

But, as we were driving in the car one day, I asked her what might be a problem that the team could solve that would make a difference for students at her high school.

"Oh," she replied, "that's easy. We don't know what is going on at school. Develop a mobile app for that."

"What do you mean?" I replied incredulously. "Don't you get the daily email of all of the activities at your school? Don't you hear the morning announcements in your first period?"

"Yea," she said, "I get them." And then she continued. "But we can't hear the announcements very well and as for the email, don't you also get it? How often do you read it?" I admitted that I got that email but never read it. She asked why. I told her that I didn't read it because it was long and most of the information wasn't relevant to me.

"Exactly, that's why we don't read it either," she responded. "Solve that problem. Find a way that students can get the information that they need, when they need it. If they are interested in the Spanish Club, don't tell them about events in the Chinese Club."

And then she quickly twisted her body around and grabbed a notebook from her backpack in the back seat. By the time we reached our destination, she had sketched out the screen designs for the mobile app, one that allowed students to set filters so that they only saw announcements that were relevant to them.

When I floated this idea with the students the following week, they lit up and said yes, that was a problem worth solving. They then jumped up to the chalkboard and started sketching out the screens for this mobile app that were almost identical to the ones that my daughter had done.

As digital natives, they shared a common understanding of how to solve that problem with this new, ubiquitous technology.

So now we had the problem to solve. But the team didn't know how to solve it. The students didn't know how to code. The developer had never made a mobile app. But that didn't stop them. They launched their first **Sprint**[1], with a commitment to release a beta version by the time school started in the fall.

The team committed to meet once a week throughout the summer to learn together and deliver a solution.

And then, as the next term was beginning, they delivered it.

Launch of Tech for Tomorrow

That following fall I was asked to give a talk to Franklin High School seniors at their Career Day. This day consisted of the students sitting in the stands in the gym and listening to people talk to them. Or, should I say, talk *at* them.

The person before me on the program was from the local workforce development office. She talked about trends in the regional economy. She highlighted that growth in our local economy was primarily being driven by two tech-based industrial sectors, advanced manufacturing, and software.

Then it was my time to talk. In front of me were about 350 students. I started by referencing what they had just heard from the previous speaker. Advance manufacturing and software as the drivers of new economic opportunity.

I then asked how many of them might be interested in going into software development. Three hands were raised, way up in the back – less than 1% of the students. We were so screwed.

I had to quickly shake them up. I began, "We are living in the center of one of the most dynamic tech communities in the country. Companies powered by creative software development."

I then asked them to pull out their mobile phones. "How many of you are interested in learning how to create something that used these phones?" I noted that many raised their hands. "This is the future," I told them.

Then came questions including one I hadn't expected: "Mr. Morrison," the student said,

1 Page **205** - **Sprints** are short, focused bursts of work focused on a specific goal. Often they are two or three weeks in length, where teams quickly define what they will deliver within that time frame and use frequent team check-ins to ensure that they deliver their goal.

"we get it, we know where the future is going. But we're seniors and will soon be graduating. How have you adults prepared us for that future?"

I looked out into the stands at the kids of my community. Some I had known since they were learning how to walk, and one was a fearless truth-teller. My heart sank.

Sheepishly, I admitted that he was right. We had failed them.

Quickly, on my feet, I began to spin up some ideas. And I made a promise that, before they graduated, we would do something that helped introduce them to this future. We would launch something.

"What might the program be called?" I asked. Another student raised their hand and suggested we call it "Tech for Tomorrow." "Okay," I promised, "Tech for Tomorrow would be launched in six weeks."

Our First Sprint

We are industry people, not educators. We don't really understand the world of education. But we do understand how to innovate. And how to learn.

The agile culture of our tech industry continually challenges us to do something audacious, an **Audacious Aspiration**[1]. Fast. Six weeks was to become the 'timebox' for many of our sprints. Now I just had to figure out what Tech for Tomorrow was and how to pull together a team to launch it.

I organized a group of industry professionals and teachers whom I knew into a meeting at the Portland Development Commission's offices. What could we pull off in six weeks that would give these seniors a taste of the opportunities to be found in this new creative economy?

We recognized quickly that most of these students had never seen our passion. What excites us? Why it is that we are not just working for a paycheck, but, for most of us, something much more. We realized that, to begin with, we needed to tell our stories so they could see and feel our passion.

Over the next six weeks, we mapped out a series of lunchtime presentations by

---

1 Page **120** - **Audacious Aspirations** call us to boldly walk into the unknown. Into challenges that take us to heights we never thought were imaginable. Ones that brings out our creative genius and our potential greatness.

passionate leaders from a wide variety of companies in our community.

To promote these lunchtime talks, we would partner with the students. We were, after all, organizing this program because they asked for it. My daughter stepped up to lead this effort.

The school administrators told us, based on their past experience, we might have, at best, twenty or so students show up. So we reserved the largest classroom in the school, one that could fit thirty, and hoped for the best.

The days ticked by. But I saw no evidence of any communication at the high school. No signs, no mentions in any publications or calendars, nothing. I had committed an amazing group of professionals to pull off this series of talks and I began to worry that no one would show up.

The night before our first talk, my daughter came up to me and said, "Dad, I think we have a problem." I turned to her and said, with no small amount of irritation, "I know, I am really worried that no one will show up." "No," she said, "that's not the problem. That room isn't going to be big enough."

I explained to her that we had booked the largest classroom in the entire school. The only other room that was bigger was the auditorium. "Well," she said flippantly as she went back to her room, "you're going to have to talk to the principal in the morning to see if you can book that."

The First Presentation

I had to move mountains that morning to book the auditorium. And it brought a whole set of challenges. Classes were held in it before and after the lunch period. We had to be in and out within the lunch period with no overlap. We had to set up the pizza, get people seated, finish the presentation and get them out with a clean-up in 35 minutes.

When the bell rang for lunch, we opened the doors to the auditorium and the kids began to stream in. More and more students. Over 200.

Sure, the pizza helped, but it was more than food that brought them there.

In that first presentation, we decided that, rather than start with a story of creative passion from an industry professional, we would start with a story of creative passion closer to home – from those students who had been working with Gage to develop the new mobile app for the school.

The students did an amazing job telling their story and demonstrating the app. You could begin to see the gears turning in the other students' heads. "Griffen and his friends did that?" was whispered around.

At the end of the program, we asked the students to give us some feedback and to find out if they, too, might be interested to learn some coding skills. More than half of the kids said they wanted to.

Reframing Tech for Tomorrow

After that presentation, we brought our planning group together for a **Retrospective**[1] of the first sprint. We had a plan in place for ongoing presentations from industry leaders, but we now realized that we had to quickly expand Tech for Tomorrow to provide an opportunity for students to learn how to code.

So, for our next sprint, we had to quickly spin up an after-school coding program.

We reached out to other programs we knew and asked if we could use their curriculum. We then organized volunteers to work with the students. Three weeks later, we launched an after-school program.

This program held sessions twice a week and focused on game design and web development skills. We would have about twenty kids show up with about half a dozen industry professionals for each session.

The sessions were held twice a week in the library at Franklin. Now I understood the teachers' frustrations that they expressed at the earlier site council meeting. The computers were so decrepit that we would have to get to the library thirty minutes early just to try to boot them up. And even then, we couldn't get all of them to work.

There was another problem. The slice of the student body that was showing up was very limited. Kids from lower-income homes weren't there because they often had transportation problems or family obligations. Many kids of color and girls weren't there either. It was mostly white boys who self-identified as techno-geeks. We were facing the same problem with inclusion that afflicts our entire tech industry.

1 Page **196** - **Retrospectives** are meetings where teams gather to identify insights that help shape the next sprint. They are a core piece of many agile frameworks.

But we also began to appreciate the potential of intergenerational co-learning.

Each high school in Portland is assigned a full-time police officer. They were referred to as School Resource Officers (SROs). Their job is to help the administration when there are situations that might impact the safety of the school. Needless to say, they are well known by a select few students but have little interaction with the general student body.

We invited Franklin's SRO to join us with our after-school program. He would sit with the students and learn to code with them. As the students could learn much faster than he could, he would continually ask them for help.

But the students would start to ask him for help in other areas. A relationship between them began to build through this learning partnership. He was no longer the uniform, but a curious and warm-hearted man.

Despite our successes, we had to once again reimagine. We needed to reframe what we were doing to clearly communicate that *everyone belongs at the innovation table.* In fact, the more diverse the participation, the more creative the solutions that can be developed.

So planning soon began for another launch.

Launch of Innovation Academy

We began to realize that a lot of kids feel that they don't belong to a 'tech table'. Tech is for 'those kids', not us, we heard. Girls didn't feel that they belonged at that table. Kids of color felt that they didn't belong there either.

So we had to stop talking about tech.

But we did see their eyes light up when we talked about the possibility of solving problems – problems that they and their community cared about. Everyone wanted to be at that table.

As the summer was fast approaching we had to come up with another name and another structure – a program that could keep nurturing this learning process.

On May 18th, the anniversary of the Mount St. Helen eruption, we launched the Innovation Academy, our boldest experiment yet.

It was a Saturday. More than 150 people showed up at the Franklin High School auditorium: students, parents, community members. I kicked off the gathering by telling everyone that we were going to do something amazing that day.

We started by talking about who we were as a community – the **Core Values**[1] that defined us. We crowdsourced these values and began to group them on a screen, identifying those key ones that appeared to be at the center of who we were.

We then asked people to reflect on those values and to think about areas of the community they would like to reimagine. Again, we put the crowdsourced ideas up on a screen. Then we grouped them together into major themes. Three emerged.

Now it was time to get to work. We had three different spaces defined in the building. Everybody had to go to one of those spaces, depending on which theme most intrigued them.

In the spaces, we had set up discussion tables, each with an assigned facilitator and recorder. The facilitator led the discussion and the recorder would capture the ideas on a shared Google Doc. The team's job: develop project ideas aligned to their chosen theme that would be pitched to the whole group.

When each table had around eight people, the facilitator asked everyone to introduce themselves and briefly explain why this theme was important to them. From there, the teams began to explore ideas for projects they might be able to prototype over the summer.

These discussions went on until lunch. During this time the teams had to select one project that they felt more strongly about and prepare a pitch for it. One caveat: the pitch had to be made by one of the students on their team.

After lunch, the whole group gathered back in the auditorium and the pitches were made. Through a rudimentary voting system, interest in the projects was gauged and the top seven projects were identified.

The group then dispersed again, this time going to one of seven rooms where projects teams would be organized. These teams had to map out roughly what was needed for them to deliver their prototype in six weeks.

---

1 Page **130** - Our **Core Values** define us. They are not negotiable and express our truth. They bond us together to create the bedrock of our communities, a foundation from which we can aspire to reimagine.

After a final gathering to reflect on the experience of the day, the Innovation Academy was launched. Each Saturday through the summer, the library of the high school would be open for the teams to meet in preparation for a demo day in front of industry professionals.

It was the beginning of a creative eruption.

Summer of Learning

Each student team was assigned an adult who helped coordinate the weekly gatherings at the library. Although we didn't use the terminology, we ran these teams with agile principles and practices. For many of the adults, these practices required new learning. But it came naturally to the kids.

Often these Saturdays fell on beautiful summer days. And, after a winter of cold rain, these days made it even more enticing to be outside. Yet the kids kept showing up at the library. There was something special happening there and they wanted to be a part of it.

They all were stretched; there was so much to learn in order to deliver their prototypes, many of which were mobile apps of one kind or another.

One team had a middle schooler as their creative leader. He envisioned making a mobile app that would allow home gardeners to be able to list produce that they could give away to those in need. He was a painfully shy boy, but when he pitched his idea on the stage at Franklin, everyone knew he had a winner. His mom couldn't believe it – she was profoundly touched by seeing her son begin to find his voice.

We paid the school for the use of their library that summer. We wanted this creative work to be done not outside of the school, but at its core. We wanted to see what might happen if students began to associate creative making and learning with a building they knew as a place of rules and obedience.

Teachers would occasionally stop by, wondering what we were doing. They would see their students engaged and excited about what they were learning. Some of them started asking questions. How might they begin to bring this energy into their classrooms?

At the end of this summer sprint, the student teams gathered down at a science museum, where TechFestNW, an industry conference, was being held. There, the students presented prototypes of their mobile apps. Industry professionals gathered around them and asked engaging questions – impressed by what they saw.

All seven teams delivered their prototypes.

Maintaining the Flame

Over the next school year, we continued the after-school program and helped launch another one at Madison High School, a nearby school. These programs were focused on creating projects that were important for the community in one way or another.

We aligned with teams coming from two other schools, and the next spring held a regional demo day where we again invited members of Portland's tech industry to come and hear their stories. Around twelve or so student teams participated in that gala.

But something was wrong.

I knew that there was a magical energy surrounding what happened the previous summer, feeling that we were tapping into a powerful creative energy that could transform how students learned. Something we began to call **Purpose Driven Learning**[1].

But the administrators in the Portland school district didn't understand. They didn't even seem to want to understand it. Multiple times I would invite them to participate and they would never show up. There was little willingness to support teachers who were curious about what we were doing.

The administrators were putting us into a box – another after-school program for the special interests of a small group of students. A club.

If we were trapped in their box, our experiment would fail. Because what we were exploring was much deeper and more profound. It was about the very nature of the culture of learning – not about attending to special interests.

That was when Gary, a board member of the Technology Association of Oregon (TAO) Foundation and the CEO of a winery in Dayton, challenged me. What might happen if you took this aspiration to transform education to a rural community?

---

1 Page **193** - **Purpose Driven Learning** clarifies the reason to learn. It focuses curiosity on a problem that is important to solve and that ignites a passion to learn.

The Transformation

A Crazy Idea

That is how I found myself sitting in the meeting room at Stoller Vineyards in Dayton, Oregon.

I walked in and found every seat of the table, except one, filled. I really had no idea what I was walking into.

Gary jumped right in without any introductions and asked me to share my idea. Having no choice, and everything to lose, I did.

The idea was to reimagine how we could educate our kids to unleash their creative genius. The idea was to do this in a small rural community that could become an innovation hub. The idea was to create a national model.

I explained that in order to do this transformation we needed everybody on board: the school, the community, and businesses.

Then I paused. At first, there was silence.

And then people started talking. Something in their response struck me: a lack of doubt. It was simply, "Sure, let's do that." I was expecting either a strong pushback or an enthusiastic endorsement. Neither were there. It was simply, "Sure," as if what I had asked was nothing out of the ordinary.

So I pushed back. I asked if they really understood what I was asking: that they all really had to be committed, particularly the school district. Then they went around the table and introduced themselves. The school, business, and community leadership were all represented. And they were all on board.

Realizing that there was only one way – forward – I explained that we worked in six-week sprints, which meant that we had to immediately launch our first sprint with a deliverable in six weeks.

And that would be launching Dayton's Innovation Academy, to see if we might replicate the experience at Franklin High School from the previous summer. I heard a slight audible gasp from the group, but we all agreed to press the button.

Dayton's Story

Before I continue with my story, let me share a little bit of Dayton's history. Learning it helped me understand their response to my ideas that day at Stoller Vineyards.

Dayton sits on the Yamhill River in Yamhill County. It was founded in 1850 by Andrew Smith and Joel Palmer. Smith named it after his hometown, Dayton, Ohio.

This founding was a mere seven years after the formation of the Provisional Government of Oregon where the settlers laid claim to the Oregon Country from Britain, a vast new land that extended west of the Rockies from California to Canada.

The site that established this provisional government was Champoeg, on the eastern banks of the Willamette River, just a little downstream from Dayton. The connecting point of these four new administrative districts was where the Yamhill River met the Willamette River. That place, which would soon be known as Dayton, was defined as the nexus for this entire new land of opportunity and was to become an important region of the US, the Northwest.

The Willamette River is the last major river that had to be crossed in order to reach some of the best farmland on the entire continent. This land was rich with topsoil that was scraped from Eastern Washington in massive floods, some 15,000 years ago, at the end of the last ice age. The Missoula Floods.

This river was uncrossable by wagon all the way north to where it flowed into the Columbia. But Dayton's future was defined by a sandbar, just upstream from where the Yamhill River met the Willamette.

That sandbar was important for two reasons. It created the Dayton Landing, the first place on the entire length of the Willamette where wagon trains could cross the river. It also hampered the navigation of boats further up the river. Steamboats were diverted up the Yamhill River to Dayton's docks.

Early settlers used that landing to lay claim to land that some might describe, within the context of the Manifest Destiny, as the promised land.

After indigenous tribes were forced into a reservation in the coastal range, the land was settled and farmed. The produce from this rich valley was shipped from Dayton's docks back to the mills and markets in Oregon City and further north to Portland.

Dayton's settlers had great plans. They hoped that it would become the seat of the new Yamhill County and in preparation they built their city around a grand square. But their hopes were soon dashed by the railroad. The railroad company chose to bring their tracks into McMinnville, further up the Yamhill River.

McMinnville soon became the primary hub of the Yamhill Valley and the county seat, leaving Dayton without even a major state highway running through it. It was left behind. And, for many, still to this day, largely overlooked.

Today Dayton has around 2,500 people. About two-thirds of its students come from families facing real economic challenges. A third of the students are Hispanic.

Despite its size, this town is proud. Their school mascot is a pirate and they wholeheartedly embrace that image of themselves, referring to themselves as the Pirate Nation. Over the years they have continued to win numerous state championships in sports. They also have one of the country's best Future Farmers of America (FFA) programs, and commonly win at the national competitions. They have multi-generational family ties and a fundamental belief in themselves and their potential. It's a place where people feel a strong sense of belonging.

The aspiration of building an innovation hub that could become a model for rural communities around the country felt completely possible.

Besides, their story was inextricably tied back to Dayton, Ohio, the birthplace of flight, where a couple of bicycle mechanics courageously thought differently about the nature of balance. These rank amateurs dared to change the world.

Dayton's Innovation Academy

Six weeks later we launched Dayton's Innovation Academy. Our launch event was held at the end of the school year, bringing together students, teachers, and community members. We had about eighty people show up in their community center.

During our day-long gathering we followed a similar format to the one at Franklin, where we began by talking about values. What were Dayton's non-negotiable values that defined them?

It was a powerful discussion. From there we went to themes – areas of potential transformation in the community – and eventually to projects. Three projects were launched that day, each with a six-week commitment to demo a prototype.

One project, in particular, stood out. This team sought to build a prototype of a mobile app that would allow farmers with excess crops to sell directly to restaurants in nearby urban areas. The team discovered that it was not uncommon for 20-30% of a farmer's crop each season to be plowed back into the ground – crop that was greater than the amounts they had under contract with local packing companies. These fresh vegetables would be welcomed by restaurants and provide additional revenue for the farmers.

Six weeks later a presentation of these projects was held in Courthouse Square, during one of their Friday night community events.

The experience was powerful for the community. By quickly aligning, committing, and doing, something amazing happened. Everybody felt it.

The experience got people wondering: could you create a similar experience with kids in a typical classroom or was this experience only available to self-selected students who were already motivated to learn?

That question became the focus of the next experiment, in many ways, the most important one yet.

Breaking In

The walls of schools are thick.

The education system is a world unto itself. It has its own rules, its own culture. Most people who are in that world have spent their entire life in education since they were six years old. It is relatively rare to find an educator who has ever worked outside of the realm of education.

For an outsider like me to be given permission to come into a classroom and teach is highly unusual – particularly since I didn't really know what I was doing.

But Debbie, a recently retired teacher and trusted community member from Dayton, was involved with our experiment from the beginning. She saw that there was an opportunity to swap out a six-week module of their Careers class with an agile sprint. Debbie pitched the idea to the career teacher and she agreed.

This class was required for all 11th graders. It consisted of two back-to-back periods, held in the first two periods in the morning, involving half of the students in that grade level. In the spring term, the other half of the 11th graders would take the class. I was to model a new learning approach in the fall and then their teacher would try to replicate it in the spring term.

They slotted me in as the middle curriculum module. I had only a few weeks to prepare before the launch.

To be honest, I was terrified. When you enter a classroom, you have to follow a whole new landscape of academic accountability – curriculums, learning targets, and grading rubrics – none of which I deeply understood or had previous experience with.

And then I had to figure out what I would teach and how the students would learn. On top of that, I knew that after six weeks we had to deliver something that was truly amazing.

Finally, there was the thought of standing in front of two classes of thirty students each day and keeping them engaged and focused. I was in way over my head.

But the fact that I was invited inside their walls was a powerful testament to the power of trusted relationships – this would likely never have happened in a larger district. I needed to take advantage of this opportunity and walk courageously into the experience.

Getting Ready

I knew that, as part of this unit, I had to help the students develop a base level of programming literacy, something called computational thinking. I also had to create a framework for them to do a sprint that allowed them to prototype a solution using the principles of **Design Thinking**[1]. All within an **Agile Experience**[2].

I am a business manager, not a software developer. In all of the previous sprints, I had a team of professional developers who would actually work directly with the students.

But this time I was flying solo.

I realized I would need to find an online teaching program that I could use for

1 Page **139** - **Design Thinking** is a creative process that was originally used for product design but has now been widely deployed in other areas, including education. It utilizes the process of iteration to co-create solutions with users.

2 Page **108** - It is difficult to describe the **Agile Experience**. But once it has been experienced, what is seen cannot be unseen. It integrates courage and joy to significantly increase the speed of learning,

introducing coding skills. I would also need to find some kind of prototyping tool for mobile apps that I could provide to the students.

As for the rest, I figured that I would just wing it.

Finding Purpose

On the first day of class, I laid out our experiment. I talked to the students about how we were going to do something in the next six weeks that was going to be amazing. But that we had to do it together, as a team.

We first had to find a purpose worthy of the challenge.

I asked them to pull out their phones. Most of the kids had smartphones. Then I asked them if they might be interested in prototyping an app for that phone to solve a problem that was important to them and their schoolmates. They responded with a few unconvincing head-shakes.

I then asked if any of them knew anything about coding. No one raised their hand.

We talked about values and we talked about making the school a better place. I thought at that point we would brainstorm some ideas of possible apps they could create to benefit their community based on the values we had just discussed.

Silence.

I made another attempt, trying to find a way to spark ideas.

Nothing. This was not going well.

I had never had this experience before – standing in front of thirty faces that just blankly stared at me. I had a feeling of complete irrelevance, like I was just wasting their time.

I had to find a way to crack through their indifference. I tried one last time.

These were kids. I knew that they were very passionate, but had learned to keep their feelings hidden from their peers and adults. So I asked them, "Here at school, what do you hate – you know, what really feels stupid?"

The dam broke. Oh, there were a lot of things that they thought were stupid, things they hated. But it quickly became clear there was one thing they all agreed upon: the binder.

"What's a binder?" I asked. They explained that last year the principal started requiring them to carry around a binder containing sections for all of their classes. Here they would keep the learning targets and their assignments for those classes. These notebooks were big and clunky and didn't fit easily into their backpacks.

The binders were stupid.

"Huh," I responded. "Any way that you could keep that content in a mobile app so that you could have all of that information available on your phone?"

Their eyes lit up. We had our project.

Now it was time to organize into teams. Each team would be commissioned to pitch a prototype of their solution to the principal and superintendent within six weeks.

But first, we had to learn a little about coding – the underlying language of this new economy.

Beginning to Code

I had no expectation that in six weeks these students would become computer programmers. But I wanted them to begin to understand how problems are solved with logically structured instructions. I wanted to demystify coding and help lay the cornerstones for **Computational Thinking**[1].

I had identified two online courses that I was going to try to use. One used videos to help guide the learning process, the other was just text-based. I started out with the video course since I thought that it might better engage the students.

But I quickly confronted a problem I wasn't expecting. Thirty students streaming videos simultaneously ground the entire school network down to a halt. The website wouldn't load correctly for the students and when it did, the videos would constantly freeze.

It wasn't pretty. When technology fails and you have thirty kids in a room who are

1 Page **129** - The term **Computational Thinking** was coined by Seymour Papert, the founder of MIT's Media Lab, to describe the algorithmic thinking required to program computers.

getting frustrated, everything starts going sideways. The noise increases, the interactions increase, attention fragments and you have classroom chaos – a teacher's greatest fear.

Later I found out that the entire district only had a 40 Mbps internet connection. Given that each video stream needs about 5 Mbps, there was no way that a classroom of students could stream videos. I began to wonder how kids from a rural community like Dayton would ever be able to participate in the global economy shackled with such poor internet connections.

So a quick pivot was needed, Plan B. We were all going to use the other online course.

CS First

The year before, Google had piloted a learning curriculum for students called CS First. It was a simple platform that used something called block-based programming. More important, it had an easy interface enabling me to be able to track the progress of each of the students.

To prepare the teacher, I explained the plan to move everyone over to this new learning platform and to give the students a little history of block programming – how it was originally developed by the MIT Media Lab as a language called Scratch.

"Oh," she replied. "I wouldn't mention MIT – these kids will have no idea what that is and likely never will."

I was shocked.

The implication was clear. Just because a student grows up in a small rural community, they would never be able to even dream of going to a world-class university like MIT. That was like cold water in my face. It felt so wrong.

I followed my own guidance and shared with them the story not only of MIT Media lab, but MIT itself and its critical role in developing the technology and culture of the computer age.

Organizing Teams

We now had to organize into teams to build the prototypes. Each team had to have a lead.

They had to present their progress to the entire class once a week.

They first had to go through a process of exploring the problem, then articulating the problem, then brainstorming potential solutions, then prototyping one of them. A basic **Design Thinking**[1] cycle.

We quickly settled into a rhythm. Monday and Wednesday would be 'learning days' where they would be learning how to code, Tuesday and Thursday would be their 'creating days' for working on their project. Friday would be set aside for their presentations, where they would report back their progress to the entire class.

For five minutes at the beginning of each class, I'd talk about the larger story of what we were doing. I talked a lot about the word *reimagine* and how computer technology is empowering their generation to become makers of new solutions.

I shared with them Apple's famous 1984 ad that launched the original Macintosh computer. I talked with them about creative genius that was inherent in each one of us.

I was trying to **Blue Plane**[2] their consciousness.

The Discipline of Learning

But first, I had to focus on the discipline of learning.

The days that the students had to work on the coding were difficult for many of them. They struggled to keep their attention focused on their coding tasks for more than a few minutes.

1 Page **139** - The key aspect of **Design Thinking** is the starting point. A time of deep, empathetic listening to someone to understand what they need. Only then can one be able to understand and begin to ideate and prototype a potential solution.

2 Page **122** - The metaphor of the **Blue Plane** was coined by Alan Kay based on the ideas of Arthur Koestler. This plane is perpendicular to the plane of our current reality. It is a space where the constrictions of our current reality are removed and we are free to dream and reimagine.

The computers were along the walls in the room and around an island of tables in the middle. This created a circular path in the classroom that I used to observe the students' progress.

My job, on these learning days, was to walk around and around on that path. My shoes were leather-soled, and so the students could hear my footsteps, almost like a metronome. Around and around. I almost always walked counter-clockwise, perhaps to be a little more disruptive.

As I walked the path I could see students whose screens were on Facebook or other social sites. As I approached, they would quickly flip back to the course. And I would just continue walking by them. This pattern would be repeated, but they always knew when I was walking by. Each time, they would have to refocus on their coding task.

Over and over again.

On those walkabouts, I began to more deeply understand how hard it was for students to deeply focus on a task. That self-discipline is critical for deep learning – for them to potentially experience the **Flow**[1]. So I kept walking.

Team Dynamics

Weekly reporting of the progress to their classmates pressured each of the teams to perform. For the most part, they held themselves accountable.

It was not about a grade. It was about looking good in front of their peers. Or, at least, not looking bad.

That performance expectation gave me an opportunity to coach each of the teams. I challenged their thinking, questioning if they were, in fact, doing the best that they could do.

I told them I was expecting greatness. Nothing less.

---

1 Page **150** - Powerful creativity happens when we become hyper-focused and the world fades away. We are in the moment, a time difficult to describe. But once felt, is understood. That is known as the **Flow**, a term coined by Mihály Csíkszentmihályi. Ask a jazz musician to describe that moment when riffs interweave and you will get a hint.

The Struggle

Some of the students were struggling, particularly in my second class.

The difference between the two classes was pronounced. The first class was much more focused, while the second class would often teeter at the edge of chaos. This contrast came into stark relief on the day I invited a consultant from Google into the classroom to discuss the best practices of their recently released Google Classroom, software that we had begun using to help manage assignments for our project teams.

When the consultant presented in the first period, there was rapt attention. But not in the second period. Far from it. It was embarrassing, bordering on being disrespectful.

I was livid.

I shared my feelings afterward with the teacher. I asked her if I could have a frank conversation with the students the next day. She said it was okay.

So, the next day I came in and did some honest truth-telling. I talked about what employers would expect of these students when they entered the workforce. I shared with them how important character is for defining success. That we expected greatness from them. But that we weren't seeing it yet.

It was a passionate, pointed talk. I looked directly at each one of them. There was no middle ground here.

Judging by the expressions on their faces, I don't think they had ever had anyone talk to them that way. And it made a difference.

The Deeper Issue

This experience forced me to ponder why the dynamics of these two classes were so different.

I realized that the composition of these two classes was different. The first period had some of the best students in the school. These were the leaders in the FFA program and the student council. They were the kids who were expecting to go on to college. While there were some students who were struggling in that class, there was a cohort of confident learners that defined the atmosphere of the class.

They expected to learn. They wanted to learn. They were a natural learning community.

Not so in the other class. There was no pre-existing learning cohort. The class felt fragmented. Most of these students were either struggling or, at best, apathetic. They were the ones who were just showing up for school. They didn't think of themselves as successful learners.

What I was seeing was a segregation of students similar to what I had seen before at my daughter's high school. This segregation happens largely because of math class.

Those students who are confident learners are often put into accelerated math courses. The scheduling of all of the other classes, then, often has to be done around those classes. As a result, these students tend to have all of their other classes together. They also become labeled the smart students.

Then there are the other students, ones who are either average or struggling. They go to the grade-level math classes, or below, and are grouped together for their other classes.

So my first class had several students who expected to be successful in high school and beyond. The other class largely comprised students who might, at best, simply graduate.

And the students all knew their labels – they had internalized them.

But then I began to notice a larger dynamic – an implied classification of students in every class. Particularly classes that had a diversity of students. Many times a teacher would have two or three high achieving students that might be labeled as Talented and Gifted (TAG) students, and two to three kids who were struggling and disrupting the learning of others.

The daily challenge typically faced by teachers was to keep the TAG students engaged and keep the struggling kids from disrupting the class, while incrementally moving the learning forward for the rest of the students. It often felt like pushing a mound of jello.

When I used that metaphor to describe what I was seeing to other teachers in the building, we locked eyes and they let out long, deep sighs. Yes, they would tell me, it's exhausting.

The Bell Curve

What I was seeing was a bell curve; that's how the teachers were grouping the students in their classes. The mound of jello was the middle of the bell curve. And pushing that middle incrementally forward was sucking the life spirit out of them.

I began to realize that our entire education system was based on this bell curve paradigm. The underlying purpose of our system seemed to be to sort students into groups along that curve for employment in an industrial economy.

The really smart people become academics and industry leaders. They sit out on the far right shoulder of the bell curve. Next, moving toward the center, are the middle managers that make up the majority of the right side of the bell curve. Those in this right half of the curve are known as 'white collar' workers.

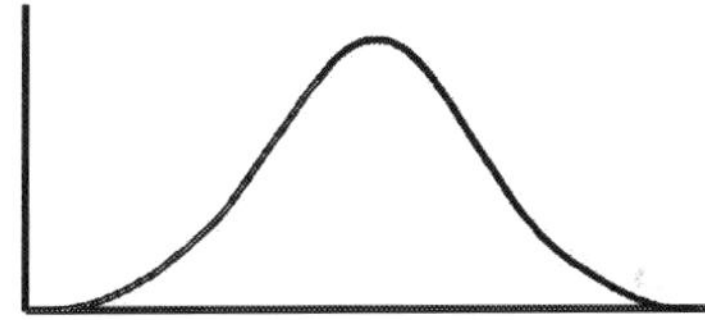

On the left side of the bell curve are our students destined to be our blue collar workers. First, our skilled laborers, and then our unskilled laborers on the far left shoulder of the curve.

It all made sense. What I was seeing in the classroom was mapping to the original intention of our educational system, a system designed using the philosophies of scientific management that came to be called **Taylorism**[1] – that model that underpinned the entire industrial economy.

The only problem was, these students were not going into an industrial economy anymore. We needed to prepare them for a new economy, a tech-enabled creative economy.

The Power Curve

If the bell curve is the underlying paradigm of the industrial economy, the power curve is the model that defines our new tech-enabled creative economy.

1 Page **208** - **Taylorism** was a paradigm of industrial production that focused on efficiency. It fundamentally shaped how we designed our current educational system, turning it into a production line to create workers for an industrial economy. As we seek to reimagine education to prepare students for the new creative economy, we must replace this underlying paradigm.

It all started with Moore's Law that predicted the exponential growth of the computational power of computers.

Then there is Koomey's Law that predicted the exponential shrinking of the battery size, and thus the decreasing size of electronic devices.

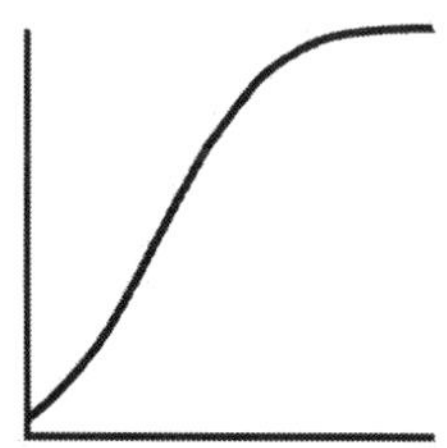

And then there is Reed's Law that predicted the exponential increase in the size of social networks that connect all of us together.

Combined, they become the three laws that underpin the new economy.

The power curve defines our new economy. An economy that is driven by innovation that is increasing at an exponentially faster rate.

My challenge, then, became modeling the power curve in the classroom.

Unleashing Creative Genius

It starts with trust: trusting others with your vulnerabilities.

The students knew that we had committed to present prototypes in six weeks. They also knew that I didn't know how to code. That we all, together, had to figure out how we were going to deliver these prototypes.

While I could coach them on how to learn and how to manage their projects, I wasn't in control of the process. I was only a guide. We wouldn't be successful unless they were all actively contributing to the solution.

This was the same authentic approach I used with the software development teams I managed in my company. I decided to treat these students with the same respect and expectation.

They realized that I was serious, and they quickly stepped up. We developed a powerful learning community.

To help support their learning days each week, I would put up on the screen the relative progress of each of the students in the online coding course. I told them that this wasn't a race, but that they should look at the names of students who were further along than they were. These were students that they could reach out to for help. I then asked them to look at the names of those who were not as far along. These were all of the students whom they had a responsibility to help. We were all in this process together.

On the creating days, they began to realize that I was serious not only about believing in their greatness but expecting it. They weren't used to an adult talking to them this way. And most of the teams began to deliver each week, on schedule, what they had committed to. As they did, their confidence and creative genius began to flow.

Katelyn's Story

Katelyn was in my first-period class, the one with all of the highest achieving kids at Dayton. She wasn't one of them: she struggled. She was two years behind them in math. She was behind in her credits and graduation was uncertain. But graduation really didn't matter that much to her, as she was planning to become a hairdresser.

Little of what she was learning in school had any relevance to her planned future. Certainly not computer programming. She would sit, slumped in her chair, chewing her gum. When I would come around, she would look at me and roll her eyes. "This is so boring," she would tell me, elongating the "o" in "so" in a way only a teenage girl can do.

Another lap for me around the classroom. The same roll of the eyes. I would tell her that this wasn't about coding, but about learning. She wasn't buying it. "Come on, Katelyn," I would urge, "you can do it!"

But then I began to notice something. Every week, her team had their project update ready to share with the rest of the class. She made sure of it by clearly defining tasks and responsibilities. Her leadership of that team was clear.

Near the end of the sprint, a reporter from the local paper called and asked if she could stop by with a photographer and write a story about our Innovation Academy in the Careers Class. I arranged for her to come and visit the first-period class.

The writer spent the morning floating around the classroom interviewing different students.

The article appeared on the last day of our class. I asked the students to read it online. I told them that they had done something special and that others were noticing.

After the bell rang, the kids streamed out of the classroom. But I stopped Katelyn before she left. I asked her if she had read the article. She nodded. Then I asked her if she had noticed anything about that article. She didn't know what I was talking about, so I continued. I talked about how the writer had come to her class to hear the story of something amazing that the students had done, this class that had the best and the brightest of Dayton's school.

But one student had more quotes in that article than any other. They were her quotes. It was her voice that most impressed the writer.

I went on, "Perhaps that writer saw something in you that you are not yet seeing in yourself." She looked at me. This time there wasn't an eye roll. She quietly asked if she could take a copy of the article home to show her mom.

That moment dented her universe.

I bumped into Katelyn right before graduation the following year. I had been following her story: how she had passed all of the math classes she needed to graduate, how she had joined the varsity softball team – a team that had gone all the way to the state finals – and how she had a new confidence that marked her stride.

When she told me she was planning to go to a beautician school after graduating, my heart sank. But then she continued, explaining how she was then going to go down to LA and become a make-up artist. Then her plan was to return to Oregon to start her own cosmetic company. She was on a mission. She had found her purpose. She was a force to be reckoned with.

She believed in her greatness.

Caleb's Story

Caleb was in my second-period class. He sat in the corner of the room and never said a word. He was autistic.

Mainstreaming. That's the name for it. It used to be that students with special needs would have their own classes. But then the decision was made to incorporate these students into regular classrooms to remove their isolation and stigmatization.

For teachers, mainstreaming has been incredibly challenging. Not only did they now have to balance the needs of the high achieving students and the disruptive ones, but they also had to find the time to support those with special learning needs. A Herculean task.

But as long as Caleb sat quietly in the corner, this challenge could be managed, if only by often ignoring him.

As with the first period, we ran a pattern of interleaved coding and project days. As we shared the progress each of the students were making on their coding lessons, the teacher noticed that Caleb was learning faster than the other students.

She asked me about the speed of Caleb's advancement. I told her I wasn't surprised. Coding, for some students on the autism spectrum, comes quite naturally. In fact, there is an organization in Texas called the nonPareil Institute established to teach coding specifically for these young adults.

Well, it surprised her. So she mentioned it to Caleb's counselor. The counselor then asked if she could take me aside and talk with me.

Caleb's counselor asked me if there might be classes at a community college that he could take to learn programming. Was there hope for him?

I told her that she was thinking about Caleb in the wrong way. She was looking at him as a social liability to be managed. I challenged her to, instead, think of him as a community asset. One that had special gifts to give.

She was taken aback. She had never thought about Caleb that way. "Well," I replied, "you should."

A couple of days later, while I was doing my rounds during their coding day, I stopped by Matthew's computer. He was about to punch out the monitor. He was frustrated. He wanted out.

Matthew was a great athlete and socially well-liked. But he also had trouble focusing on school work. Coding, with its demand for logical thinking, was difficult for him. I knew that I couldn't help him – all I could do was reassure him. But then I thought about asking Caleb to come over and help him.

I held my breath because I knew that Matthew had, in the past, led others in making fun of Caleb. What would he think about being helped by Caleb?

Softly, he responded, in a slightly defeated tone, "Sure." I then went over and asked

Caleb to go over and help Matthew. Caleb quietly got up and walked over, pulled up a chair next to Matthew, and started to explain to Matthew how to solve his coding challenge.

As this conversation was going on, the teacher suddenly pulled me aside. "What's going on over there?" she asked. "Caleb is helping out Matthew. Why?" I replied. "But Caleb can't communicate with other people," she explained. "Well, it looks like Caleb is doing a good job communicating now," I responded.

She was shocked, but I wasn't. In fact, quickly Caleb became my wingman. Anytime I had a student who needed help, I would send Caleb over. Soon, he was spending most of the period bouncing from student to student.

After a few days of this, Caleb came up to me. "Mr. Morrison," he started in his slow, methodical diction, "if I am spending all of my time helping the other students, when am I going to have time to do my own course work?" I told him that this was a great question and that I wasn't sure. I then asked him if he had a computer at home. He told me that he did. "Well," I said, looking him straight in the eyes, "it looks like you are going to have to do your coursework at home because I need you here to help me."

Caleb finished the entire course that next weekend.

I attended the graduation of the students the following year. Caleb's mother came up to me, with tears in her eyes. Caleb was heading off to college to study computer science.

Parents of autistic kids carry a huge burden of worry that other parents will never know. Theirs is a worry about how their kids will be able to function in society once they can no longer take care of them. This fear is real. For Caleb's mother, there was now a promise that all might be well for her son. That there might be the potential for an independent, self-sufficient future.

For me, I just knew that Caleb had found his calling.

Demo Day

After six-weeks, demo day arrived. Each team had to present the prototype of their mobile app to the district superintendent and the principal.

One by one they presented. In truth, as they were all solving the same problem, their solutions were quite similar. But it didn't matter. Each team was proud of what they had accomplished. They had done something that they never thought they could have done.

This pride in their work was contagious. There was a lot of joy and laughter that day.

Then it was my turn. To close, I wanted to provide a short reflection on this experience. As I had never met either the superintendent or the principal before, I wanted to share with them some of what I had learned in this sprint.

The only time I had previously seen the principal, Jami, was when she stopped by the class about mid-way through the sprint. She stood in the back, unannounced, for about five minutes. And then left. That was it. But the next day the teacher took me aside and said, "Jami gets it."

As I only had a few minutes to share my learning, I realized I needed to find a visual that could help explain this practice of interleaving that I had been using during the sprint. I wandered around the web, then found it: the dual sine wave. An image of one sine wave that has an inverted mirror, where the two continually intersect in the middle.

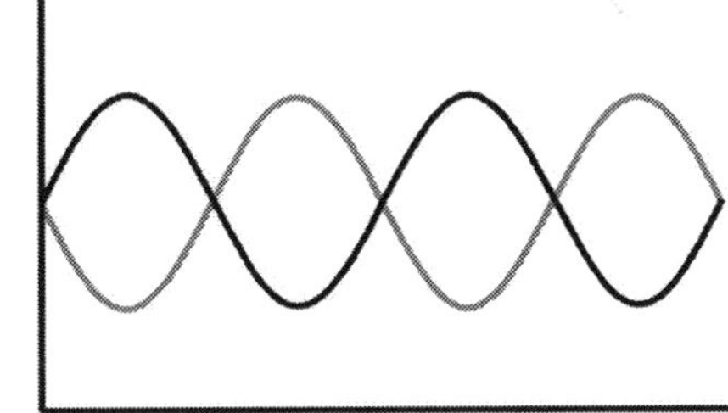

I talked about the power of integrating the act of creating with the act of learning – how in my software team, learning was always tightly integrated with creating.

By structuring the classroom experience to interleave the two acts, the students could be empowered and learn faster – **Purpose Driven Learning**[1]. While these theories could be tied back to Dewey, Montessori and Piaget, it was important to find new practices that brought these theories to life. That was what I was doing in this sprint using an agile framework.

I was not teaching these students about mobile apps, I was showing them a new way to learn.

Of course, I was learning as this process unfolded. I am not, after all, a professional educator. And I wasn't really expecting the superintendent or the principal to understand what I was doing – I was mostly putting these ideas together for my own benefit

1 Page **193** - For learning to have meaning, it must have a purpose. This purpose empowers our curiosity and guides our passion. It must answer the question, "Why?" It must become **Purpose Driven Learning**.

in order to synthesize the meaning of what I had just experienced.

But I didn't get the response I was expecting. Instead, Jami pointed at the graph of the dual sine wave and said, "I want that everywhere."

And thus the partnership began.

The Partnership

Every once in a while, a special person enters your life. That is what happened to me when I met Jami.

Jami's life and professional experiences have been very different from mine. But we quickly found that we shared the same **Audacious Aspiration**[1] – to reimagine education.

Jami is one of the most courageous people I have ever met. She needs to be, in order to drive change in a system defined to control.

We began to meet together, through a Hangout, once a week. These meetings would start at 7:15 in the morning and would often stretch over an hour. I learned more deeply about her world as an educator and she learned about my world as a technologist. We found our worlds had different vocabularies; I learned hers and she learned mine.

Over time, we dubbed these sessions our 'Innovation Therapy' – a time that we could come together and, in a trusting friendship, explore new ideas.

We started talking about how we might test this learning experience in a core class. She wanted to first pilot something in math. Dayton had some of the lowest math scores in the county.

Jami knew that the confidence that a student has in their math skills directly impacted their graduation prospects. And that math, more than any other academic area, has left many adults scarred by shame.

So we dived into our next experiment.

---

1 Page **120** - An **Audacious Aspiration** reaches beyond our current world. Into something that can only be imagined. Great leaders not only hold this imagined realm in their mind's eye, they also learn to use it to inspire others to walk into the unknown with them to achieve it.

The Challenge of Transformation

There are many schools that model a creative learning environment. High Tech High and others come to mind. But the vast majority of them are either charter or private schools. Schools that were built from the ground up with a new paradigm of learning.

The problem is that about 90% of our students in this country are in traditional public schools. The challenge of *transforming a public school from a conventional teaching institution to a dynamic learning organization* is far more difficult than simply building a new one from scratch. There are many internal and external barriers to change that challenge almost every step. It is a hard road, but an essential one.

That is the transformation that Jami set about to do in Dayton. She committed to sharing her path as a framework that might guide others in this process. A commitment for Dayton to become a **Positive Deviant**[1] for other school districts.

White Knuckles

I will never forget the image of Michelle sitting outside Jami's office. She was clutching the arms of the chair, her knuckles white.

Michelle was a very dedicated math teacher who had been in the school district for many years. She loved math and tried to impart that love to her students.

But she also only felt safe coloring within the lines. She found comfort in the predictability of a math curriculum. One section led to the next. It was orderly. If she followed the curriculum and followed the rules, she knew that all was fine in her world.

She had no idea why Jami had asked for this meeting. Had she done something wrong? She was worried, and her knuckles showed it.

When we sat down in Jami's office, Jami shared her idea. Could we find a three-week unit in any of her classes that could be used for an experiment? Michelle's eyes began to dart all over the place. What if the experiment didn't work? How could the kids find the time to recover if the experiment failed? How might she be judged?

---

1 Page **189** - **Positive Deviants** are individuals or groups that have adopted new mindsets and skillsets that others notice and begin to follow. We used this model as a key foundation of our strategy for reimagining education.

It took Jami almost an hour to walk Michelle back from the cliff. But then Michelle shared a story about how, early in her career, she had integrated math with a forest survey and it was a wonderful experience. She then agreed to the experiment.

We decided that we would do the pilot in Michelle's trigonometry class sometime in the next month.

Later I asked Jami why she chose to do this pilot with Michelle. Jami slyly smiled and said it was because she knew Michelle would be terrified. If this worked, the other teachers would know. If Michelle could do it, anybody could.

Not too much pressure.

The Meaning of Math

It has been said that math is the language of the universe. Fluency in that language helps us unlock its mysteries. But for many students, there is little reason to learn math. They don't see the correlation between what they learn in math class and their day-to-day life.

And they are right.

In order for this pilot to work, we had to find a purpose for the math that the students were learning – not a simple challenge.

I started asking the teachers and education professionals that I knew how, as the students were learning trigonometry, they might apply those math skills to solve real-world problems. I found many blank responses. So I kept asking, my concern increasing as I went along.

Finally, I reached out to an education specialist at the Oregon Department of Education. "Oh," he told me, "you need trig for trusses. By the way," he continued, "Dayton has a truss manufacturer just a few miles away."

I had no idea what a truss was, but I took his word for it. We had a lead.

I then talked to Debbie about our plan and asked for her help. Could she go out to this truss manufacturer to introduce me and our project? The following day, she knocked on their door and set up an appointment for me to meet them.

The following week, I went out to the company. Scattered around their yard were, what I now recognized, trusses that are used for supporting the structure of roofs.

I sat down with their general manager and explained that we were going to do a three-week sprint with trig students and needed a problem for them to solve that involved the application of their newly acquired math skills.

He was hesitant. He knew little about schools, didn't know what problems students might be able to solve, and hadn't used trig for many years because computer programs now did all of the math for him.

I sighed. I jumped back in and explained that this was an experiment. We had no idea how it might turn out, but it was really important to find a reason for their math learning. Finally, he agreed to come to a meeting with Michelle and me to find a problem for the students to solve that required their trig.

The Vacation Home

We went around and around looking for a problem for the students to solve. But then we found it: a vacation home.

Here was the challenge that the students would be given: the students had recently inherited some land from an uncle and they wanted to build a 1,000 square foot vacation home together with a couple of their friends. They needed to figure out how much money was needed to build it.

An important cost was going to be the expense of the roof. They would learn that a roof sits on trusses and that there were several different ways that you could design a truss. They had to develop a floor plan for the house, decide on a truss design, then calculate the material cost for the trusses.

They would be told that lumber comes in eight and ten-foot lengths and that it costs 35 cents per linear foot. That was all the information they were given. Their trig would come in handy for the truss design.

Three weeks later, they would have to present their designs and costing calculations. The principal and the general manager from the truss manufacturer would attend this presentation.

The next week, the general manager came to their class and explained the different types of truss designs to the students. The students then organized into teams and launched their sprint.

They were told that for the next three weeks, they would have two days each week to work on their project. They would continue to learn their trig curriculum on the other two days. The fifth day would be set aside for presentations of their progress to the class.

The Mysteries of Conic Sections

This sprint was being inserted into a three-week unit on conic sections, something I knew nothing about but would have to teach.

I had to model a learning process radically different from the traditional model that Michelle knew so well – a model commonly referred to as 'sage on the stage'.

I quickly searched Khan Academy for lessons on conic sections. Lo and behold, they had them. The students could learn conic sections on their own.

My job, as I had done in the previous experiment, was to be there as a guide and community builder. I would identify those students who were learning faster than others and designate them as the resources for other students who needed help: a learning community.

Michelle had never experienced this learning style before. At first, she was very skeptical. But she began to walk around the room with me, listening and watching the process as it unfolded. As a skilled teacher, she was able to see quickly dynamics I couldn't. She then would gently interject herself to nudge or support students, helping them along the way.

She was also able to identify a handful of students who really weren't ready for this unit on conic sections. They had missed some key concepts from the previous section that were a building block for this unit. So she took them back to that earlier unit and was able to help them put those missing concepts in place before they continued with conic sections.

She was beaming by the end of each class. This was so much fun.

The Way

What Michelle was experiencing was something new. She was not in control of their learning; she was observing it. By doing so, she could gently support and guide it.

This model of leading a learning journey was fundamentally different from traditional teaching.

Our responsibility was to define a clear intention for the learning and then empower the students as learners. From there we had to support that process.

This experience is at the core of Agile. Leaders do not control. They define the purpose, remove impediments, and enable teams to achieve an experience of **Flow**[1]. In this way, agile management, is, at its best, an expression of **Wu Wei**[2].

A Cluster in the Making

The project days were not going well, the teams were unfocused. Several of them were not excited by the challenge.

Unlike the previous sprint where the student had defined the purpose of their learning, this project was given to them; for many, its purpose wasn't sparking their curiosity.

But we had to see it through. The days of the sprint ticked by until the final week. The day before the demo I prepped Jami. Failure was okay – we had still learned some great lessons. "Please don't feel disappointed," I urged. Internally, I was heartbroken.

And then came demo day. We walked in and the students began. Our jaws nearly hit the ground.

They must have stayed up all night. They all had completed presentations and walked through their designs and the corresponding calculations of the material costs for their trusses.

---

1 Page **150** - **Flow** happens when an individual or a team enter a state that becomes hyper-focused, igniting neurotransmitters that allow deeper, more empowered learning.

2 Page **222** - **Wu Wei** is a Confucian, Taoist, and Buddhist concept, each a variant form of the other. In the Confucian meaning, it is a way of leading and in the Taoist meaning, it is a way of being. In the Buddhist meaning, it is a way of non-being.

One of the teams projected on the screen a complex computer-generated modeling of their home and truss design. It was beautiful.

The teacher turned to me, shocked. "How did they learn to do that?" she asked.

It turned out that, unbeknownst to her, one of her students had a 3-D printer at home and had taught himself how to do modeling on the computer. He then taught all of his teammates how to do it – and they went to town.

Looking Good

Jami and I learned some important lessons that day, including the important motivation of looking good to one's peers.

Even though the project that these students were given wasn't particularly compelling for many of them, they felt it was important that they deliver. They needed to look good in front of their peers. They needed to look good for the adults, particularly if those adults were from outside their school.

The need to look good pushed them to exceed their own expectations.

Another important insight from that demo day was that you never know, when you have a room full of students, what will spark their curiosity.

While most of the students were not very interested in the challenge, there were two girls whose eyes just lit up. They found the challenges of construction design fascinating. They loved it and wanted to learn more.

When something sparks curiosity in a kid, it's truly a magical moment. Jami saw that and realized that it was critical for her to create a learning environment that nurtured these newly ignited embers.

The final insight was the untapped potential of students teaching students. Learning could be a far more dynamic process than a simple one-way street between a teacher and the students. That one team had shown us the hidden potential of students not only as co-learners, but also as teachers.

Internal Alignment

With these two classroom experiments, Jami now had evidence of something real. As the year was drawing to a close, she asked me to come in and share what we had learned with her entire teaching staff.

The teachers trusted Jami. She had built that trust over the preceding couple of years. She knew that deep cultural change could not happen without that trust.

This trust had been built through a very painful process of moving to a proficiency-based grading system. The transition had almost pulled the entire staff apart, but they got through it.

Proficiency-based grading requires much more of teachers. Grading a student is no longer based on averaging a set of test scores, but individually assessing specific skills that have been defined as learning targets for that particular subject. It's hard and time-consuming. But it's really important. Most schools who attempted the transition gave up. But not Dayton; they pushed through.

The courage that Jami demonstrated in that process forged with her staff a deep trust in her leadership. So when she introduced me, an outsider who had been experimenting in their school, they were willing to listen.

Without directly experiencing this new culture, most didn't fully appreciate what we had learned. But they knew something different was happening. They all knew Katelyn. They all knew Caleb. And they all knew Michelle. Something was happening.

The school year was now drawing to a close. Normally, teachers by the end of the year were exhausted, ready to crawl out the door for their summer reprieve. But Jami noticed something different. There was a sense of anticipation in the air. The teachers were more energized going into their summer break than she had ever seen them.

They were beginning to align to a new vision.

A Summer Party

The time had come to step out and lay claim publicly to this new vision. So we formed a team and set about to organize a gathering that would bring industry leaders and educators together. This event would be the launch of Innovate Oregon, a movement to transform education in Oregon.

We knew we needed a bold vision. Incremental improvements would never allow us to catch up with school systems in other states. We needed to **Leapfrog**[1].

So, on a beautiful day in August, under a tent in the rolling hills of Stoller Vineyard, a hundred people met. Half of them were industry leaders, the rest educators.

We began by introducing twenty middle and high school students from Umatilla, Oregon, a small community in eastern Oregon, where many families lived in poverty.

While the adults were meeting together, the students were going to be in a tent next to the main one, working on a challenge. Their job was to deliver, by the end of the day, presentations of their solutions.

We presented them with a practical scenario: given that their community currently had no recycling program, how could they prototype one using a $10,000 seed grant? They had six hours to organize into teams, research, ideate and develop pitches for a pilot project.

In the main tent, we had a keynote presentation to frame our aspiration. Then the real listening happened as business leaders and educators talked to each other at their tables.

These were powerful conversations. For many of the educators, this was the first time that they had ever had an opportunity to sit down with CEOs and discuss their hopes and aspirations for their companies. What became immediately clear was that these CEOs were all facing difficult times and desperately needed employees who were creative problem solvers.

The challenges facing these CEOs were intense, as market dynamics required fast iteration of new solutions using technologies that may not have been imagined just a few years before. And tomorrow's challenges had to be met with technologies that hadn't yet been invented.

The discussions were eye-opening – particularly for Jami. She came to deeply understand that the current teaching institutions that rewarded compliant learners created compliant workers – failing both the needs of students and their future employers.

---

1 Page **170** - **Leapfrog** is a term used for marketing technology products that strive to introduce a radically new offering, one that leaps beyond the best current product or practice of a specific industry.

In this new economy, an entirely new student needed to be nurtured, one who was empowered to solve complex problems. She heard it straight from the CEOs.

The day ended with the student teams presenting their prototypes, one by one. Their ideas were creative and powerful, impressing everyone, particularly the CEOs.

Teaching Innovation

What I love about Jami is that she is fearless. She challenges everyone around her to go courageously into the unknown – including me.

Soon after that event she asked me to help her write a job description for a new teaching position at her school. This new hire was going to teach innovation.

I was taken aback. How does one teach innovation and what were the teaching qualifications needed? I had no idea.

I helped her write a broad description and off she went to post the job.

A week before school was to start, she asked me to come down to meet Patrick, the new innovations teacher. Patrick's previous experience was teaching social studies. This was to be his first full-time teaching position. He had limited technical background. He was perfect.

Patrick was curious and confident, and he was fine making things up. Because that was exactly what we were going to have to do.

But first we had to find a classroom for Patrick to teach this new class. We walked around the main school building, going into each of the available rooms, some of them old computer labs that I figured would work well. Then we walked out to the ag shop, a separate building behind the school.

This was Mitch's building. Mitch was the agriculture teacher. He had many amazing attributes, but organizing things was not one of them. This building was filled to the roof with old projects, old equipment. Just stuff, several feet deep. In the center of this mess was one unused but cluttered room. The school had turned it into a graveyard for broken and mismatched chairs and tables.

Patrick walked into the room and smiled. This is where he wanted to teach his Innovations class.

Jami and I looked at each other, shrugged and sat down in the middle of the mess. He continued, telling us how he could use these tables and chairs. There was something about this building that felt right. He could make it work.

What he was feeling was, undoubtedly, Mitch's spirit. Mitch, through his ag program, had been teaching kids to think, to be creative problem solvers. That was why his students were continually bringing home awards from national competitions. But Mitch was an outlier. Like many vocational education teachers, he had to teach differently, because he had to inspire those kids who didn't understand why they should sit in rows all day while someone talked at them about things that didn't interest them.

He had created a place in his building for those students to learn. And Patrick felt that.

While we sat there an idea came to me. I turned to Jami and asked a 'what if' question. What if this entire building was reimagined from an ag shop to a center of creativity? A place where all students felt empowered as makers? A place of inspiration, innovation, and invention?

Something that we might call the **i3 Center**[1]. Jami looked at me and her eyes said it all. The i3 Center was launched.

But then, she turned and asked me a very practical question: "So how do we teach innovation?"

I had no idea.

Making it Up

Experience had taught me that when facing a vast array of unknowns, one must start by defining the knowns and work from there.

I knew that a term was eighteen weeks long. Those weeks could be divided into units of different lengths – typically two, three or six weeks long. The previous year we ran two sprints: a six-week unit and a three-week unit.

I also knew that when talking about innovation, we often talked about different ways of

1 Page **157** - The **i3 Center** was envisioned as a creative space for all students. It would become the hub for all of the learning in the school, and a model for supporting independent learning initiatives of the students.

thinking. There was **Process Thinking**[1]. There was **Systems Thinking**[2]. There was **Design Thinking**[3]. Creative problem solvers need these three core skills.

With only a few days before classes were to start, we roughly framed out the class: three units, each six weeks long, focusing on one of those areas of thinking. If we started with process thinking, we could leverage the experience of the previous year, using CS First, the computer science curriculum developed by Google.

That would buy us a few weeks before we had to figure out what we were going to do for the next two units.

And off Patrick went.

Reaching Out

I know when to ask for help; I do it all the time. I might have crazy ideas, but often I don't have the answers. Ideas are very different from answers. Answers are where ideas are turned into practices that then make something real. And I had no idea how to turn the idea of this innovation class into a reality.

But I knew people to ask. So I called up Derek, who leads education initiatives for SparkFun, an open-source circuit board manufacturer based in Boulder, Colorado. Could he work with Patrick to put together a six-week curriculum to introduce systems thinking to students? He agreed and off he went.

Then I called Don, known for thinking in new ways about learning. Don was a master teacher for the Lemelson-MIT Program, a joint venture between the Lemelson Foundation and MIT to support the development of young inventors around the country. He also was the one who opened my eyes to the potential of creating empowered learning communities in classrooms.

On my first visit with Don, I walked into a drafting class he was teaching at Hillsboro

---

1 Page **191** - **Process Thinking** allows us to understand what needs to be done and how to do it. When programming computers, we are challenged to structure process steps into algorithms of increasing complexity.

2 Page **207** - **Systems Thinking** allows us to understand how we can build and maintain relational networks of increasing complexity.

3 Page **139** - **Design Thinking** allows us to develop new solutions for others by deeply understanding their needs and co-creating solutions with them.

High. He had a vast classroom space, filled with about sixty students. I found Don and we started chatting, looking out over this sea of students. He started explaining to me that there were five levels of drafting being taught simultaneously in this class period, from intro to advanced.

All of the students were working independently, focused and engaged. Occasionally a student would come up to him with a question. He would gently direct them to another student who could help them, and then returned to our conversation. This happened several times that period. Sixty students were clearly learning, while the teacher was standing along the wall, chatting quietly with a visitor.

He had created a self-managing learning community using an online curriculum that he had developed. It was amazing.

Don was also a farmer. His family's farm was just down the road from Dayton. His parents, in their eighties, were still working that farm and he was helping them out on the weekends, even though he was nearing his own retirement. I knew we could count on him.

"Lemelson-MIT has a curriculum for an after-school class that helps students develop design thinking," he explained, when I reached out to him for help with the i3 Center. He would contact them to see if they might be willing to pilot this curriculum for an in-school class. This would be the first time in the country they had done this. They agreed. I connected him with Patrick, and off they went, building the third unit of this class, focused on design thinking.

We now had an Innovations class.

Going Deeper

Jami and I continued to experiment together. One of those experiments was with the Ocean of Data Institute (ODI), based in Boston. IBM, one of our strategic partners, introduced me to them. Ocean of Data, an initiative of the Education Development Center, was at the forefront of efforts to develop data literacy curricula for schools.

They were intrigued by Dayton's exploration of agile learning in classrooms, and Dayton was intrigued by the potential of empowering their students as data storytellers. Jami just needed to find a teacher willing to experiment. She found Carrie, a science teacher.

We connected Carrie to ODI and the planning for the sprint began. She came up with a three-week sprint where the students had to tell a story through a data analysis that answered one of the environmental questions she had given them – all drawn from the local ecosystem. ODI would send one of their staff members out to Oregon to observe.

Carrie added an important piece to the puzzle: standards mapping. She launched, and the students delivered.

One of the challenges of bringing new learning practices into high schools was the requirement that the learning aligns with nationally defined standards. There are two sets of standards that teachers have to work with: one called Common Core, focusing on English and Math, and the other, Next Generation Science Standards (NGSS), focusing on science education.

Carrie had a deep understanding of NGSS. She would constantly challenge herself to defend how the learning that was being done mapped against these standards. She went through this same exercise with this sprint. It was impressive to watch.

What's Next

As the fall term came to a close, we had no idea what to do with the Innovations class. Should we just repeat it? What about the students who wanted to keep going further?

There are few things worse than disappointing a young person, yet it happens all the time. They have an experience that ignites their curiosity only to be told that the experience is over. Time to move on to the next topic or the next class. The disappointment in their eyes says it all: "But I really liked doing that..." Over time, they become cynical about their learning experiences, just like adults. We are used to disappointment.

Patrick and Jami faced this challenge at the end of that first term. For some students, Innovations was just another class. But others were on fire. They were excited and wanted more.

But there was no clear way to teach them – so Jami came up with a new idea. Rather than find a way to teach them, they would be given a different opportunity to keep learning. Patrick would help guide and support them, but it would be the students' responsibility to learn.

They would be assigned to a new class, Innovations 2, that would be held at the same time as the core class, Innovations 1, for new students. While Patrick would lead the main class, they would be given tables in back to work on projects as an independent study. Patrick would be teaching both sets of students, in the same room, at the same time.

The more advanced students were doing all sorts of projects, driven by their personal interests. The students in the introductory class saw them working away, which inspired their own learning. They could see how they could apply their new skills to complex problem solving that was exciting the more experienced students.

Patrick's space was being transformed by the students. It was still messy but now filled with creative energy. The art students wanted to get involved – they painted the walls and the ceiling tiles. The space certainly wasn't pristine, but it was alive.

It was also way too small. So Jami began to work on plans to reconfigure the classrooms to create a much larger room for Patrick: an Innovation Lab. She applied for a grant from the Department of Education, but her vision for this new i3 Center was well beyond the imagination of those who wrote the grant guidelines.

So she worked with her superintendent to cobble together some funds to help pay for a small renovation. She also needed volunteers to pull it off, and for that, she had to develop community support for this vision.

Pirate Night

School open houses – many of us have been to them. It's a time to talk to your children's teachers and to be reassured that your kids are in good hands. Many parents don't show up. Typically, the parents who come tend to be more affluent, better educated, more socially successful. Their kids tend to do better in school.

It's not that other parents don't care. For many of these parents, school was not a place filled with fond memories – it was a place where they didn't feel successful. A place, for far too many, of shame.

Jami hoped the evening would open the door to a new way of thinking about school.

She had a big story to tell and wanted everyone to hear it. Postcards were printed and sent out to the community. Students canvassed neighborhoods. Come to Pirate Night, they beckoned. We are Pirate Nation – we all need to be there.

On the night of the event, tables were set up in the gym where students could share stories of projects that they had done that excited them.

Jami and Grace, a middle school student, stood at the top of the gym stands watching people come in the door. Grace had been part of the initiative from the beginning as a member of Dayton's Innovation Council.

The people kept coming in. The stands filled up. People who couldn't find a seat were standing along the edges or in the hallway outside – more than three hundred people. Jami and Grace looked at each other. They each knew what the other was thinking. Something magical was happening.

It was now time to watch Cate's video and for Jami to tell the story to her community. It was the story of a new beginning, a story about creativity, possibility, the i3 Center and reimagining education. A story of Dayton's future.

The Innovation Council

The Innovation Council was helping shape the future that Jami described that night.

We had started the Innovation Council at the beginning of the previous term. Each month we brought together teachers, students, and community members to help shape the new strategic direction of Jami's school.

It was at the first meeting that we met Kathy. At the start of the meeting, everyone went around the table introducing themselves. When Kathy introduced herself as the CEO of OnlineNW, she mentioned that they were the new internet provider for the school district and had built a fiber optic line to the school over the summer.

Jami and I looked at each other. Neither of us knew of this construction of fiber to the school building. But we both recognized immediately the importance of this news.

If Dayton's school now had fiber, there would virtually be no limits on future bandwidth. That opened up the door to all of the online media content of the web to support student learning. For a small rural community, this access leveled the learning playing field.

After the meeting, Jami and I took Kathy aside to learn more. Over the next few days, we expanded the conversation. Two weeks later we put in place an agreement for the company to build a world-class internet network for the entire city that included a revenue-sharing plan to fund student projects.

As the Council continued to meet, more community resources were discovered. But also the initiative in Dayton became more focused. The students on the Council wanted this to be Dayton's initiative, not just a part of a larger state initiative.

So Innovate Dayton was launched, the first of what would become many initiatives to embrace a new innovation culture to support the local community.

To guide the development of Innovate Dayton, a new student-led group was needed. It was called the Innovate Dayton Leadership Team.

Innovate Dayton Leadership Team

The Leadership Team included both junior high and high school students. Jami knew that an authentic cultural transformation in her school would need to be guided by the students.

This team began to develop outreach initiatives, both within the school and in the community. One of their first challenges was to define the messaging for their campaign.

A Portland-based marketing firm agreed to help them. The students all got on a bus and spent an afternoon in a workshop led by Kerry, the firm's CEO. She took them through the same brand-messaging process that she used for her corporate clients. The adult chaperones from Dayton sat quietly in the back of the room watching the students and Kerry engage in thoughtful discussion.

At one critical point in the discussion, Kerry asked the kids that if Innovate Dayton was successful, what might that success look like?

The adults in the room held their breath. Would it mean that these students, their kids, would finally be able to leave Dayton? For that was how success has often been defined for students in rural communities – that they can escape to cities where there are more opportunities.

But that is not what these Dayton students wanted. They wanted to stay in Dayton close to their families and in a community that they loved. Success for them was to have the opportunities of this new economy while still living in Dayton. They wanted to build this new opportunity in Dayton.

So the tagline for their marketing campaign quickly came together: "I am Dayton's Future."

Soon posters started appearing all over the school with photographs of different students that included a quote from each one of them, all under a common headline: "I am Dayton's Future."

The Launch of Innovate Dayton

The company that was providing the electronics for Dayton's new fiber network got wind of the story and asked if they could fly out to Oregon to create a short promotional video about Dayton. They had worked with hundreds of communities around the country but had never heard a story like this one.

The company flew a film crew and its creative director from its corporate headquarters back East. They spent a few days filming, including a session of the Innovate Dayton Leadership Team.

The creative director came out of that meeting amazed. He had never known that students could be so mature, so capable. He went on to note that there were three students that really impressed him – so much so that he would gladly fire some of his staff in order to hire them onto his team.

I pointed out that two of the students he just mentioned were junior high school students – 14 year olds. He couldn't believe it. But it was true.

We knew that we had something special happening with the initiative, so Innovate Dayton needed to be officially launched at a special event. The planning for this event was turned over to the students.

The event was scheduled for May, right before the end of the school year. Every single student in the district was going to be brought to the gym. They would all wear identical t-shirts with the Innovate Dayton logo on the front and the words "I am Dayton's Future" on the back.

For the first time in Dayton's history, all of the students in the district were gathered together. Over 1,000 students were in the gym. The students ran it like a pep rally. The energy was electric. The future was being made.

Capacity Building

Jami recognized that changing how her teachers taught would require a tremendous amount of courage. They would need to experience the reason to change.

For years teachers have been continually buffeted by new models of education. With each new model, they were told by their administrators to change how they were teaching. There was a new way, a better way, to teach. And then that model would be discarded, replaced by another model. They would be told once again to teach in a different way.

After teachers have gone through several cycles of these mandated methodologies, many become cynical. They also feel increasingly powerless, feeling that their own experience and expertise is not being valued by their leaders.

Jami understood that she was not introducing a new teaching model, but a new way of experiencing learning – one that mirrored the culture of innovative companies.

That spring, she invited her teachers to a two-day workshop on **Design Thinking**[1]. This was a voluntary workshop, but one that she hoped they would attend. Most of her teachers agreed to come.

While the elements of design thinking have been around for a while, it was a product design firm in Silicon Valley, IDEO, that defined and promoted this multipart process that included discovery, ideation, prototyping and testing in an ongoing, iterative process of product development.

This concept of design thinking was embraced by Stanford's design school, the d.school, who then began to bring this thinking into elementary and secondary education through its K12 Lab. The workshop leaders had been trained by Stanford.

This training introduced a fundamental shift in the mindset of teaching. Typically teachers are taught to design and implement curriculum – a fixed path of teaching that extends through the length of an entire term. Much like a production line.

---

1 Page **139** - **Design Thinking** is an adaptive process to co-create new solutions in partnership with users. It begins with the premise of understanding. Deep, empathetic understanding of user needs that launches cycles of creative exploration.

Design thinking uses iterative **Learning Cycles**[1] that continually morph, based on what is learned. They are highly adaptable, requiring a new agility for both the teachers and the students.

Each class or each unit becomes, in a sense, an experiment. But, in this process of experimentation, learning rates accelerate.

The workshop was remarkably successful, opening the door to a new way of learning. Jami knew, however, that there would only be a few teachers who had the courage to fully implement what they had learned.

But she also hoped that other teachers might begin to experiment, particularly if they knew that they would not be shamed by failure.

A Culture of Shame

Shame is very effective for society or organizational control, but it destroys the potential for creativity.

Spending time in schools, I began to more deeply appreciate how shame permeates the entire culture of traditional education.

Failure meant shame and rejection. Failure was to be avoided at all cost. Students knew this. It was the fear of failure that created obedience.

But in this agile learning paradigm, you have to fail. Failure is how we learn. For each time we fail, previously unrecognized false assumptions are illuminated. We **Know the Problem**[2] better.

We try again, this time emboldened with deeper understanding. We may not know what is true, but we now know what is not true. We are incrementally smarter with each progressive cycle. Do those cycles fast and we learn fast.

The faster we understand the problem, the faster we are able to design solutions.

---

1 Page **174** - The concept of **Learning Cycles** lies at the heart of Agile. The faster we can move through those cycles, the faster and deeper we can learn.

2 Page **168** - When we venture into the unknown, our intuition guides us. This intuition is based on assumptions built from our past experiences. When we fail, we discover assumptions that were wrong, illuminating a previously hidden part of the problem, allowing us to **Know the Problem** better.

But if failure leads to shame, we will not experiment. And for teachers, the fear of being shamed was also hard to break. Jami understood this.

When there is failure in a classroom, everything can break down and the entire class can quickly dissolve into chaos. Pounded into teachers from day one is the importance of classroom management. That means order. The worst fear of a teacher is for their principal to walk into their classroom at that moment when everything is spinning out of control.

So it is extremely difficult to ask a teacher to experiment with new ways of learning with their students when it carries real risks of lessons that might not work.

They will only do it if they truly trust their leadership. Trust that their leadership will not shame, but will, instead, allow them to reflect on the learning from the failure to help shape the next experiment.

The Right People

Jami quickly found that not everyone was up to this challenge.

Some of her staff were near retirement: they were looking at the finish line. The personal work for this transformation required more energy than they had. So Jami had to have some difficult conversations.

Perhaps it was time for them to retire and to move on.

She knew she needed the right teachers. She needed teachers who were curious, creative and courageous. With new positions now opened, she began to interview. Borrowing a technique used by a tech company she read about, she decided to provide the interview questions before the interview. Her last question was about Design Thinking: “Using the principles of design thinking, how might you structure a learning plan?”

She was surprised by the result. The candidates came in better prepared than she had seen in the past. They also had almost identical responses to that last question.

None of them knew what design thinking was. They started asking around and none of their colleagues or former professors knew what it was. So they had to search the web to learn about it. But when they understood it, they were so excited. They wanted to come to Dayton and to be a part of this experiment.

Jami picked the best candidates and launched into her next school year.

Learning Cohorts

Our tech world is largely shaped by the **Rogers Curve**[1]. This bell curve describes the market adoption of new technology and is formally called the Innovation Adoption Lifecycle.

This model describes how innovations are gradually embraced by a market, one segment at a time, until they become widely adopted. It describes how different segments of a market will adopt a new technology or innovation. In the initial stages of market development, there are the **Innovators**[2] and the **Early Adopters**[3].

This model was modified by Geoffrey Moore when he identified a gap between the Early Adopters and the Early Majority. He called this gap a 'chasm' and identified that crossing the chasm was the greatest challenge facing the introduction of new technologies or innovations. It has become known as Moore's Chasm.

The same is true for the adoption of new cultural paradigms. Jami's challenge was finding a way to cross the chasm in her school in order to create a **Paradigm Shift**[4].

She identified a couple of teachers who were Innovators and then developed a handful of Early Adopters. She knew that, to cross the chasm, she would depend on the bridge built by those teachers.

Wide adoption happens once an innovation is embraced by the Early Majority. Unlike the Early Adopters, they are more cautious; they don't believe a pitch. But they will watch others. If they see real value obtained by those whom they can identify with, they will be willing to adopt.

---

1 Page **197** - The **Rogers Curve** lies at the core of strategies to bring new technology to markets. This model also effectively describes how new paradigms can transform a culture.

2 Page **162** - **Innovators** are risk-takers. They are curious and are willing to play with new technology even when it is not stable or fully formed.

3 Page **141** - **Early Adopters** are willing to change their behavior to adopt new solutions, once they are reasonably well-formed and stable.

4 Page **187** - Thomas Khun coined the term **Paradigm Shift**. It describes the point in which we understand the world differently. At that point we have a new reality, we see everything differently and there is no going back.

Jami began to carve out time for her Innovators and Early Adopters teachers to share their learning with each other. By doing that, she was strengthening the practices and encouraging them to keep experimenting.

She then began to provide opportunities for those teachers to share what they were learning with other teachers. She also created events for all of the teachers to come together on design challenges to further experience the joyfulness of this learning. She was creating opportunities for teachers to become curious.

Learning begins with **Curiosity**[1]. Jami was not mandating change, she was creating a culture that encouraged it.

Telling the Story

Stories began unfolding in her school, more and more stories. Stories of new learning discoveries, new learning opportunities, new excitement.

When Jami and I embarked on this journey I shared with her that it felt that we lived in two worlds. As a technologist in this new creative economy, mine was defined by a **Paradigm of Abundance**[2]. Hers, as an educator living in a world defined by the industrial economy, was defined by a paradigm of scarcity.

In my world, we were always running as fast as we can to take advantage of new opportunities. School districts, on the other hand, were always dealing with the next budget crisis, and struggling to make do with less.

When we began this journey I wondered: if Jami began to live in my culture, might her world transform from scarcity to abundance?

It happened. Not only was there abundance flowing from within her building, but from the outside too. For instance, one day a set of boxes arrived from Tektronix. Jami called me up and asked me if I knew anything about them. I didn't.

But, after digging around, I found out that one of their senior executives had heard

1 Page **136** - **Curiosity** unlocks real learning. It guides our passions and changes our neurochemistry. It brings us joy.

2 Page **185** - The **Paradigm of Abundance** underpins the new economy. More than anything else, it was the radical premise held by Open Source software community that opened the door to the idea of creating a commons where value could be freely shared - an idea that transformed our technology world and unleashed immense new potential.

Jami and me speak at an event and wanted to donate an entire set of testing equipment to the school. Then there was a massive crane donated by Nike. 3D printers showed up one day from another company. And the list went on.

There were many other stories. But they weren't being told.

We set up the Innovate Dayton website to post articles, but we were struggling to find resources to write them. Jami felt that it was important to empower the students as the storytellers. But how?

Living with Failure

Many times, success does not come easily. You try something, and it fails. You try again, and it fails. Over and over again. It is easy to become discouraged. But you have to be committed to trying again and again. You have to be bullheaded in your commitment.

That one characteristic separates a true innovator from others. True innovators never give up on their vision. Thomas Edison lived with multiple failures when inventing the incandescent light bulb. Norm Larson lived through thirty nine failures when inventing WD-40. Each failure illuminates a different nature of the problem so that we can better imagine the solution.

Jami lived with failure when figuring out how to empower students to tell Dayton's story – over and over again.

She started by working with one of her star students. He was to be the lead writer and develop a band of other writers. That didn't work. The next year she formed a special team of students called the blog squad and gave them the space and time to write, mentored by a volunteer who was a corporate media specialist. That didn't work.

The story of Dayton needed to be told because there were so many exciting things going on. But everything on their website was stale and dated and she had no writers.

But then one day she was listening to a presentation about an event that a team from the Design Thinking class had put on for elementary students. One of the team members was a young student she didn't know well, someone who kept quiet and lived in the shadows of the school. But she noticed something special in Bevin's work.

Jami began to explore Bevin's gifts by asking her to do some design projects for her. Then she learned that this young student wanted to write. Working with a corporate partner, Bevin was trained up as a professional writer through an internship, and the school gave her a class credit for her writing. The student grew in confidence and then began to train other students.

She was able to build the student writers team that Jami couldn't. And the stories began to flow.

Inspiring Others

Telling stories is one thing, but we knew that the **Agile Experience**[1] was difficult, if not impossible, to describe, like asking someone to describe the flavor of an exotic fruit. It was something so profoundly different that it could only be understood by experiencing it.

So we set about finding a way to share the experience.

One afternoon we were with a group of educators and community members from around the county, grappling with this question: How could we share this learning experience with others?

And then, Derek hit on it. He simply said, "What if we hold a make-a-thon?" We then asked him what a **Make-a-thon**[2] was, and he simply replied, "I don't know, we will need to figure that out."

But it was a brilliant idea that quickly morphed into a plan. We were to bring sixty students, teachers, administrators, and community members from surrounding school districts to a gathering at the local community college.

We were then going to mix them up into teams of different ages and backgrounds. Next, launch into a three-hour boot camp to introduce the concepts of programming and circuit board design. Then, in the afternoon, each team would plan and construct a solution to one of three challenges before a final presentation to the rest of the group at the end of the day.

It was a crazy idea. We would be bringing together people who had no programming

---

1 Page **108** - When the mindsets and practices of Agile are truly integrated, there is an **Agile Experience** of learning that unleashes creative genius like never before. Once seen, it cannot be unseen.

2 Page **178** - **Make-a-thons** have been used throughout Oregon to introduce schools and their communities to the potential of learning in a new way, one that mirrors the experience in our most innovative companies.

experience or any understanding of electrical engineering, challenging them to create something astonishing in one day.

It was crazy enough that it just might work.

And it did. What came out of the day profoundly dented the universe of everyone in that room. The educators saw – many of them the first time – that kids could learn faster than they could be taught, often pulling the adults along in their draft. But more rewarding than the product at the end of the day was the exuberant joy of this co-learning process. Laughter filled the room. This extreme challenge did not daunt them, it exhilarated them.

Everyone returned to their schools knowing that there was something special happening in Dayton. And they wanted to learn more.

The Power of Partners

A supporting ecosystem began to form around what we were doing in Dayton. Working with a local foundation, the Construct Foundation, Jami was able to introduce the concept of Design Thinking to most of her teachers. But it was when Dayton connected with the Stanford d.school that the **Positive Deviant**[1] model really began to bear fruit.

A year before, Stanford d.school's K12 Lab had launched the School Retool program to introduce the **Hacking**[2] mindset to school administrators. They recognized that in order for innovative educational practices to be introduced into a building, principals needed to give their teachers authentic permission to fail.

To fail forward to learn. To try something, understand it might fail, then quickly learn from that experiment, and to try again, creating fast, iterative **Learning Cycles**[3].

Through the Construct Foundation, Stanford wanted to bring this three-month fellowship program to Oregon. We realized quickly that the groundwork laid by Dayton in the Yamhill Valley was a perfect testbed for this fellowship.

---

1 Page **189** - The **Positive Deviant** model encourages others to quickly adopt new behaviors by providing a tangible example of success.

2 Page **152** - **Hacking** refers to a process of creative discovery that involves rapid trial and error experiments.

3 Page **174** - **Learning Cycles** are at the core of Agile.

So it was launched, bringing together nearby school districts for playful, courageous learning to transform school culture. Most of the administrators immediately got it. But when they all went to Dayton for a day-long immersion into an 'inspiration site', they really understood the profound implications of reimagining education.

The Secret Sauce

I have given many talks about the Dayton Experiment. But the one that most terrified me was to a management team from New Relic.

New Relic is a large software company that provides analytical tools for managing complex cloud-based server deployments. It is a public company, based in San Francisco, but has over 500 developers working out of its offices in Portland.

The management team for their engineering group was holding a day-long conference on innovation. They asked me to be their keynote speaker. They wanted to hear a story of innovation from beyond the walls of industry.

These managers were leading some of the most innovative teams in the industry, knowing far more about Agile than I did. I had to tell the story of what we were doing in education in a way that was meaningful and compelling to them.

And I had to walk into my own fears of being an imposter. This fear is not uncommon. Most of us have it. It is just that many of us are good at denying it.

After my talk, five managers came up to ask me more questions. Oddly enough, the one that I wasn't prepared for was, "What can we do to help?" My talk had no ask - I wasn't looking for their support. I was just telling a story.

When that question was asked, I realized that I had a decision to make. Would I be authentic and honest, or to give them an answer that I thought they might want to hear.

I decided to take the risk of being authentic and honest. I decided to walk into my own fear. To trust these strangers with my vulnerability.

I shared with them that my biggest concern was that we could not replicate the Dayton Experiment in other schools. Because, key to this experience, was my commitment to meet with Jami once a week to talk, reflect and ideate together. As other schools began to embark on this journey, I couldn't make that same commitment to their leadership. And I couldn't clone myself.

So here was the question that I shared with them: Was this type of creative relationship between an industry agilist and an educator unique to just Jami and me, or was this life-giving relationship possible for others?

I asked them if they might be willing to help answer that question with me. It would be messy as I didn't know how we might do it, but would they be willing to explore this question through a quick sprint we spun up together? They agreed.

I now had a rock-star team of industry agilists to help figure out the next step in our journey.

Leaping into the Void

Jim, my system architect, taught me many things in the fifteen years I worked with him. He introduced **Extreme Programming (XP)**[1] to me. He also instituted our practice of three iteration release cycles.

I would share with Jim an aspiration for a new software solution that I had envisioned. It was normally only a vague idea, but it had a clear purpose. He would listen and ask questions to better frame out the intention. And then he would set to work on the first version. He called this rough prototype a 'kludge'.

He would quickly slap together pieces of the solution. Some might be pulled from other codebases or just manually built in spreadsheets. It was a mess, totally jerry-rigged. But it had all of the elements of the experience that we were trying to create.

He would share that with me and I would use it. As I did, I would notice pieces of the solution that were missing. He would add that. I would notice process steps that were clumsy. He would redefine those. We hacked on that kludge as fast as we could.

Finally, I would let him know when our first version contained the solution we needed. Then he set out to do the next version, where he would properly architect the solution. He would then give that to me to use. That would be further tuned.

When that second version felt solid, he would set out to build the third version, one that was designed to scale. Scaling required a lot of supporting functionality. Once that version was built we were good to go on to the next solution we needed to develop.

1 Page **147** - **Extreme Programming (XP)** is a set of practices that empower software developers and were instrumental for the launching of Agile.

We were able to turn out solutions in record time with this three-iteration model: kludge, architect, scale.

It takes courage to jump into that first version – the kludge. You really have no idea what you are jumping into. And you know, whatever it is, it isn't going to be pretty. It will be a mess.

But you need to leap into the unknown, the void.

That's what I was doing with the New Relic agilists. I had no idea what we were going to do or how we were going to do it. But I knew, as they lived in an agile culture, that if anyone would be okay with the leap, they would.

So we jumped.

Defining a Partnership

I floated the idea with Jami. She thought it was great and went to Portland the following week to sit in a conference room at New Relic with the five managers who wanted to participate in the pilot.

We started out with introductions. Each of the managers shared a little of their story and why they wanted to be involved. Jami listened deeply. She had to find the thread in each of those stories that could then be matched with five of her teachers.

Would this be a mentoring or partnership relationship? We quickly agreed that the managers were not coming into this relationship as experts but as co-learners. As partners.

We then started framing out what a six-week sprint might look like. It was going to start with a liftoff held in Dayton. It would end in a **Retrospective**[1] back at New Relic. Between the two events, we were going to ask the partners to do one thing: find a time to talk to each other every week.

That was all. A thirty-minute check-in once a week in a video call. No agenda. Just a conversation.

What might happen?

1 Page **196** - A **Retrospective** (sometimes just called a "retro") is a meeting at the end of a sprint where the team reflects on their experience to help identify and incorporate insights. It also helps shape the next sprint cycle.

The Liftoff

Two weeks later the New Relic team was down in Dayton. The plan was to have a ninety-minute kick-off meeting, called a 'Liftoff', and then have the managers go to the classroom with their partners to experience a typical day with students.

Brent led the Liftoff. He's an expert at these, having led many of them with teams at New Relic. It started with each member of the group introducing themselves, sharing a little of their story, then making a formal commitment to the sprint by hitting the table while proclaiming, "And with that, I'm in."

We were sitting at a set of tables that had been formed into a circle. We had to share one thing that was going well in our work, and one thing that wasn't going well. Then we had to do the same thing for our personal life. Brent started off.

What he shared was startling in its honesty and the vulnerability he demonstrated. Wow, we all thought, now we have to do that?

And we did, each one of us. Deeply personal stories were revealed in those introductions. At the end of each, was the courageous bang on the table. We were all in.

We talked about our values, identifying three key ones. We then defined the behaviors that would make those values real. We were committing, over the next six weeks of the sprint, to live and breathe those values.

Then the managers went off to the classrooms with their partners.

The Calls

Several of the teachers struggled at first with the idea of these weekly calls. Jami was able to help them find the time – always a challenge for teachers – but that wasn't the problem. They struggled to understand what the reason was for the weekly call.

There was no pre-defined purpose, no agenda. The teachers were concerned that they would get on the call and have nothing to say. Perhaps, for some, there was a little bit of guilt – taking the time of someone they respected but not being able to give anything in return. But Jami kept encouraging them. And slowly, their walls of resistance began to fall.

The managers would ask them about their week, their successes and their failures, what was working and what wasn't. And they would listen.

When they found dynamics that they recognized from their work, they would help the teachers put names to those patterns. And then they would share some practices that they might try that could change the dynamics.

Soon all of the partners were having their weekly calls, the highlight of their week. The teachers would ambush Jami in hallways wanting to share new ideas that they were trying. Their excitement was infectious.

The pilot was then over and it was time for the retro. It was time now for Dayton to experience the world of their New Relic partners. So they piled into cars and drove up to Portland.

The Retro

New Relic's offices in Portland are much like those of other high tech firms. They are sleek and beautiful. For the Dayton teachers coming from a small rural community, the offices were a different world.

But as the teachers and the managers came into the main conference room – one that overlooks the entire city – it felt like a homecoming. Something had happened over these past six weeks. Their worlds had become one. It felt like a family gathering.

During the retro, stories were told. Stories of deep learning. Stories of creative problem-solving. Stories of real friendship.

In six weeks?

Ward and I were in the room, listening to the team. We recognized that something powerful had happened, but we were not sure exactly what it was. It felt like the retro was just scratching the surface of a more profound experience.

At the reception after the retro, Ward suggested that the two of us go deeper into this experience. So we started asking the teachers and the managers if they would be willing to do follow-up interviews with us. They agreed.

Deeper Meaning

Ward and I needed to find the deeper meaning of that experience for the participants. So we started scheduling hour-long interviews.

Ward asked me to put together an interview guide. I decided to try another experiment. The week before we had been discussing deep learning from systems failures through a progressive exploration of the underlying assumptions used for making decisions. By identifying these incorrect assumptions, systems can become more robust.

I thought that it might be interesting to use this technique to more deeply understand the meaning of experiences. So we developed a **3x3 Reflection**[1].

What we found was that many of the partners had experienced the same life-giving magic that I had experienced in my calls with Jami.

The teachers found it very validating to have professionals outside of education help them experiment with new practices. The managers, too, were deeply affected by the powerful impact of their small commitment on classroom experiences – potentially touching hundreds of students.

Most importantly, the walls separating their two worlds had dissolved. They recognized that they had far more in common than not, even though their professional lives were so different. They had found a shared purpose and shared meaning.

The Next Iteration

The next fall the partners were asked if they wanted to do another round to help us architect a replicable process. All of them agreed. This time we defined a nine-week sprint. We did another liftoff and off they went.

This second sprint ran smoothly but had a different energy. The partners were now like old friends. While we didn't have the freshness, there was much more comfort. Some of the partners pushed new learning, but by now some of the teachers were moving forward on their own with a lot more comfort. The calls were not as critical for their creative explorations.

---

1 Page **223** - a **3x3 Reflection** is a powerful tool to identify insights and the meaning behind those insights. By diving deeper into the deeper meaning, the insights are better understood

When we came back for the second retro, it was now clear that we were ready for the next challenge: expanding to other schools.

Making Matter

When Jami and I embarked on this journey together, it was only an idea, a concept, a thought. An **Audacious Aspiration**[1]. Little else.

It was not real – just a fiction, an illusion. But in four short years, that illusion would manifest, become reality, become *matter*.

The evidence was clear. First it was the experience of the Dayton team that went to MIT as part of the Lemelson-MIT Inventeam challenge.

Dayton was chosen, from hundreds of schools from around the country, to be one of fifteen participants in a design challenge sponsored by Lemelson-MIT. Their entire team of a dozen or so students was flown to Boston to present their project – an automated chicken coop – to judges and professors from MIT.

The team was classic Dayton. Just normal kids that represented the entire student body. Girls, boys, techie kids, farm kids, Latinx kids. Just kids.

On the surface, they were totally outclassed at the event. Most of the other schools were wealthy private or charter schools that had sent their best and brightest students. The most privileged.

But the Dayton kids stole the show. Everyone wanted to hear their story, intrigued by the ingenuity of their chicken coop. Months later the program leaders were still talking about them.

Then the graduation rates were announced. In four years, Dayton had improved their graduation rate by fourteen percentage points, while the state, in that same period, had only improved by five. At 97%, Dayton now had one of the highest graduation rates in the state.

---

1 Page **120** - An **Audacious Aspiration** can be thought of as a Vega star – a future north star. Not Polaris, the North Star of today, but Vega, that star which will, in the future, become our North Star. That is the North Star that the courageous use to lead others.

But one afternoon, when I observed what Jenni was doing in her Genius Hour class, I knew that this transformation was real – and powerful.

State of Ri

Japanese martial arts has the concept of **Shu Ha Ri**[1].

These are three stages of proficiency. In the *shu* stage, one is just learning the mechanics of the form. In the *ha* stage, the form becomes natural and intuitive. In the *ri* stage, the practitioner goes beyond the form as their own creative expression.

Underpinning this progression is the increased flow of life energy through the practitioner, known by some as *qi* or *prana*. The source of this life energy is a mystery. But as this energy enters the world, it manifests through our actions. It becomes real. It becomes matter.

As I sat and listened to Jenni that afternoon, I realized that she was not only a master teacher but had become a master agilist. She was developing new practices in her classroom that I had not seen elsewhere, practices that were unleashing both her creative genius and her students'. But not only in this classroom – throughout the school.

Practices that are likely to have an impact well beyond Dayton.

She had reached a state of *ri*. It was now my turn to learn from her. She, with a team of her colleagues, had developed, what became known as **The Dayton Practice**[2].

The Reckoning

All experiments end; they have to. That is their nature, that is their fate. But none of us thought that it would end in this way.

It started one morning when Jami was asked to come to a meeting with her new superintendent. He presented her with a three-page document itemizing all of her administrative infractions. Although all of them were minor, he felt they were violations of policies that he had been putting in place.

1 Page **202** - The metaphor of **Shu Ha Ri** can be applied in many areas, helping us to better understand the deep transformation potential of subtle practices when undertaken with clear intention.

2 Page **210** - **The Dayton Practice** is a learning practice that is based on agile mindsets. It challenges students to become empowered meaning makers and creative problem solvers.

As a result of these infractions, he would tell the school board the following night that he would not extend her contract when it ended the following year.

This decision put Jami in a very difficult position. After consulting her lawyer, she felt that the only way to protect her career was to sign a separation agreement, resigning her position as principal, before the school board met. So she did.

The board accepted her resignation with little discussion. The school and the community, however, were outraged.

The many attempts to engage board members in the transformation that was going on in the Junior High and High Schools had been unsuccessful. The board, which pulled largely from influential families in the community, did not understand what was going on in the building. They had had a good school experience when they were young and saw that there was little reason to change.

Jami's license to innovate had been granted to her by the previous superintendent. She had trusted Jami's expertise as an educator and while she did not fully understand the full nature of the experiment, she believed that Jami and the teachers would always do right by the students.

But then, two years into the experiment, she retired. Jami was encouraged to apply for her position, but the board rejected her, deciding instead to hire someone who knew the rule book, would play by it, and make others play by it.

In public education, the rule book exists, and it is extensive. It is a powerful tool to control the behavior of others.

After two years of working with Jami, the new superintendent decided he had had enough. She was not the type of leader he wanted, and he told her that.

The school and the community, however, had a very different opinion. When her resignation was announced, the students staged a walkout and went over to the administration offices and held a demonstration. The school board meetings became packed as teachers, students, and parents berated the board. They knew whom they wanted as their leader and the school they wanted. And it was not one that rolled back the clock.

What was seen could not be unseen.

They had found their truth, their voice, their path. And they were not to be denied.

In the midst of this struggle that was ripping the community apart, I received an email from Debbie. She was still on the school board, the sole member who understood what Jami was doing, and the only one who voted against her resignation.

She simply assured me: "Just don't forget that Truth always wins."

That next May, when the majority of the school board was up for re-election, voters summarily removed the old guard and replaced them with ardent supporters of Dayton's new path – education reimagined.

But that was only the beginning, a new beginning that is still unfolding.

In Jami's last school board meeting as principal, she finally spoke her truth. Until then, she had been quietly observing the furious winds flying around her.

Her words were powerful. They were then amplified by community members, teachers and students. There was a larger, shared truth that was being spoken, that could not be denied.

The next day the chair of the school board resigned. Two weeks later, the remaining board members negotiated with the superintendent to terminate his contract.

That day Dayton's school district began the process of rebuilding. Rebuilding trust, based on a new, shared truth.

They say that this work of cultural transformation is not for the faint of heart. That is a gross understatement.

Jami knew that at some point she was going to have to leave Dayton, to carry this story to educators in other school districts. She just didn't realize that this was going to be her path. But she walked through this journey with courage, empowered by what she knew deep in her heart to be an undeniable truth, one that was unleashing the creative genius in each and every student.

At the graduation a week before that final board meeting, as she hugged each of the graduates, she knew that not only had every student in that class graduated – yes, 100% – they had each been empowered as makers and creators of their own future.

Making Meaning

Reflection

A critical element of agile learning is reflection. Each learning cycle is defined by three steps: define, do, and decipher. At the end of a sprint, we typically call the deciphering step a retrospective.

But by whatever name you use, this last step is a critical time of discernment. It is that time when the experience sits within us. It sits there waiting. Waiting to be understood. Waiting to provide insight. To provide some wisdom that helps illuminate our path forward as we move into our next learning cycle.

So it is with this story.

For in this discernment one deciphers the meaning of the journey. Something that can be shared. Wisdom that can help guide others. An ultimate boon, perhaps.

Let's start our reflection with a single word, the beginning of creating meaning to share with others. The definition of a word matters. And so let's begin with the meaning of 'matter'.

Matter

It is a noun and a verb. As a noun, it means something that is physical. That which is not mind. That which is not spirit.

Something we can touch. Something that is real. That which makes up the material world. Our world. Baryonic matter.

And then there is its definition as a verb: something that it is important. Something that has significance.

When Jami and I embarked on this journey, there was nothing but an aspiration, an intention, a dream held in the realm of ideas. We both believed, in our hearts, that we could reimagine education in her school. But, at the outset, there was nothing real. Just the belief that this aspiration was critically important, not only for our students, but for our country and beyond.

What then, were those elements that were important in this journey, that enabled it to become real, something that could be seen and felt by others – such that it became, in a sense, matter.

Purpose Matters

In this experiment, certain terms that we began to use seemed to resonate with the vibrations of a deeper, more universal truth. One of these terms was *purpose-driven learning*.

Not just project-based, but something more.

Project-based learning is a common term associated with many innovative learning institutions. But it didn't feel strong enough to describe what Jami and I were seeing at Dayton when students were becoming truly engaged as co-learners with their teachers – when they knew the purpose of their learning and that purpose was personally important to them.

But what is the nature of purpose? How might we unleash its potential?

Purpose has three core elements: the center point, the north star, and the journey to try to connect the two that challenges us to become meaning makers.

It's critical to understand the center point, which is often overlooked. Each of us has a unique center point. This center point is based on our values and has been shaped by our past experiences. It is from here that we understand the world and how we can interact with it. It defines our personal truth.

As I watched teachers at Dayton work with students, I began to see them engaging with their students differently. They were becoming more present with their students, recognizing that each student had their own unique story to tell, and that each story was vitally important.

Even if it was only for a few minutes at a time, in those moments, teachers and students locked eyes. There was deep empathetic listening. There was validation. A validation of a student's truth.

It was powerful to watch. And profoundly empowering for the students. For in that moment, they felt that there was someone who truly believed in them and in their potential.

This center point is where authentic learning begins. And the Dayton teachers began to appreciate that it was essential to understand that each student launches from a unique point: from their truth.

Then there was the north star – the important aspiration to focus their learning.

By offering different aspirations and also allowing students to develop their own, Dayton teachers were able to launch journeys that ignited curiosity that guided the learning process.

Most students would work in teams, allowing personal learning journeys to be interwoven with classmates who had similar interests.

And then there was the journey itself.

Structuring these learning journeys was critical for students to be successful. It was here that Dayton teachers were able to leverage agile practices borrowed from industry.

Each journey existed within a clearly defined period of time. These journeys were called sprints and the length of a sprint was its time-box, which could be a single class period or two to three weeks depending on the learning aspiration. Each sprint's time-box had to be short enough to create a sense of urgency that would motivate immediate action. The tighter the time-box, the better.

Each sprint would end with a 'deliverable' from their learning journey that could be shared with the rest of the class. This deliverable created a sense of accountability, for both the team and each of its members.

At first this learning approach felt foreign for both the teachers and the students. But as the students became more empowered, what they were delivering at the end of each sprint went far beyond what they, or their teacher, could have imagined.

And they became more confident and courageous as they entered into their next learning cycle.

Everyone could see and feel this new reality.

Purpose made real, made matter.

Genius Matters

Another term we used when describing this experiment also resonated with us. It expressed a deeply-rooted intention we owned in our hearts and ardently proclaimed to others. One that felt radical and liberating. It was *unleashing creative genius*.

Unleashing

The old teaching paradigm was defined by control. Controlling behavior, controlling performance, controlling process. A system that used fear, the fear of rejection, as its primary cudgel.

Eliminate control and you have chaos. Or so we have been told.

The first and foremost skill that teachers are taught is classroom management.

Learning in this new paradigm is messy, really messy, but it isn't chaotic. The difference is that chaos has no focus, whereas, in agile learning, students have a clear focus, defined by purpose.

Get purpose right and teachers can begin to let go of the reigns of control. They can begin to unleash the potential of their students. They can become co-learners in a dynamic learning community.

Creative

We are all creative beings. What holds us back is a fear of being judged, of being shamed.

As students find their creative confidence, they begin to hold themselves differently. This shift is subtle, yet powerful. It is unmistakable.

They also begin to appreciate that there is no single form of creativity. In fact, creativity has an infinite number of dimensions. They can discover those dimensions that channel their strengths and how their creativity can complement the creativity of others.

Genius

We all have genius. Every person. Every teacher. Every student. It is time we reclaimed it.

Genius is the manifestation of our innate spirit. It is the mystery of life that flows through us. It is our unique experience. It is our gift to others, and, ultimately, our legacy.

For far too long the word "genius" has been used against us. By those who sought to use a questionable measurement of intelligence to claim creative and social authority.

At Dayton the genius of every student began to be recognized, even in those who were struggling to show up each day. For all students were seen as worthy, filled with potential brilliance, even if it was not yet recognized by themselves and others.

The audacity of this conviction was felt throughout the school. It unshackled the chains of shame. Brilliance began to break forth. Everywhere.

Jami modeled this conviction and others followed. Within a short period of time it defined a new reality.

Genius made real, made matter.

Joy Matters

Call it the five-second rule.

That is how long it takes for an experienced educator to walk into a classroom and to know if there is authentic learning happening.

They don't need to see the curriculum. They don't need to see the test scores. They know it by the eyes. Of the students. Of the teacher.

The sparkle. That mysterious thing called joy.

Real learning is joyful. And it's obvious. And it can't be faked. Hard learning. Deep learning. Real learning.

As educators came to visit Dayton, they immediately knew that what was happening there was truly a profound transformation of a learning culture.

They walked into the building and could immediately feel the joy.

Brené Brown talks about how joy is our most vulnerable emotion. And she is right.

In joy, we are in our most egoless, unprotected state. It seems to flow through us. We feel it, we are vitalized by it. But we really don't understand it. Yet it is real.

Once Jami recognized the importance of joy, that became what she looked for and judged success by. When she walked into a classroom, did she see it? If not, she would ask, why not?

By courageously naming and claiming joy, she empowered her staff and the students to do the same.

One evening, beers in hand, Jami and I were reflecting on this journey with a group of educators. At the table with us was Ward, one of the original signers of the Agile Manifesto.

We were exploring parallels between the experiences in Dayton with the experiences that he and Kent Beck had when they were working together back in the mid-nineties. Experiences that led to the development of Extreme Programming (XP) and, ultimately, to the launch of the Agile movement.

What was that shared experience that bound together different worlds and different times? And then Jami named it: **Joyful Sandboxes**[1]. I looked over at Ward and his eyes beamed.

Yes, that was what he was experiencing with Kent as they experimented programming together using Smalltalk, Alan Kay's radically new software language that was designed to usher in a new way of thinking and creating with computers. That experience which became the catalyst for a profound transformation in the software industry and underpins our entire creative economy.

And that was what was happening in the classrooms at Dayton.

Joy made real, made matter.

Beyond Matter

We live in a world of matter. A material world. Our senses and our consciousness are defined by it. But we now know that matter is a mere fleck in the vast tapestry of the universe. The rest is a mystery.

Cosmologists estimate that matter makes up less than 5% of the universe. And that galaxies, which includes our planet, constitute only 10% of matter – a mere half percent of the universe.

The vast majority of the universe is dark energy, dark matter, or perhaps, even

1 Page **165** - When joy flows in the learning process there is a experience that feels playful and magical, one we call **Joyful Sandboxes**.

something we might call dark fluid. Non-matter. Non-being. A mystery they call zero-point energy that, some physicists believe, is even beyond the realm of time.

We don't have to understand joy; we may never. Perhaps that energetic flow we feel is part of this mystery of the universe. A mystery that has been named by multiple cultures over thousands of years. Some call it spirit.

But if we are to truly empower ourselves and others, perhaps we must strive to become whole once again, in body, mind, *and* spirit. And to claim joy at the core of our human experience. As our birthright.

Jami knew this. And it gave her the courage to walk into the unknown.

Truth

As I said, this has been a deeply personal journey for me. I am really not sure why I was called to embark on it, but I knew that I had to. There was a truth I needed to discover. A truth for me. A truth, perhaps, for others.

It was a truth that would give me the courage to walk through my fears into joy, a joy that would become my new truth which would guide me inextricably back into the journey. A joy that could not be denied – a truth that I could not deny.

This was a journey that I hoped might inspire others to find their truth. To give them the courage to walk into their fears so that they, too, might find joy. A joy that had the power to transform. The joy that became their truth.

A truth which I found to be expressed in a simple, elegant gesture of Zen – what is called the *ensō*. A circle, a practice. A way of being. Painted with a brush, it forms a circle. A graceful circle that is imperfect and incomplete.

To understand that circle is to understand Zen, arguably one of the most elegant expressions of Buddhism. An expression that began with a flower.

For the root of Zen goes back to a sermon that Buddha gave. It is known as the Flower Sermon. The story goes that one day Buddha sat with his disciples and they waited for his sermon, his dharma talk. They sat and waited. And Buddha just sat there, saying nothing. In his hand, he held a flower, a lotus flower. Perhaps, some thought, he was ill, unable to speak.

And they waited.

And waited.

And then it happened. One of his disciples understood and smiled. Understood that the beauty of a single lotus flower held the entirety of his teaching. That disciple was called Mahākāśyapa and it was from his lineage that Mahayana Buddhism was born. That lineage that was to be taken to China by Bodhidharma. There, the wisdom of Buddha was woven with that of Laozi to form what was to become Zen Buddhism.

This wisdom was expressed through the simple gesture of the *ensō*, a gesture that tells the story of a path, a learning cycle, where truth gives us the courage to walk into fear to find the joy. The joy that becomes the new truth to inspire the next adventure.

The *ensō* is also a hole through which something mysteriously flows from a place beyond being – the breath of life the Greeks called *psyche*, Jewish mystics referred to as the *sefirot,* and early Christian mystics called the *pneuma*.

My journey had begun in that library of Franklin High School. When that switch had gone off, something shifted in me. As I spoke at that site council, I felt that I was giving voice to a truth that was deep and real, as if it was flowing through me. It felt like a sacred wind.

What was that spirit?

It unsettled me. But it also empowered me. I could not deny it. It gave me the courage to walk into the unknown, into my fears. I felt I didn't have a choice.

Over and over again, this journey has challenged me to walk into my fears. But each time, something so profound, so real, so joyful has been revealed, something that once seen could not be unseen. It became my truth that compelled me to venture out again.

And then Jami began to walk with me. She, too, was being empowered by her truth to courageously walk through her fears into the unknown. She was finding joy that could not be denied, joy that allowed her to find her voice, to illuminate her path.

And then I watched as her courage was inspiring teachers and students in her school. It was becoming infectious. It was becoming powerful. It was becoming a movement.

This journey has been challenging – at times extremely challenging. But to see teachers, students and the community find their truth, their voice and their path has been a profound experience – making trivial any discomfort.

A path even found by my daughter, who went on to graduate with a degree in electrical engineering and is now in the process of launching her first company.

The truth.

The truth of our spirit, our unique human spirit. This mystery that is beyond our comprehension. But a truth that cannot be denied – a spirit that flows through us, that gives us life, that gives our life meaning.

That is my truth. But it is also a universal truth, a truth that makes each of us both whole and part of something much bigger than us. A truth formed by love that unleashes our creative genius. A truth that transforms.

A truth that gives us the courage to continually walk through our fears into joy.

The Garden

Into the Garden

Welcome to *The Garden.*

The Story introduced many concepts. Each has been given a name, a label. These ideas can be further explored here in *The Garden.*

Ideas never sit in isolation. Instead they are connected to, and informed by, other related ideas. That is how we create meaning.

The Garden, then, is a place to wander among these ideas that have been introduced. You will find, at the end of most concepts, a diagram of connections to other concepts.

I recommend that when you finish reading about a concept, pause.

Take a moment and explore the diagram. You will find there a guiding map, an illustration of how that concept is a part of a larger pattern of meaning that might unfold for you, one flowing from your **Curiosity**[1].

There are three levels in these diagrams: the current concept, the linked concepts, and the concepts that are then linked to them.

These ideas become new patterns of thought, each a **Meaning Matrix**[2].

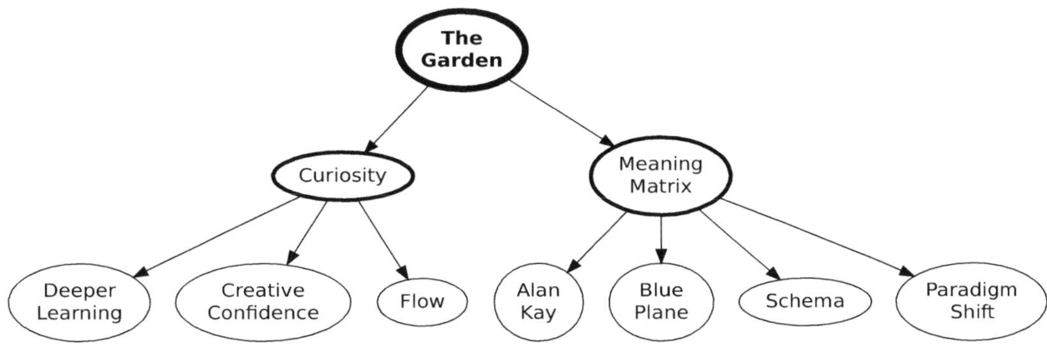

1 Page **136** - **Curiosity**

2 Page **181** - **Meaning Matrix**

Garden Index

Agile

We use 'agile' as an umbrella term to mean at least four different concepts that all emerged together and continue to influence how we work and learn.

The **Agile Experience**[1] where commonly-faced problems find fresh solutions that are hard to understand but easy to experience.

The **Agile Mindset**[2] where one learns to look for similarly fresh solutions in diverse activities.

The **Agile Practices**[3] where specific solutions are assembled into a framework supported by available training and coaching.

The **Agile Paradigm**[4] where recognizably similar solutions are used in distinctly different activities.

Agile has a complex history going back several decades. Even at its founding, many of Agile's solutions were well known but not yet widely applied together. See the **Agile Story**[5].

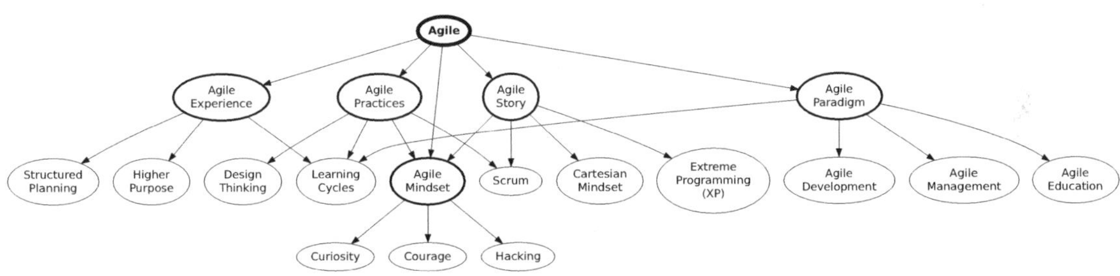

1 Page **108** - **Agile Experience**

2 Page **112** - **Agile Mindset**

3 Page **115** - **Agile Practices**

4 Page **113** - **Agile Paradigm**

5 Page **117** - **Agile Story**

Agile Development

Back in 2001, seventeen software developers came together to share their stories of reimagining how software could be developed.

In that gathering, they found a common understanding and crafted a manifesto to express it.

They adopted the term 'agile' for their movement and wrote the Manifesto for Agile Software Development:

> *We are uncovering better ways of developing software*
> *by doing it and helping others do it.*
>
> *Through this work we have come to value:*
>
> ***Individuals and interactions*** *over processes and tools*
> ***Working software*** *over comprehensive documentation*
> ***Customer collaboration*** *over contract negotiation*
> ***Responding to change*** *over following a plan*

Along with the Manifesto, 12 Principles were defined. The last two principles were arguably the most radical and guided the **Agile Story**[1]:

> *The best architectures, requirements, and designs*
> *emerge from self-organizing teams.*
>
> *At regular intervals, the team reflects on how*
> *to become more effective, then tunes and adjusts*
> *its behavior accordingly.*

1 Page **117** - **Agile Story**

These principles fundamentally challenged the paradigm of scientific management known as **Taylorism**[1] that underpinned the Industrial Age.

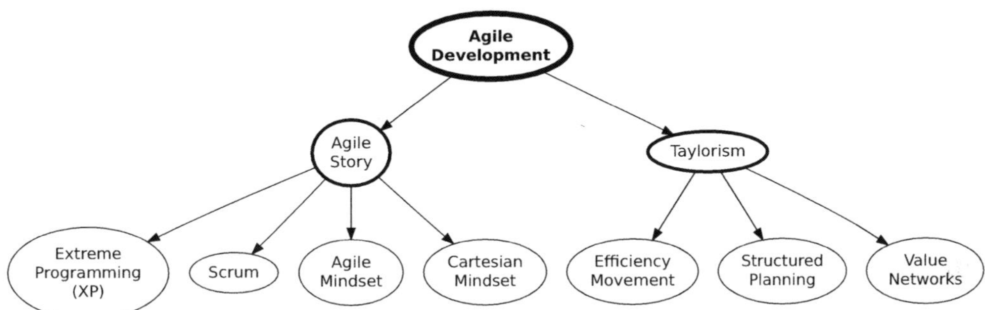

1 Page **208** - **Taylorism**

Agile Education

We are entering into, what many are now calling, the Age of Agile, defined by a new mindset that is profoundly transforming software development and business management. And now, potentially, education.

The current model of education in most schools today was defined over a hundred years ago – an industrial model designed to prepare workers for industrial jobs.

This design of the education experience was based on the concept of production efficiency derived from the principles of scientific management known as **Taylorism**[1]. These principals shaped the thinking of leaders of the second Industrial Revolution in the late 19th Century and early 20th Century.

A key model of the industrial economy was the production line. So we made our schools look like production lines.

The industrial economy is now quickly being replaced by a new economy, a creative economy, fueled by digital technologies.

In this creative economy, competitive advantage is no longer primarily defined by production efficiency but by the creation of new products and solutions. Competitive advantage is now based on the rate of innovation.

We need to prepare our students to be empowered makers and creators in this new economy. We need creative problem solvers that are able to integrate **Design Thinking**[2], **Process Thinking**[3] and **Systems Thinking**[4].

To prepare our students, we must reimagine education in a way that reflects the new culture of our companies – a culture being shaped by the principles and experiences of Agile.

1 Page **208** - **Taylorism**

2 Page **139** - **Design Thinking**

3 Page **191** - **Process Thinking**

4 Page **207** - **Systems Thinking**

We are adopting best practices from **Agile Development**[1] and **Agile Management**[2] to develop what we are calling Agile Education. It is meant to be applied as a philosophy and practice for the education community.

Agile Education is not a single practice; it is an integrated paradigm of how we learn.

By embracing common experiences, mindsets and vocabulary we are tearing down the walls between education, communities and industry, allowing us to reimagine radically the nature of learning in our society.

Agile Education combines this industry perspective with best practices emerging from the education community for Proficiency Grading, Project-Based Learning, and Deeper Learning.

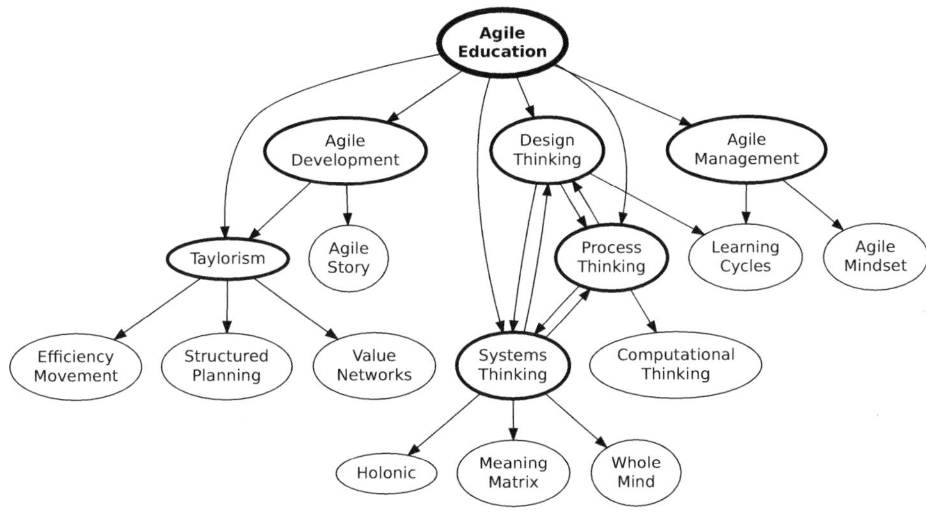

1 Page **104** - **Agile Development**

2 Page **111** - **Agile Management**

Agile Experience

The word "agile" is difficult to understand without the experience of it.

> *ag·ile*
> able to move quickly and easily.

At its core, Agile is an experience of fast, iterative learning with a **Higher Purpose**[1] that unleashes new creative potential.

By breaking complex problems into small pieces and then working with others, passionately focusing on each piece, solutions can be created much faster than traditional process models that utilize **Structured Planning**[2].
164
When a group of software developers came together in 2001 to find a common ground and shared language that embraced new methods of software development, they published the Manifesto for Agile Software Development.

With that manifesto, agile now had a new meaning – one that was intended to capture not just the form but, far more importantly, the process, practices and, ultimately, the mindset of creating in a radical new way.

An experience of self-managing teams working together to create with clear and meaningful purpose; co-creating with end users in iterative **Learning Cycles**[3].

---

1 Page **154** - **Higher Purpose**

2 Page **206** - **Structured Planning**

3 Page **174** - **Learning Cycles**

It is very hard, if not impossible, to understand this agile experience without personally experiencing it. But once you have had this experience which accelerates dramatically the learning process, you are never the same.

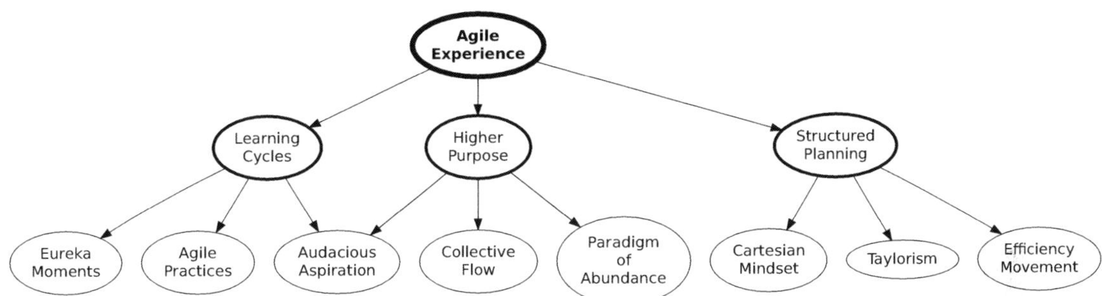

Agile Learning

Agile Learning is the shared experience found in the **Agile Paradigm**[1].

At the core of Agile Learning is the concept of **Learning Cycles**[2].

This experience of accelerated learning creates **Joyful Sandboxes**[3] as teams of committed people focus together to solve meaningful problems.

As we seek to reimage education, we are guided by an **Agile Learning Manifesto**[4].

Once people have felt the exhilaration of this type of learning experience, it is very difficult, if not impossible, to return to the old way of learning and creating.

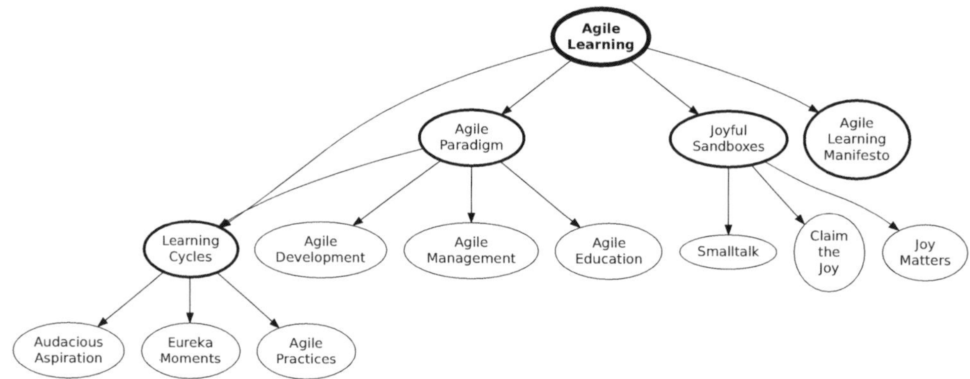

1 Page **113** - **Agile Paradigm**

2 Page **174** - **Learning Cycles**

3 Page **165** - **Joyful Sandboxes**

4 Page **v** - **Agile Learning Manifesto**

Agile Management

Agile management, in contrast to the traditional "command and control" model of the Industrial Age, allows companies to innovate faster, helping them be more competitive in increasingly competitive markets.

The concept of agile management entered the mainstream in a 2016 article in the Harvard Business Review, "Embracing Agile". Over 75% of US companies are now using agile practices – including companies such as IBM, Microsoft, AT&T, and 3M.

Steve Denning has written extensively on this topic. He builds his framework for Agile Management around three "laws":

- Law of the Small Team
- Law of the Customer
- Law of the Network

The key to Agile Management is the **Agile Mindset**[1], one that utilizes rapid **Learning Cycles**[2] to empower a creative culture.

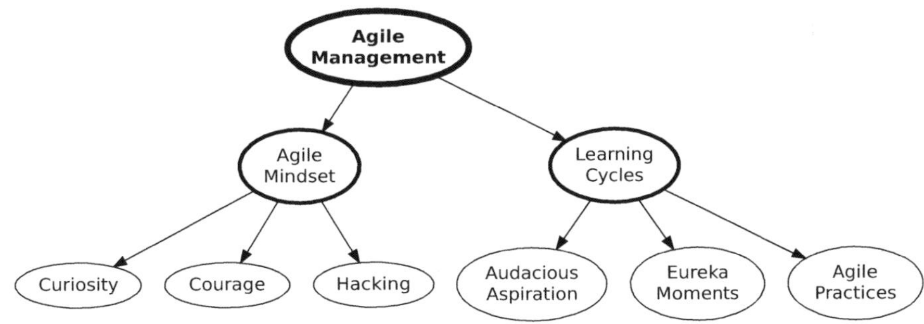

1 Page **112** - **Agile Mindset**

2 Page **174** - **Learning Cycles**

Agile Mindset

Once someone has had the experience of Agile, they cannot unsee it, cannot unfeel it.

The Agile mindset is defined by **Curiosity**[1]. It is a path of discovery that is led by questions which start with "What if...?"

It is a mindset that is defined by **Courage**[2] to walk into the unknown. To know that to fail is not to be shamed and rejected, but an opportunity to understand a problem more deeply.

It is a mindset that embraces the experience of **Hacking**[3] in a process of iterative learning.

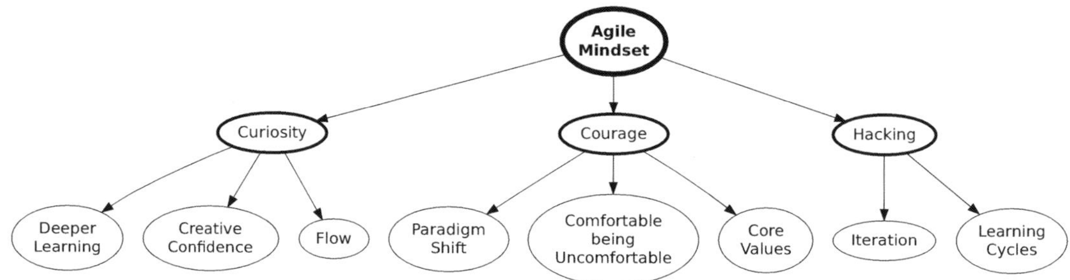

1 Page **136** - **Curiosity**

2 Page **131** - **Courage**

3 Page **152** - **Hacking**

Agile Paradigm

The Agile Paradigm is where recognizably similar solutions are used in distinctly different activities.

When the **Agile Development**[1] movement was launched in 2001, it set out to transform the process of developing software. It was so effective that managers in other parts of organizations began to adopt it.

Agile Management[2] is now transforming how companies are being managed in the new creative economy. This new management model, organic in nature, allows companies to innovate faster in order to compete in increasingly complex markets.

Our traditional model of education is based on the industrial economy's paradigm of the production line. A new paradigm is needed.

Agile Education[3] is now unleashing the potential of the human creative spirit to prepare the talent needed for this new economy.

All three of these agile paradigms utilize the potential of **Learning Cycles**[4].

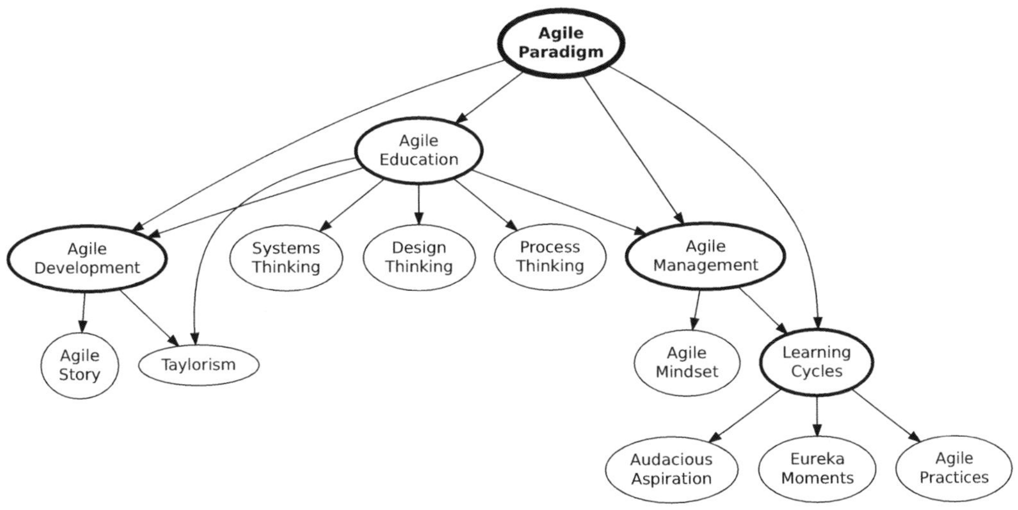

1 Page **104** - **Agile Development**

2 Page **111** - **Agile Management**

3 Page **106** - **Agile Education**

4 Page **174** - **Learning Cycles**

Agile Partnership Program

It started with a simple question: What might happen if we matched industry professionals that are managing agile teams in their companies with teachers who are exploring how to introduce new agile practices into their classrooms?

We asked industry professionals and educators to do nothing more than what Jami and I had been doing for the last five years of the Dayton Experiment. Make a commitment, each week, to simply talk. To listen. To share. To learn together.

Often we feel that those from industry live in such different worlds than those of educators. This distinction leads us to think that we can't understand each other and it creates seemingly impenetrable walls.

But we actually have far more in common than we may realize – we are all trying to create new dynamic learning environments.

In the spring of 2018 we launched our first six-week pilot which combined **Innovators**[1] and **Early Adopters**[2] from Dayton High School with agilists from New Relic.

They co-created **Agile Practices**[3] to experiment within the classrooms. This program is now expanding to include other schools.

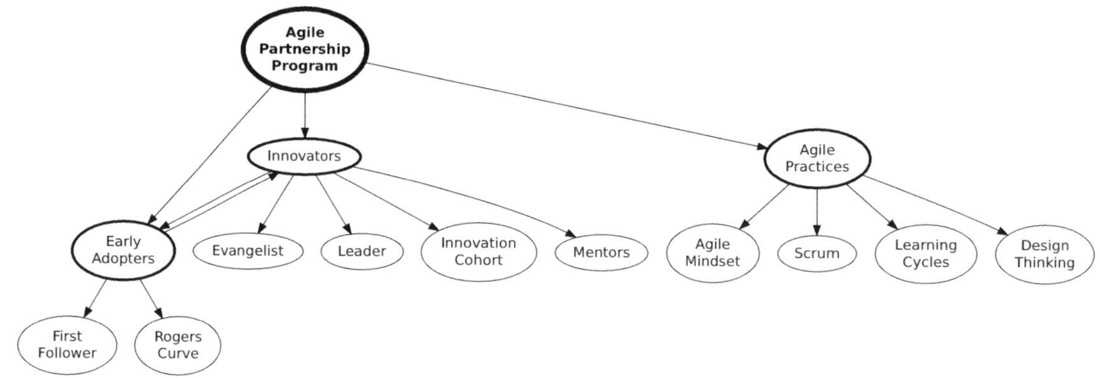

1 Page **162** - **Innovators**

2 Page **141** - **Early Adopters**

3 Page **115** - **Agile Practices**

Agile Practices

Agile Practices are specific solutions assembled into a framework supported by available training and coaching.

Once individuals began to adopt an **Agile Mindset**[1], they started developing practices to support it. These practices have been bundled into different sets of "frameworks".

There are many different frameworks that have been developed. One of the most common frameworks is called **Scrum**[2]. In this framework, **Learning Cycles**[3] are called sprints, the team solving the problem is called a "scrum", and the team leader is called a "scrum master". Sprints are generally 1-2 weeks long and they build toward a solution called an "epic".

Design Thinking[4] is another framework that utilizes learning cycles for fast product design.

But note that, in Agile, there is no single framework or set of practices that are universal – they often are adjusted by the nature of the team, its challenges, and the organization.

Agile can thus feel messy and difficult to explain. For this reason, it is critical to first understand the experience and the mindset.

1 Page **112** - **Agile Mindset**

2 Page **199** - **Scrum**

3 Page **174** - **Learning Cycles**

4 Page **139** - **Design Thinking**

For Agile to be effective, four critical ingredients must be present:

Purpose that is clear and meaningful
Trust that creates the safety for team members to risk failure
Experimentation that is always supported
Commitment to deliver new value quickly

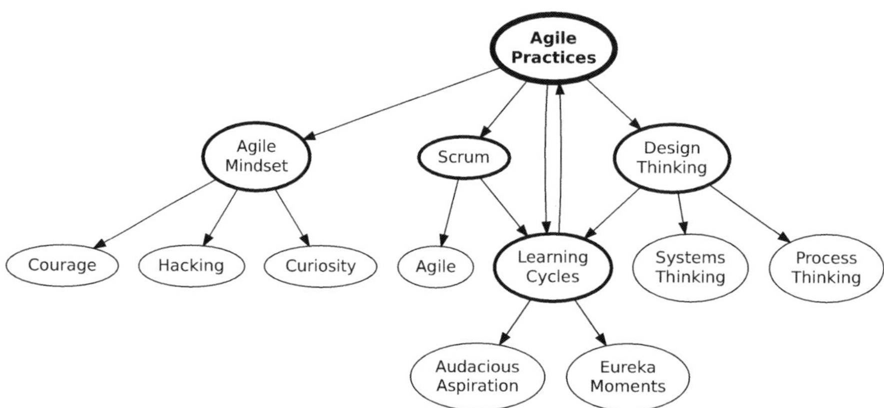

Agile Story

The Agile Movement was launched in 2001 when seventeen software developers came together to find common language and purpose for a radical new idea.

They called this movement Agile Software Development and published a manifesto to proclaim the values and principles of this movement.

These developers were challenging the traditional way software was developed, a process that was described as the Waterfall Model.

The Waterfall Model was based on the production process of the industrial economy. This process was called a 'value chain' where production was carefully designed with precisely defined sequential steps. Workers were trained by their managers to consistently follow these steps. This 'command and control' management model was designed to maximize efficiency.

But software developers faced a challenge: this Waterfall Model was not flexible enough to handle the complexity of software development, where needs and tools sets were dynamic and continually evolving. As a result, there was a palpable frustration that demanded bold action.

There were multiple experiments of alternative models. Two of the most significant were **Extreme Programming (XP)**[1] and **Scrum**[2].

1 Page **147** - **Extreme Programming (XP)**

2 Page **199** - **Scrum**

Together these developers began to shape a new **Agile Mindset**[1] that radically transformed how value is created and provided an alternative to the **Cartesian Mindset**[2] of the Industrial Age.

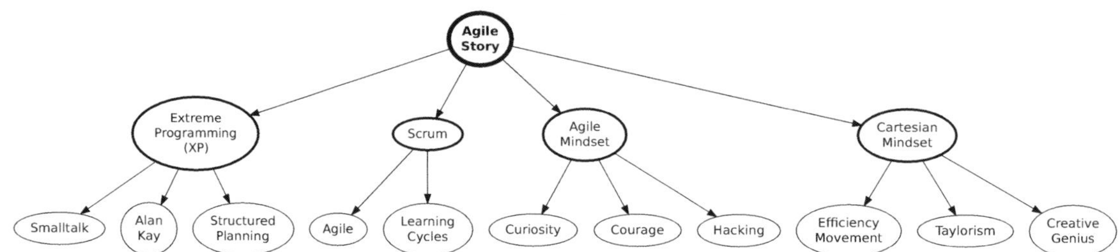

1 Page **112** - **Agile Mindset**

2 Page **124** - **Cartesian Mindset**

Alan Kay

Back in the 1970s Alan Kay helped reimagine what a computer could be. Building off the work of **Seymour Papert**[1], J. C. R. Licklider and others, he envisioned the possibility that computers could become something far more wonderful than sophisticated calculating machines.

They could become learning tools to empower our creative potential. If only we could imagine that potential on a **Blue Plane**[2].

To help unlock this potential, he created, with his team at PARC, a new software language called **Smalltalk**[3].

Using Smalltalk, his team began to learn. To create in new ways. Could the computer reimagine how we wrote? Could the computer help us reimagine how we drew? Could the computer help us reimagine how we made music?

The personal computer of today was defined by these early questions. A computer that, in each of our hands, could become a creative instrument, one that might help us unleash our genius.

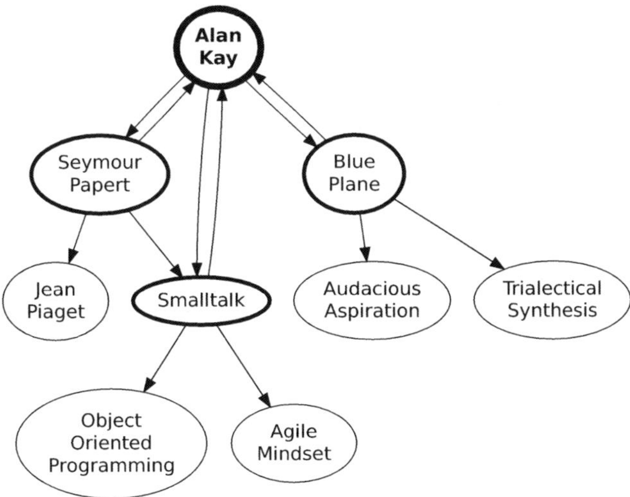

1 Page **200** - **Seymour Papert**

2 Page **122** - **Blue Plane**

3 Page **203** - **Smalltalk**

Audacious Aspiration

Change requires courage – innovation is not for the faint of heart. To be successful, one must become **Comfortable being Uncomfortable**[1].

To step out of our comfort zone, we have to have a compelling reason. We have to believe that there is something worth this risk, something bigger than us. Something that we are doing for others, that can become a legacy that we leave behind. Something that gives our life meaning.

The aspiration is a statement that creates a **Higher Purpose**[2]. It is something that is outrageous. That is important. That is worth the risk, knowing that if you fail, you will fail gloriously.

When Jami and I started working together, our audacious aspiration was to reimagine education and to help transform Oregon from having one of the worst-performing education systems in the country to a national model. We wanted to build a new learning culture that would unleash the creative genius of teachers and their students.

To fulfill this aspiration, we knew that we could not simply follow the path of others, but had to **Leapfrog**[3] with an entirely new learning model.

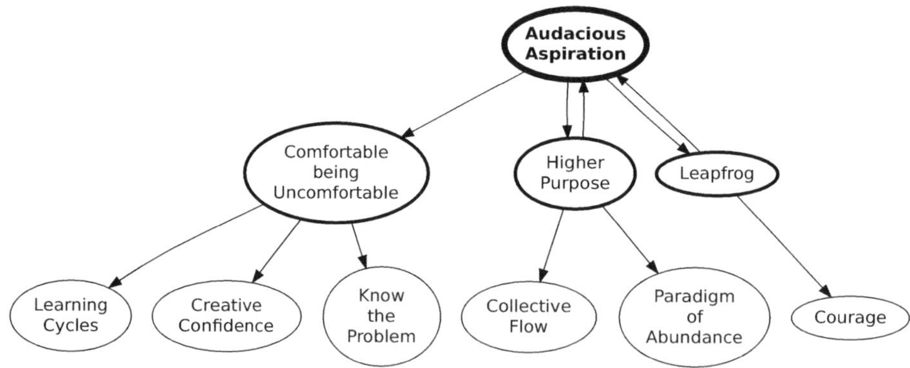

1 Page **128** - **Comfortable being Uncomfortable**

2 Page **154** - **Higher Purpose**

3 Page **170** - **Leapfrog**

Bias to Action

A bias to action is a critical first step in developing a new innovation mindset because it challenges us to step into the unknown with an aspiration, not a plan.

As planners, most of us were trained not to move forward unless we have our entire process mapped out, something called **Structured Planning**[1]. Once that plan has been defined, we execute against that plan, and judge our success based upon how well we followed that plan.

The problem is, when the challenge is very complex, we tend to get stuck. We can't act because we are not able to figure out how to develop a plan. So we don't move. We know change is needed, but we are left only with a vague hope that someone else, in the future, can create the change that is needed.

Few things are as complex as the education ecosystem. Even if we all know it needs to be reimagined, there is no one who can confidently develop a master plan for this transformation.

So it is up to individuals to try small experiments. We call this **Hacking**[2]. By just trying something, knowing it may fail, we can quickly learn, giving us insight that guides our next hack, creating fast, iterative **Learning Cycles**[3].

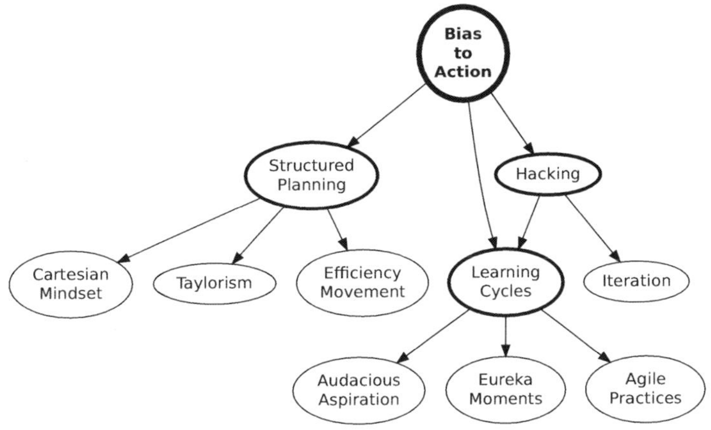

1 Page **206** - **Structured Planning**

2 Page **152** - **Hacking**

3 Page **174** - **Learning Cycles**

Blue Plane

Alan Kay[1] coined the term 'blue plane'. To explain it, he needed to tell a story.

A story of the Grand Canyon. A canyon that was slowly created by the Colorado River, etching deeper and deeper into the earth. Until it created a world unto its own.

If you have ever been to the bottom of the canyon you will understand. The journey down is a long one. As you descend, you notice that the world above drifts away. You enter another world, the world of the canyon. It is a profound experience.

There, at the bottom, is a new reality. You also notice that the light down there is different. It has a pink hue, as the sunlight reflects off of the canyon walls.

You make decisions from the context of this reality. What is possible or not on this horizontal pink plane.

Kay talks about our current reality being similar to this pink plane. The plane in which we make our decisions based on what we believe to be possible.

He then challenges us to look toward the sky above us, to that small, intense sliver of deep blue that is above the canyon walls. Where there are no limitations. Just the infinite blue sky.

If we reimagine the possible based on that perpendicular blue plane, our thinking shifts. We are no longer constricted by the possibilities of the present, but inspired by the potential of an imagined future. As we reimagine on that blue plane we can boldly aspire to an **Audacious Aspiration**[2].

With this audacity, Kay led the reimagining of what a computer is, turning it from a sophisticated calculating machine to a tool that could unleash our creativity and lay the foundation of our new economy.

For while at Xerox's research facility in Palo Alto (PARC) in the 1970s, Kay's team was not simply building a user interface for the Alto computer, but a radically new user experience for an imagined Dynabook, a simple hand-held graphical computer that a child might use in a distant future.

---

1 Page **119** - **Alan Kay**

2 Page **120** - **Audacious Aspiration**

An experience that was introduced to the general market by Apple in 1984 with the Macintosh computer, the device that changed the meaning of a personal computer.

Kay's concept of the blue plane that transforms our creative potential was inspired by *The Act of Creation*, a 1964 book by Arthur Koestler. In this book, Koestler developed a theory that creativity is derived from the tension created when two ways of thinking intersect.

He called these ways of understanding "matrices of thought", using the original Latin definition of a matrix as meaning "womb". Imagine these matrices of thought being on planes that intersect at right angles, orthogonal planes.

When these two matrices intersect they form a 'bisociation' that leads to the development of new frameworks of understanding.

An experience that inspires a **Trialectical Synthesis**[1] and new opportunities to create – in Kay's world, to create on the blue plane.

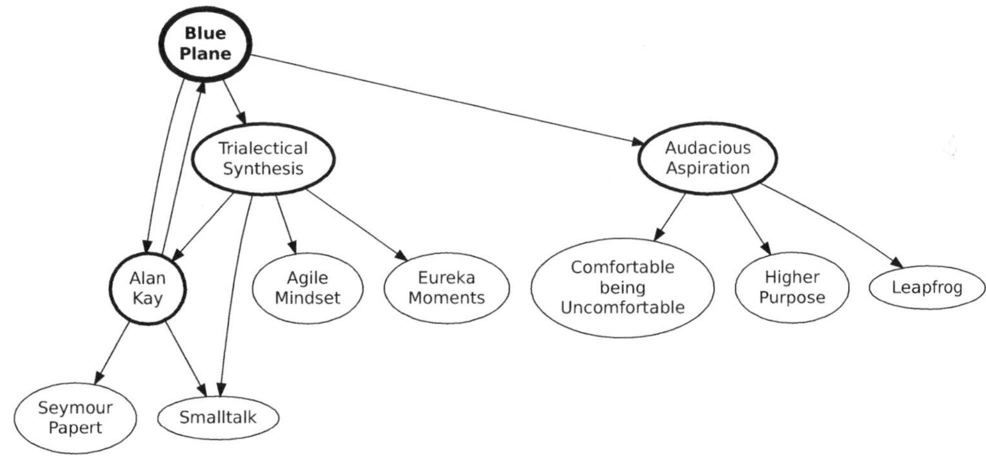

1 Page **214** - **Trialectical Synthesis**

Cartesian Mindset

Many feel that it was René Descartes, with his famous saying *Cogito, ergo sum,* that launched the Age of Reason, a worldview that continues to shape us today.

This statement, translating to "I think, therefore I am," lifted the intellect to a throne that sat above all others in the human experience. Above the body, the emotions, and the spirit. Descartes believed that, in a privileged transmission through the pineal gland in our brain, a singular and universal truth manifested through the intellect.

An intellect that allowed us to understand by taking things apart into smaller and smaller pieces. By understanding each of these pieces, we could not only understand the true nature of the whole, but we were empowered to reconfigure the parts into more efficient structures.

This mindset shaped how we created organizations and how we built nations. It lay the foundation for the **Efficiency Movement**[1] that created **Taylorism**[2].

This worldview was also used to justify the creation of new social and organizational systems that centralized power into hierarchical structures based on the premise of superior intellect. Structures of top-down authority that all too often used fear and shame to control human behavior, undermining the potential to unleash **Creative Genius**[3] throughout an organization.

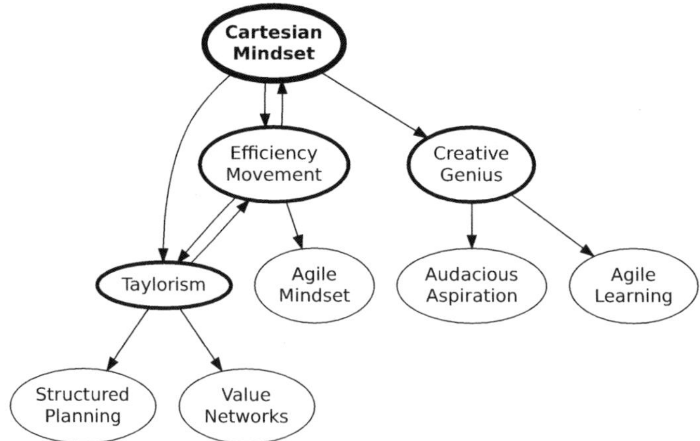

1 Page **142** - **Efficiency Movement**

2 Page **208** - **Taylorism**

3 Page **134** - **Creative Genius**

Claim the Joy

Being in the **Flow**[1] is a joyful experience. It's challenging but it vitalizes us, leaving us with more energy, not less.

Because it excites our **Curiosity**[2], it becomes almost addictive. Our heart begins to crave it.

We become fearless. Until doubt appears.

We are living in a world that doesn't fully embrace this new paradigm. Periodically, we have to come face to face with the fear that causes us to question our joy. Are we really deserving of it? Is fear more powerful than joy?

When we are confronted by our fear, we are forced to choose one or the other. If we claim the joy, we can continue to walk through the fear. With **Courage**[3].

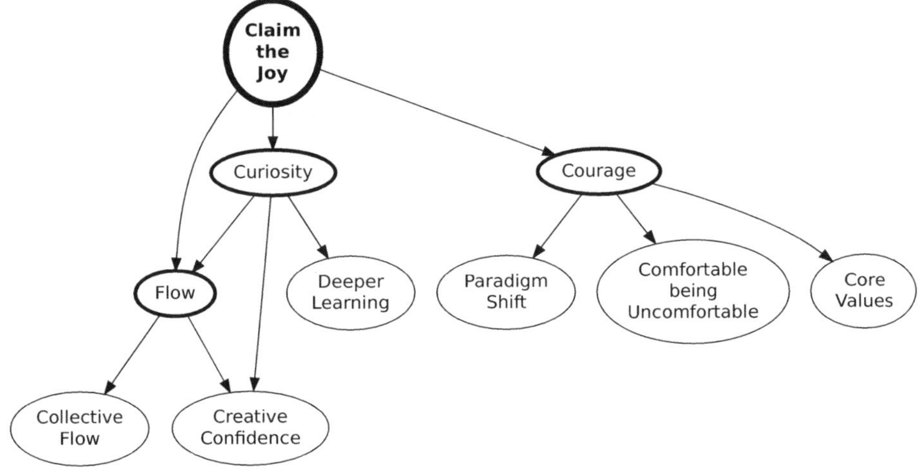

1 Page **150** - **Flow**

2 Page **136** - **Curiosity**

3 Page **131** - **Courage**

Collaboration

A key element of the **Agile Mindset**[1] is a broader understanding of the mind itself – one that is not limited to a single individual. That is, the sense of a larger, shared mind that happens when multiple people creatively collaborate.

This collaborative experience integrates multiple perspectives and skillsets to create new solutions that, quite frankly, feel magical at times.

These three elements - **Hacking**[2], **Iteration**[3], and Collaboration - create rapid **Learning Cycles**[4].

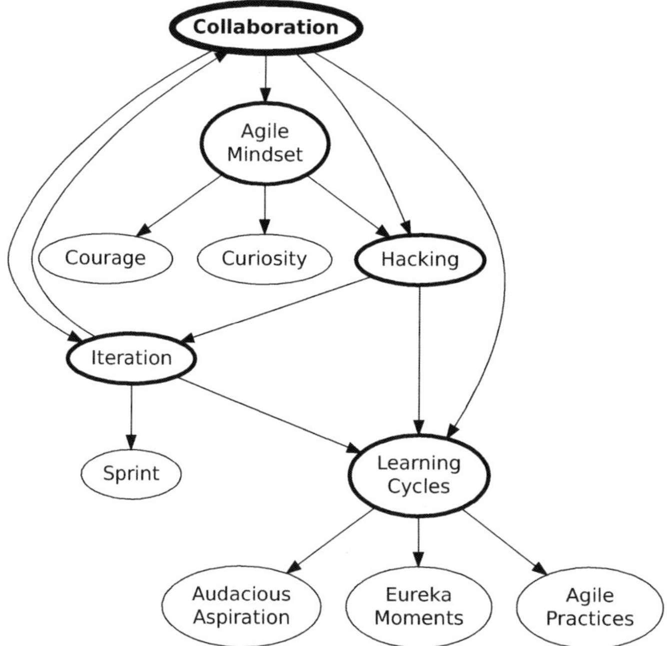

1 Page **112** - **Agile Mindset**

2 Page **152** - **Hacking**

3 Page **163** - **Iteration**

4 Page **174** - **Learning Cycles**

Collective Flow

As an individual, **Flow**[1] happens in the learning process when the rate of creativity is exponentially accelerated.

When teams work together, there are moments of shared creativity where solutions appear almost magically woven together by their shared intuitions.

The most powerful part of these interactions is often a rapid-fire ideation where team members ask "What if...?" questions that help define the next phase of their work.

The power of **Agile**[2] is that it helps individuals and teams achieve a flow state that exponentially increases the rate of learning. We have seen the impact in industry professionals and students.

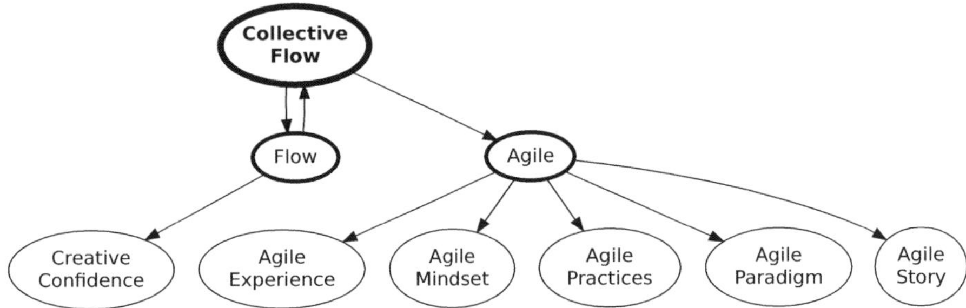

1 Page **150** - **Flow**

2 Page **103** - **Agile**

Comfortable being Uncomfortable

As someone embarks on a true learning journey, consider this rule number one: One must become comfortable being uncomfortable.

You have to step boldly into the unknown, to experiment, to fail. Then reflect, learn, and step boldly again, back into the unknown.

We call these **Learning Cycles**[1]. The faster one can go through these cycles, the faster one learns. The faster one learns, the faster one innovates. Our rate of learning is critical for success and for building **Creative Confidence**[2].

Walking into the unknown makes failure not only possible, but likely. We have been taught by our society, however, to avoid failure, for in failure we are emotionally vulnerable. We risk shame. We fear rejection.

It is important, then, to do this journey not alone but with others we trust. We need to trust them with our vulnerabilities, knowing that when we fail, they will not judge us. That they will help pick us up so that we can learn, empowering us to once again plunge back into the next learning cycle, one where we **Know the Problem**[3] better.

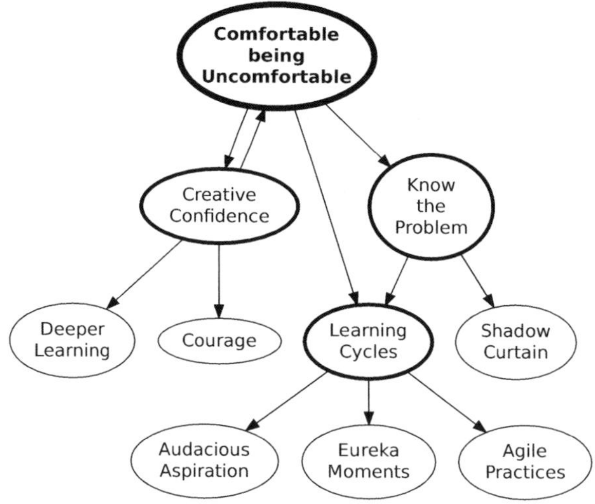

1 Page **174** - **Learning Cycles**

2 Page **133** - **Creative Confidence**

3 Page **168** - **Know the Problem**

Computational Thinking

Seymour Papert[1], from MIT's Media Lab, coined the term "computational thinking" in 1980. We use computational thinking to solve problems algorithmically, that process used to formulate a problem and express its solution so humans or computers can carry it out.

Boolean logic lies at the heart of computational thinking. This is the logic used to process tasks by a computer's CPU, the brain of a computer. The logic is primarily defined by IF, AND, and OR statements.

IF this happens, do this; OR if that happens, AND this other thing happens, do something else.

By building logic structures, algorithms can be created to help solve complex problems.

Computational Thinking is an important component of **Process Thinking**[2].

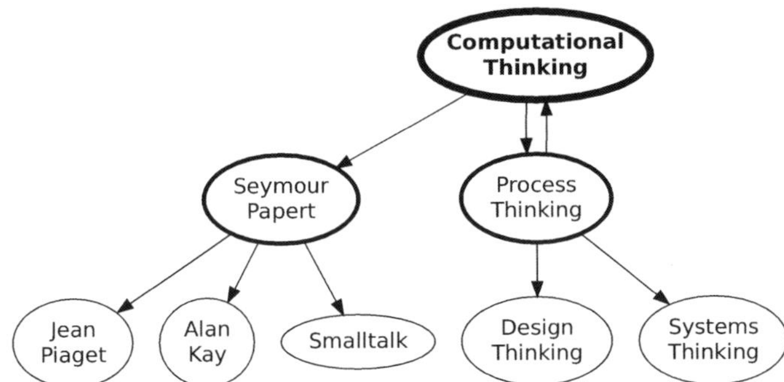

1 Page **200** - **Seymour Papert**

2 Page **191** - **Process Thinking**

Core Values

Before embarking on an **Audacious Aspiration**[1], it is valuable for a team to explore its core values. Their personal values. Their community values.

Our core values are our non-negotiables of life. They are the bedrock on which we build our families. They guide us through the most difficult times of our lives.

When we align our core values, we build bonds of trust that give us courage to venture into the unknown together.

We have found it powerful for individuals and groups to try to distill their core values down to three. Defining them can be challenging, but once they are defined, this **Trivium**[2] can be easily recalled to help maintain clarity of focus. Especially when the journey becomes difficult – because it will.

Find them. Celebrate them.

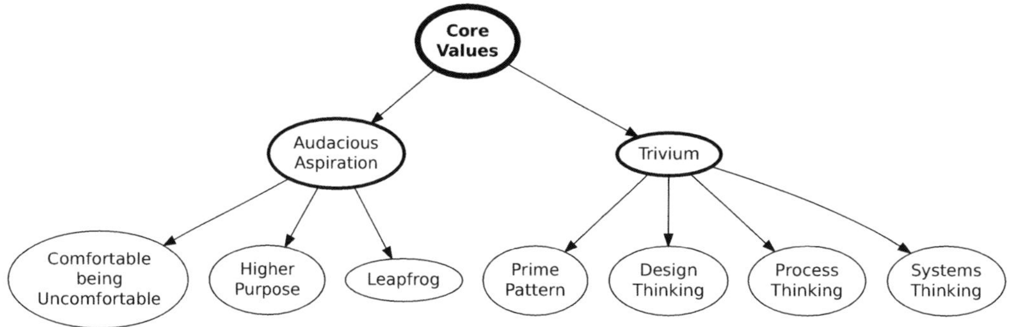

1 Page **120** - **Audacious Aspiration**

2 Page **216** - **Trivium**

Courage

Walking a path of deep learning challenges us to walk outside our existing schema. By so doing, we must face our fear of chaos.

We need to name the fear. Then have the courage to walk into it.

We have to become **Comfortable being Uncomfortable**[1].

Our spiritual, emotional, and intellectual well-being depends on the world making sense to us. That is, internalizing a pattern of meaning that provides a confidence of predictability.

Disrupting that schema through a **Paradigm Shift**[2] threatens us with chaos, leading us into our deepest fears of losing control.

For a teacher who has taught using a traditional instructional model for many years, this fear is real. For a manager who has run a company using a hierarchical command and control structure, this fear is real.

But we cannot undertake this journey unless we trust that our leadership and team members are authentically living shared **Core Values**[3].

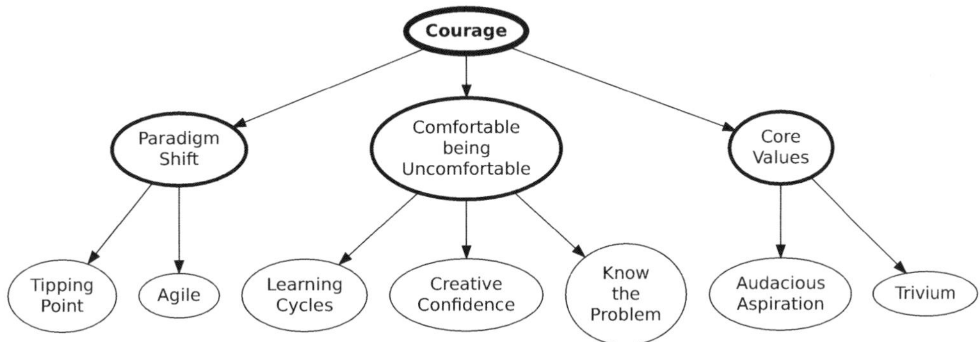

1 Page **128** - **Comfortable being Uncomfortable**

2 Page **187** - **Paradigm Shift**

3 Page **130** - **Core Values**

Create a Wake

One 'creates a wake' by moving quickly to develop a new model that can be referenced by others – a process that aligns the transformation efforts for an entire system.

Complex ecosystems have multiple power structures – each has self-preservation as its primary motivation. This dynamic discourages innovation, as change is often seen as threatening.

Trying to convince others to change is a long, painful, and, many times, fruitless process. Instead, by developing a **Positive Deviant**[1] that becomes a **First Mover**[2] who is innovating faster than anyone else, others begin to align to this new direction.

This momentum is most powerful when focused on an **Audacious Aspiration**[3] which is greater than individual territorial concerns. In this process, people become increasingly emboldened and courageous, unleashing their **Creative Genius**[4].

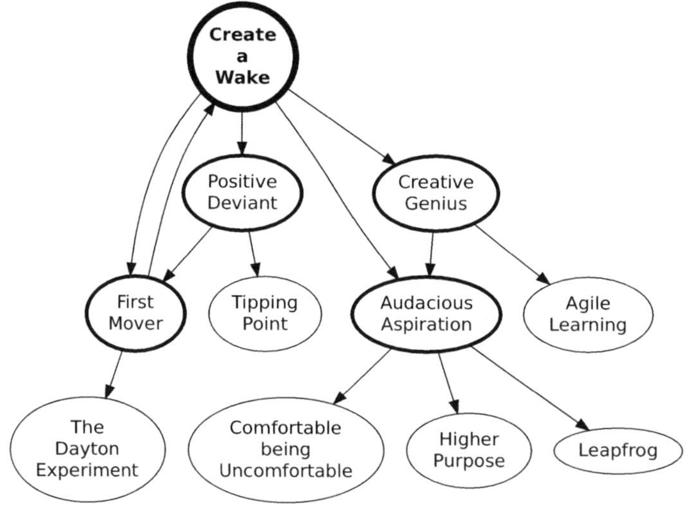

1 Page **189** - **Positive Deviant**

2 Page **149** - **First Mover**

3 Page **120** - **Audacious Aspiration**

4 Page **134** - **Creative Genius**

Creative Confidence

Creative confidence is critical for the learning process. For **Deeper Learning**[1].

It's the confidence that we need to which we walk into the unknown. To be **Comfortable being Uncomfortable**[2], to walk into the unknown with **Courage**[3].

For in that unknown, we struggle, we fail, and we illuminate – a process that allows us to better understand the true nature of the problem. An understanding that ultimately empowers us to find the solution we seek.

Creative confidence turns us into lifelong learners.

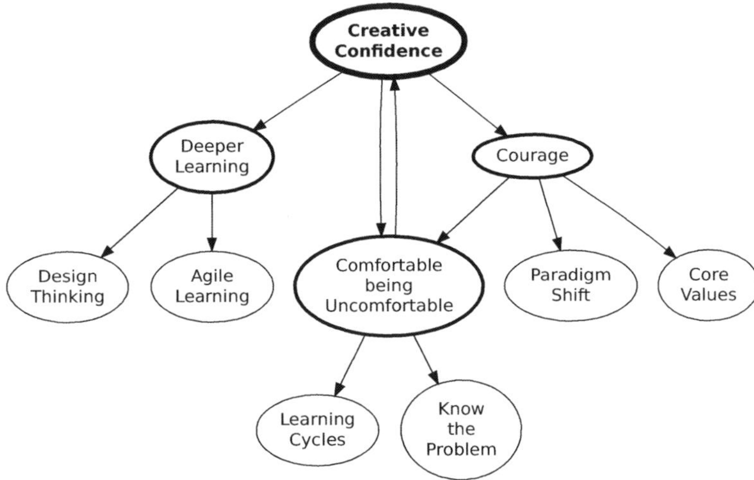

1 Page **138** - **Deeper Learning**

2 Page **128** - **Comfortable being Uncomfortable**

3 Page **131** - **Courage**

Creative Genius

We believe that everyone has the potential for creative genius, that is, creativity that springs from their innate spirit. And we recognize that everyone's creative genius is different. By working collaboratively, we can weave these geniuses together to create more valuable solutions faster.

We typically think of genius as referring to people who are deemed by society as highly intelligent. They are set apart from the rest of us 'average' people.

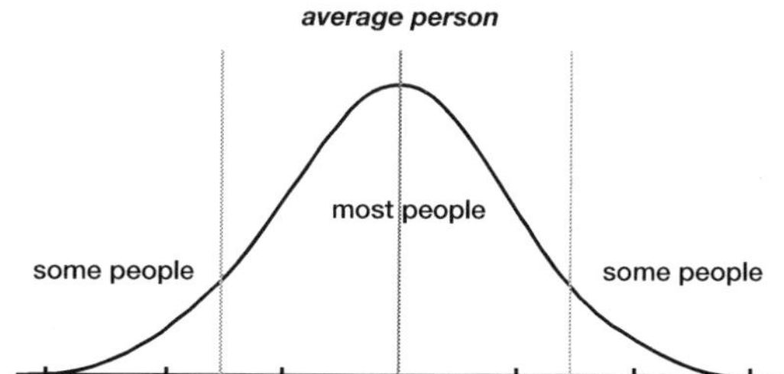

This understanding is based on the premise that intelligence can be accurately measured on a linear scale and that we can all be ranked by our relative intelligence.

This ranking forms us all into a bell curve. Those who are considered highly intelligent sit in the right foot of the bell curve. Those who are intellectually impaired sit in the left foot. The rest of us form the middle of the bell curve.

The underlying premise of this understanding is that perceived intelligence defines worth and bestows rights over others. We are to follow those who are defined as smarter than us and we have the implicit right to manage those who are seen as less intelligent than us.

But this understanding of intelligence and genius, with all of the implicit social implications, is a fairly recent concept. It only appeared near the dawn of the second Industrial Age. The concept was introduced in 1869 by an Englishman, Sir Francis Galton, who applied Carl Gauss' statistical model of normal distribution to intelligence.

Galton, as the founder of Eugenics, went on to argue that intelligence was inherited.

For the last 150 years, his model of intelligence has been embraced by many as truth – both the explicit belief in intelligence ranking and the implicit belief in genetic inheritance.

This theory has had profound implications for how social and geopolitical power was rationalized during the colonial era and beyond and profound implications for how we educate.

But genius has not always been thought of in this way. In fact, the word 'genius' is Latin and originally meant the attendant spirit present from one's birth – an innate ability or inclination.

Until relatively recently, genius was considered inherent in all of us. We each possess, by nature of our unique journey as human beings, our own human spirit with a potential for creative genius, a multidimensional genius that flows through us and is life-giving.

This reclaiming of the original definition of genius is at the core of reimagining education. Our **Audacious Aspiration**[1] is to unleash the creative genius in each student to empower their greatness.

This uncompromising conviction is the reason we are bringing **Agile Learning**[2] to education.

We believe that, through the mindsets, skillsets and tool sets of Agile, we can unleash the creative genius of teachers and students in amazing new ways.

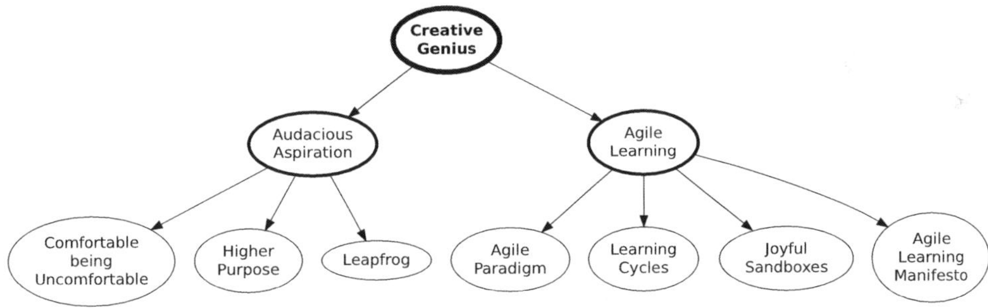

1 Page **120** - **Audacious Aspiration**

2 Page **110** - **Agile Learning**

Curiosity

Deeper Learning[1] begins with curiosity. When our curiosity is ignited, our minds are literally transformed as neurotransmitters activate key parts of our brain's analytical and memory areas. We are able to learn faster and retain what we are learning better.

According to a study by researchers at UC Davis, when we are curious, a reward system is created in our minds by the release of a neurotransmitter called dopamine. With its release, we feel more energized and joyful, and that joy flows over to other areas of learning.

> *The study revealed three major findings. First, as expected, when people were highly curious to find out the answer to a question, they were better at learning that information.*
>
> *More surprising, however, was that once their curiosity was aroused, they showed better learning of entirely unrelated information that they encountered but were not necessarily curious about. People were also better able to retain the information learned during a curious state across a 24-hour delay.*[2]

As the lead author, Dr. Matthias Gruber, of the University of California at Davis, described it:

> *Curiosity may put the brain in a state that allows it to learn and retain any kind of information, like a vortex that sucks in what you are motivated to learn, and also everything around it.*[3]

---

1 Page **138** - **Deeper Learning**

2 Eurekalert. "How curiosity changes the brain to enhance learning." https://www.eurekalert.org/pub_releases/2014-10/cp-hcc092514.php

3 Ibid.

Curiosity empowers our **Creative Confidence**[1] by igniting the **Flow**[2] within each one of us. It allows us to creatively solve problems faster.

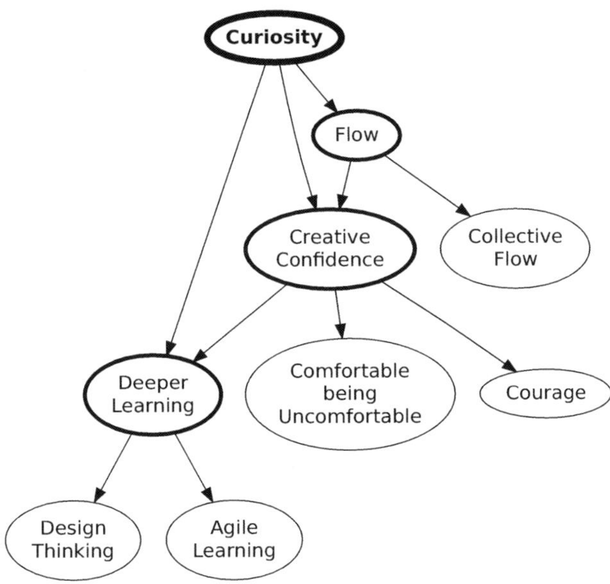

1 Page **133** - **Creative Confidence**

2 Page **150** - **Flow**

Deeper Learning

Deeper learning is a growing movement of educators committed to better equipping students with the skills needed in the 21st century.

Key to this learning approach is empowering students to apply knowledge to real-world challenges using critical thinking, collaboration and communication skills.

The Deeper Learning movement has been promoted by the William and Flora Hewlett Foundation. To help define this movement, a specific set of educational outcomes were defined:

- Mastery of rigorous academic content
- Critical thinking and problem-solving skills
- The ability to work collaboratively
- Effective oral and written communication
- Learning how to learn
- Developing and maintaining an academic mindset

The concept of Deeper Learning integrates closely with the ideas of **Design Thinking**[1] and **Agile Learning**[2].

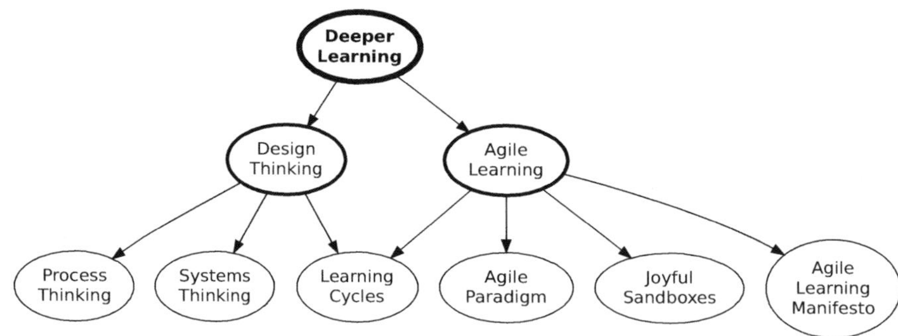

1 Page **139** - **Design Thinking**

2 Page **110** - **Agile Learning**

Design Thinking

Design Thinking is a process for creatively developing new solutions through fast, iterative cycles.

It starts with an intention that leads to a process of deep discovery through empathetic listening. From there it leads to an ideation phase in which potential solutions interplay. A synthesized solution is quickly developed that can be prototyped and tested as an experiment. Analysis of this experiment then leads to subsequent rounds of ideation, prototyping and testing, until a good solution is developed.

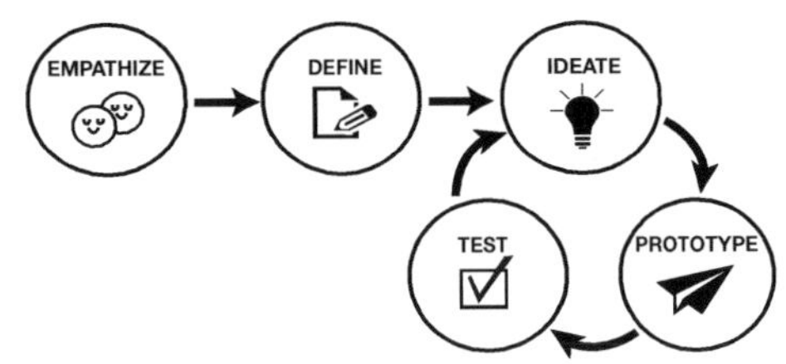

These cycles can be thought of as **Learning Cycles**[1]. The faster these cycles, the more quickly a solution can be developed.

Design Thinking has been applied to education, largely through the leadership of IDEO and Stanford d.school's K12 Lab.

It is a core skill, along with **Process Thinking**[2] and **Systems Thinking**[3], that is needed in our new economy.

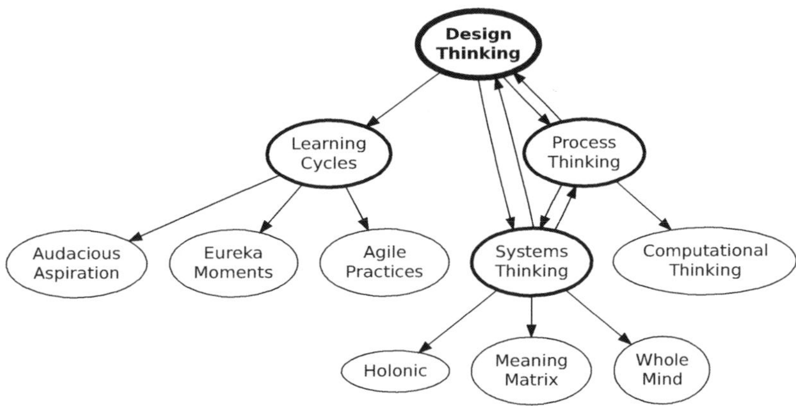

1 Page **174** - **Learning Cycles**

2 Page **191** - **Process Thinking**

3 Page **207** - **Systems Thinking**

Digital Mind

The digital mind emerges when learning from a non-linear, hypertext-based web.

Ask teachers what is their greatest challenge and they will likely tell you that kids today are just different, that most don't learn like they did.

We adults, who grew up in the closing days of the Industrial Age with an industrial education defined by **Taylorism**[1], learned in a classroom with straight rows where the path of knowledge acquisition was clearly defined. But many kids today struggle to pay attention in this highly structured environment. They struggle to be engaged.

You hear a lot of educators talk about this struggle of engagement. The lack of engagement is directly related to low graduation rates, a key measurement that educators use for evaluating their performance.

Maybe the problem is not that we need them to think *like* us, but that we need to learn why, as digital natives, they fundamentally think differently *from* us.

So, we must ask, **What if Marshall McLuhan was Right?**[2]

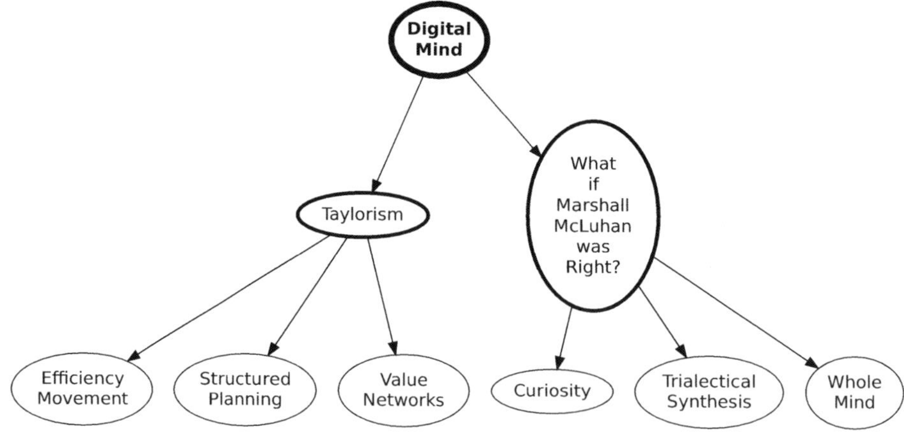

1 Page **208** - **Taylorism**

2 Page **219** - **What if Marshall McLuhan was Right?**

Early Adopters

Early adopters follow **Innovators**[1]. They pay attention to these innovators and have the courage to explore how they might be able to apply new practices based on what they have seen.

These early adopters play a critical role in the transformation of a culture. For it is they, not the innovators, that the rest of the community emulates.

For innovators are outliers. They are seen as fundamentally wired differently from others. But the early adopters are seen as practical people, who are taking those innovations and creating practices that others can use.

They are the ones of whom others will say, “If they could do it, perhaps I can too”.

It is their experiences, and the stories that they tell about them, that give others the courage to change. They are the builders of the bridge over the chasm in the **Rogers Curve**[2].

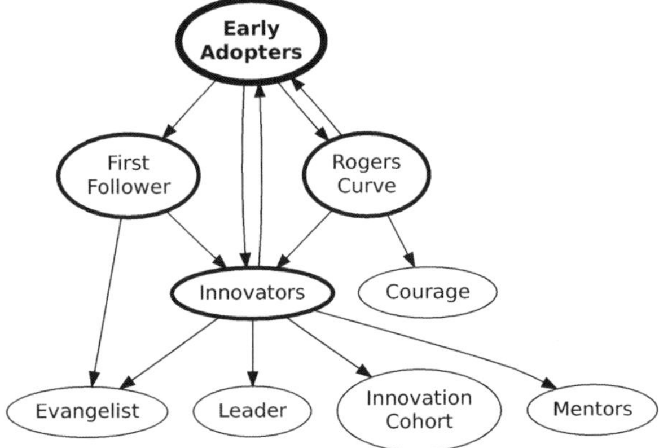

1 Page **162** - **Innovators**

2 Page **197** - **Rogers Curve**

Efficiency Movement

To understand why our schools are structured the way they are today, you have to go back to their roots, back to the early part of the 20th century when the Efficiency Movement was defining how industry and education leaders were thinking about system design.

The Efficiency Movement was embraced by leaders in the United States, Britain and other industrial countries. This movement focused on increasing production efficiencies.

This movement, which formed the foundation of scientific management, commonly known as **Taylorism**[1], was based on the fundamental premises held by the **Cartesian Mindset**[2].

A key premise was the belief that those with superior intellect could reduce complex processes to its components and reconfigure them to create more efficient systems.

Logical, *mechanistic structures* that created consistent output.

Schools were designed to produce a predictable output based on a sequential transfer of units of knowledge in discrete components.

Many have referred to our traditional school structure disparagingly as a production line – which is exactly what it is. A mechanistic structure designed to produce consistently qualified workers for an industrial economy.

---

1 Page **208** - **Taylorism**

2 Page **124** - **Cartesian Mindset**

The **Agile Mindset**[1] is based on a different understanding of systems, one that reflects the dynamic, adaptive system described in biology.

These complex *organistic structures*, called autopoietic systems, are much better suited to unleash creative genius need for the new creative economy.

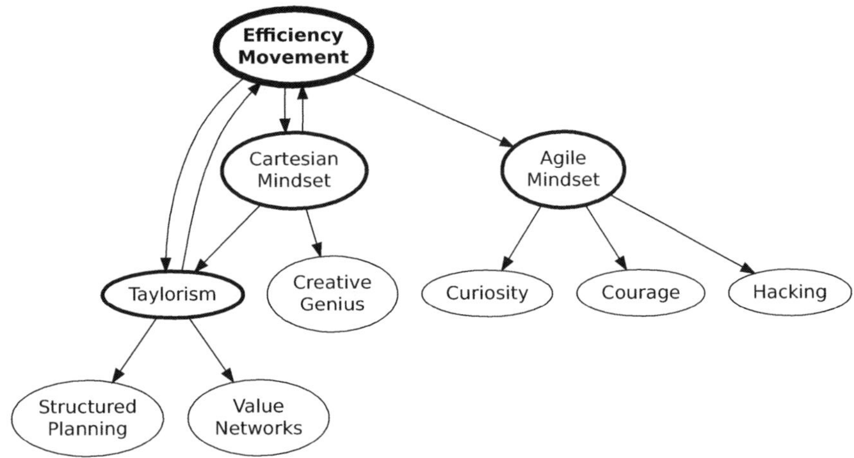

1 Page **112** - **Agile Mindset**

Eureka Moments

Eureka moments embody a sudden rush of insight by an individual or team that lays clear the solution to a complex problem or the answer to a perplexing question.

> *eu·re·ka*
> a cry of joy or satisfaction when one finds or discovers something.

This moment has several names. Some call it an "Aha! Moment".

These eureka moments feel magical – when insight suddenly manifests. There is no predicting when these moments might happen, but they are often in the midst of dark, confusing struggles. There is no rational explanation for these moments, just a clarity of insight that seems almost supernatural.

There are many theories as to why these moments are so powerful. One of the most likely ties back to the cognition theories of Jean Piaget. Piaget postulated that we live and learn using intellectual frameworks that have been based on our past learning experiences. He called these frameworks 'schemas'.

Many problems can be solved within an existing schema. By so doing, they strengthen the schema. There are times, however, when problems defy answers within the current framework. As a result, we are forced into deep discomfort as we struggle with questions that are beyond this framework – where we must "think outside the box".

The eureka moment happens when a new pattern of meaning suddenly comes together that reshapes the architecture of our existing schema.

> A new type of thinking is essential if mankind is to survive and move toward higher levels.
>
> - *Albert Einstein*

There is a huge dopamine rush during these moments as neural pathways in our mind are being rewired into a new pattern. What we see and now know, cannot be unseen and unknown.

We **Claim the Joy**[1] and are forever changed by this **Paradigm Shift**[2].

Having experienced these moments we have the courage to venture again, armed with new **Creative Confidence**[3], into the wilderness of the unknown.

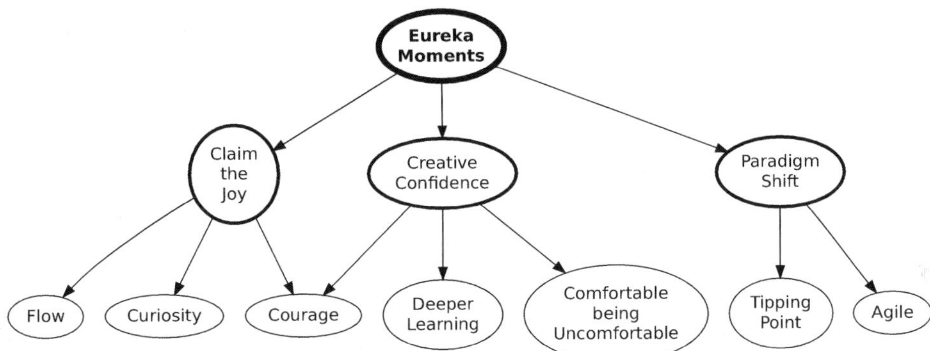

1 Page **125** - **Claim the Joy**

2 Page **187** - **Paradigm Shift**

3 Page **133** - **Creative Confidence**

Evangelist

Change often begins with one person, one who has a passionate commitment and the courage to step into the unknown.

Once someone has the courage to stand up and start the journey, others will join. The evangelist is able to identify **Innovators**[1]. They begin to form a cohort that then gathers additional followers until there is a **Tipping Point**[2], where a new paradigm becomes the dominant one. This process is organic and will be different in every organization. But it can happen far faster than anyone would expect.

It is important to just start by doing. This intention is known as a **Bias to Action**[3].

Often, an evangelist starts by learning from those in other organizations. They are the ones who have the courage to ask the 'What if' question, the ones who dare to think we can reimagine the possible.

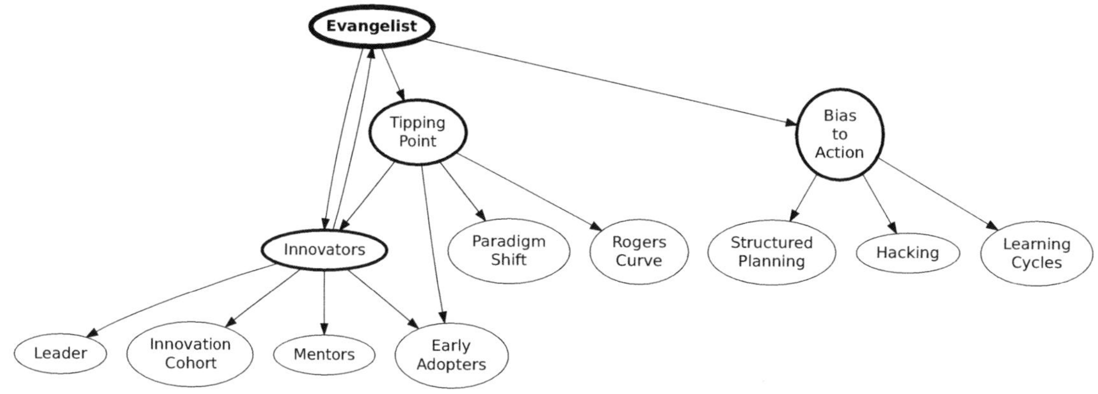

1 Page **162** - **Innovators**

2 Page **212** - **Tipping Point**

3 Page **121** - **Bias to Action**

Extreme Programming (XP)

The **Agile Mindset**[1] was shaped when Ward Cunningham and Kent Beck started playing around with the programming language **Smalltalk**[2]. They were both working at Tektronix back in the eighties. Tektronix was one of the companies that Xerox gave this new programming language to when they could not commercialize the computer technologies coming out of PARC, their research lab.

Smalltalk, as an object-oriented language with a just-in-time compiler, was conceived by **Alan Kay**[3] as a learning language for a new computer age.

Using pair programming, Ward and Kent would sit and code sitting next to each other on a single computer. They began to develop new solutions together much faster than could be done using **Structured Planning**[4], called the 'Waterfall Model', used by software developers.

One day, a package arrived at Ward's home. It had no return address. Inside was a copy of Christopher Alexander's book *A Pattern Language*.

Over the next fifteen months, Ward and Kent experimented with creating patterns of practice to begin to define and share their experiences using Smalltalk.

In 1995, Ward published a paper that defined this new pattern language of software development, which he called 'Episodes'. Kent then went on to apply these practices at Chrysler for a new payroll system they were developing. From that experience, he published, a book entitled *Extreme Programming Explained* which launched XP.

---

1 Page **112** - **Agile Mindset**

2 Page **203** - **Smalltalk**

3 Page **119** - **Alan Kay**

4 Page **206** - **Structured Planning**

Kent came up with the name “Extreme Programming” as a riff off the extreme sports movement, where athletes were beginning to challenge themselves to new heights of performance by new heights of risk.

The early leaders of XP brought a new mindset – one where they were courageous experimenting, guided by their curiosity – to their work. And it was this mindset that helped launch the agile movement.

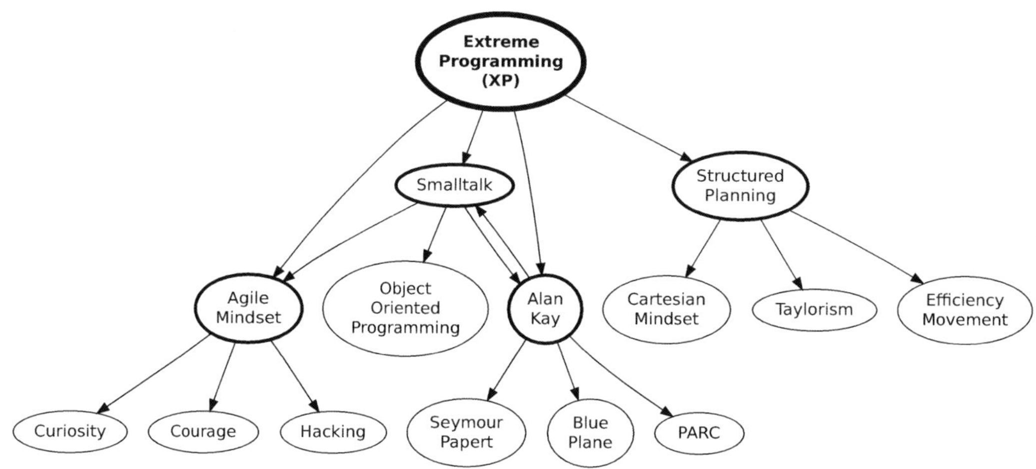

First Mover

First Mover is a marketing concept which asserts that companies that can quickly establish market leadership can create long-term competitive advantages.

When introducing a new paradigm in complex ecosystems, we have found that it is essential to create thought leadership by out-innovating others.

Complexity creates inertia that prevents transformational change. If you can learn faster and innovate faster, others begin to take note, encouraging them to follow this new model. By doing so, you can **Create a Wake**[1].

That is what Jami and I sought to do with **The Dayton Experiment**[2].

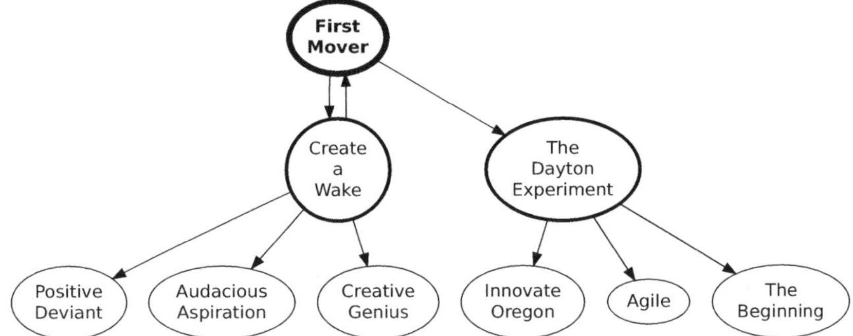

1 Page **132** - **Create a Wake**

2 Page **11** - **The Dayton Experiment**

Flow

The concept of Flow was developed by Mihály Csíkszentmihályi (pronounced "CHICK-sent-me-high-ee"). In his book, *Flow: The Psychology of Optimal Experience*, he writes:

> *The best moments usually occur when a person's body or mind is stretched to its limits in a voluntary effort to accomplish something difficult and worthwhile. Optimal experience is thus something that we make happen.*[1]

Flow, then, is a feeling and a state. A state where we are able to focus more clearly and perform more effectively. When our senses are more acute and learning is accelerated as neurotransmitters are released in our body.

Once experienced, it is a state we desire to return to, developing the **Creative Confidence**[2] to face new challenges.

Here is how he talks about this state in a Wired article:

> *Being completely involved in an activity for its own sake. The ego falls away. Time flies. Every action, movement, and thought follows inevitably from the previous one, like playing jazz. Your whole being is involved, and you're using your skills to the utmost.*[3]

In his book, he summarizes the three elements of Flow as:

- Purpose
- Resolution
- Harmony

1 Csíkszentmihályi, Mihály. *Flow: the psychology of optimal experience* (New York : Harper & Row, 1990), 3.

2 Page **133** - **Creative Confidence**

3 Geirland, John. "Go with the Flow." 09/01/96. www.wired.com/1996/09/czik/

He writes:

> *Purpose, resolution, and harmony unify life and give it meaning by transforming it into a seamless flow experience.*[1]

When a team is working together, they can enter into a **Collective Flow**[2].

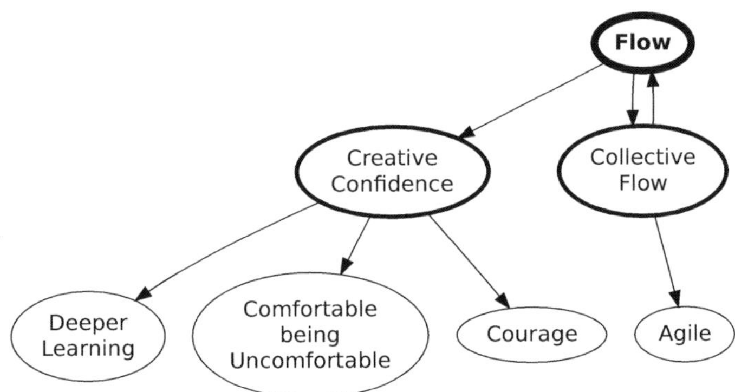

1 Csíkszentmihályi, *Flow*, 6.

2 Page **127** - **Collective Flow**

Hacking

The word 'hacking' these days often has a negative connotation – used to describe individuals who are trying to break into computer systems with evil intent.

But it wasn't always that way. In fact, the original hackers were quite different. They were engineering students at MIT who got their hands on one of the first minicomputers. They were all members of a model railroad club where they would spend hours hacking new solutions for the systems that controlled the railroad. They took that same approach when exploring the potential of this new computer.

Their experience of hacking was antithetical to traditional programming which was based on careful planning and development. Instead, it was a process of creative discovery that involved rapid trial and error experiments.

This process allowed them to quickly develop solutions through a fast **Iteration**[1] of **Learning Cycles**[2].

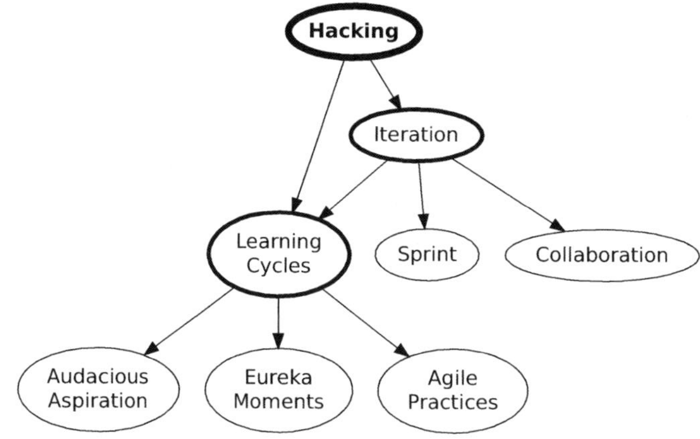

1 Page **163** - **Iteration**

2 Page **174** - **Learning Cycles**

Hero's Journey

The hero's journey is a monomyth that was first popularized by Joseph Campbell to describe the transformational journey that has been found in multiple epic stories through the ages – where a hero faces challenges, gains insight, and returns transformed.

This monomyth holds an authentic truth in the journey of personal or organizational transformation.

When you are embarking on a path of transformation, one must become **Comfortable being Uncomfortable**[1]. This journey is challenging in ways that we could not imagine. To embark, one must have the courage to walk into the unknown. That courage comes from a deep sense of purpose – that which we call the **Audacious Aspiration**[2].

There are times, though, of deep despair, which Campbell characterized as the 'abyss'. These are times when the challenges that need to be overcome seem insurmountable. An important time to sit quietly with the problem. And to wait.

But in these moments, there is a **Transmutational Experience**[3] that illuminates the true nature of the problem and its solution. This insight becomes the 'ultimate boon' that shapes transformation.

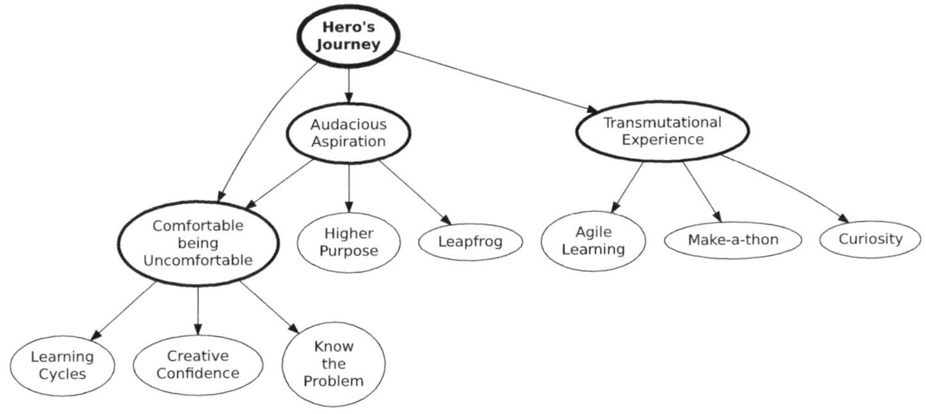

1 Page **128** - **Comfortable being Uncomfortable**

2 Page **120** - **Audacious Aspiration**

3 Page **213** - **Transmutational Experience**

Higher Purpose

Meaning is derived from purpose. When that sense of purpose is shared by others, we become empowered by a larger meaning.

A higher purpose is a goal that is bigger than any one individual, company or community. By focusing on a larger goal, an **Audacious Aspiration**[1], groups of individuals are able to align the assets and resources of others to do something amazing.

In this process, a **Collective Flow**[2] of passion is released and new potential can be realized. In this aspiration, resources align to create opportunities for increased participation that moves us from a paradigm of scarcity to a **Paradigm of Abundance**[3].

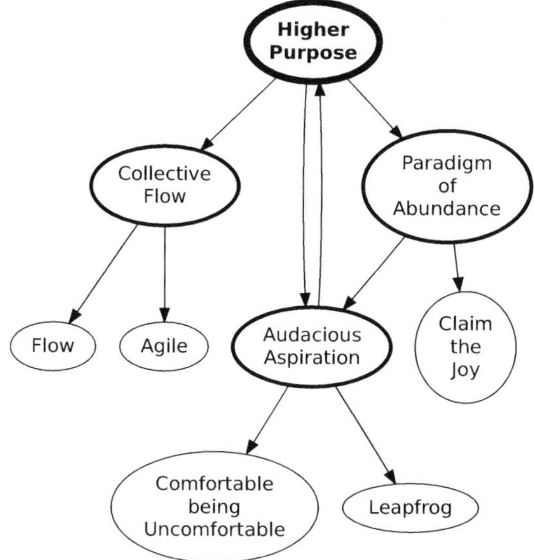

1 Page **120** - **Audacious Aspiration**

2 Page **127** - **Collective Flow**

3 Page **185** - **Paradigm of Abundance**

Holonic

Arther Koestler coined the word 'holon' for something both self-contained and part of a larger system. It means 'whole' in Greek. He then built a system theory around this concept.

He observed that nature comprises a series of parts that are both whole unto themselves and part of a larger whole.

For instance, a hydrogen atom is whole unto itself. One electron flying through a field around a nucleus. But that atom then becomes joined with another hydrogen atom and an oxygen atom to become another whole, a water molecule. And that water then becomes part of a cellular structure, and that cellular structure then becomes part of more advanced forms of life, each being a whole unto themselves.

He calls a holonic structure a 'holarchy'. Holarchies that can reach from subatomic particles to multiverses.

Higher-level holons are formed when a set of smaller holons have formed a relationship pattern that is self-sustaining and resilient. These higher-level holons then go on to form relationship patterns with other holons to form larger wholes. A holon exists in a dynamic tension between its sub-patterns and its meta-patterns, forming complex autopoietic systems.

If any part of the system breaks down and no longer supports the behavior of other parts of the system, the entire system breaks down. Cancer is an example of a system's destructive dysfunction.

Holonic patterns lie at the heart of complex system theory and are essential for us to understand the nature of **Pattern Languages**[1].

It also was at the root of Alan Kay's design for **Smalltalk**[2] that helped shape the **Agile Mindset**[3].

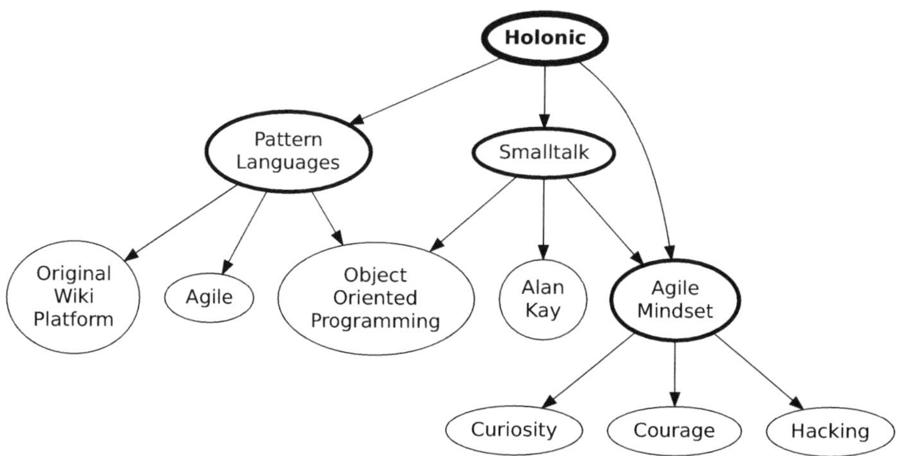

1 Page **188** - **Pattern Languages**

2 Page **203** - **Smalltalk**

3 Page **112** - **Agile Mindset**

i3 Center

It all began with a crazy idea.

What if we transformed a 10,000 square foot agriculture shop at Dayton High School into a new space, a multidimensional makerspace. A place where all students felt a sense of belonging, regardless of their interests? A place where new ideas would lead to prototypes of new solutions and **Creative Genius**[1] was unleashed.

In the fall of 2015, that idea was hatched, one that would be instrumental in helping to tear down old paradigms of education within the school. A new space that would be called the i3 Center, where 'i3' stood for inspiration, innovation and invention.

This new center was built around an Innovation Lab, where the foundational mindsets and skillsets of innovation were being taught. It was also here where teams are coming together to develop new ideas, new solutions to develop their **Creative Confidence**[2].

This lab, surrounded by fusion and fabrication makerspaces, promoted 'creative collisions' of students with different interests and skills. These collisions unlocked new possibilities and helped unleash the genius that was within each and every student.

Unlike the vocational classrooms of the past, this new center quickly evolved into a place where all students felt that they belonged and were empowered to be makers and creators in pursuit of their passion.

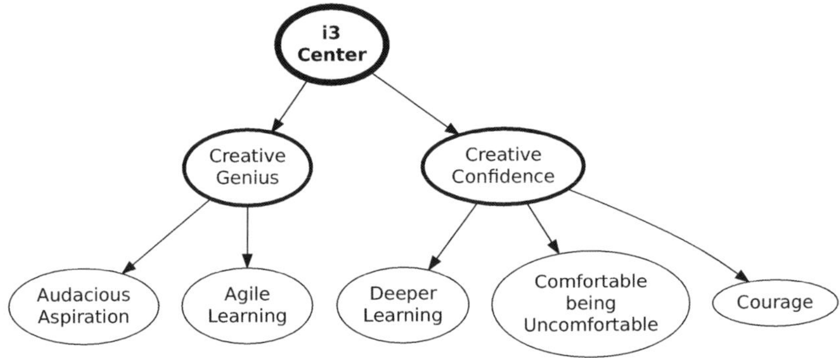

1 Page **134** - **Creative Genius**

2 Page **133** - **Creative Confidence**

In & Out Demo

At the end of each sprint in **The Dayton Practice**[1], the student teams present their findings. These presentations are done through an In & Out Demo, a practice developed by Jenni for her Genius Hour class.

The work tables in the classroom are organized into a circle. Half of the teams start out as 'Insiders'. The rest of the teams are 'Outsiders'.

The Insider teams find their seats together inside the circle of tables, facing Outsider teams that ring the outside of the tables.

The timer begins. For three minutes the Insider teams use their creation to present to the Outsiders what they learned. The Outsiders listen and then have two minutes to ask questions.

After the second bell goes off, the discussion ends and the Insiders shift to the next Outsider team. The clock starts and the process is repeated. After four or so of these presentations, the Insiders become Outsiders and the process is repeated.

At the end of the class period, the best team presentation is voted on for the da Vinci Award and that team selects the 'base' topic for the next learning sprint.

Many students find presentations in front of their classmates intimidating. This process of small group presentations helps them build their verbal communication skills. In addition, by repeating these quick presentations multiple times, teams are able to quickly learn what works and what doesn't, and make adjustments on the fly. While the first presentations are often rough, by their fourth iteration they have significantly improved.

The students are graded not only for their roles as Insiders but also as Outsiders. That is, both for their presentation skills and for the questions they ask. Through this process, these students were learning the important skill of active listening.

---

1 Page **210** - **The Dayton Practice**

By using their creation to tell the story of the findings from their research, it becomes, in a sense, their 'ultimate boon' in what has been a **Hero's Journey**[1] igniting, once again, a **Curiosity**[2] that guides real learning.

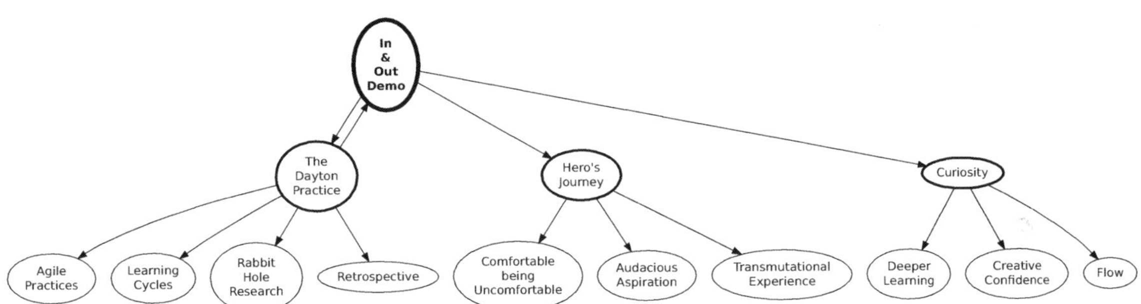

1 Page **153** - **Hero's Journey**

2 Page **136** - **Curiosity**

Innovate Oregon

Innovate Oregon was launched in 2015 as a strategic initiative of the Technology Association of Oregon (TAO) Foundation. It was designed as a north star to align shared passions for a transformational vision, that of creating an inclusive, innovation economy in Oregon – one that might become a national model.

The initiative sought to address a fundamental challenge faced by companies of not having the talent needed to sustain their growth. More than just technical skills, these companies were looking for creative problem solvers to help them quickly adapt to challenges in increasingly complex markets.

After starting the initiative in Portland, it began to focus on school districts in rural Oregon.

The primary focus of the movement was on workforce development, partnering with our K-12 education system to better prepare the next generation of makers and creators.

Innovation Cohort

Innovation carries a lot of risks and, quite frankly, can be exhausting. But the rewards of this process far outweigh the risks.

Developing a cohort allows **Innovators**[1] and **Early Adopters**[2] to know that they are not alone in this path, but that there are others who have the **Courage**[3] to take risks, to accept failure, and to learn quickly.

Each school has educators who are continually exploring how they can better teach their students. But often they are in different parts of the building teaching different subjects. By bringing them together for frequent check-ins, the cohort can not only share their insights with each other, but also get important support for their journey.

As this innovation cohort begins to tell their experiences to other teachers, they inspire others. The support from the **Leader**[4] is important for organizing and sustaining this cohort.

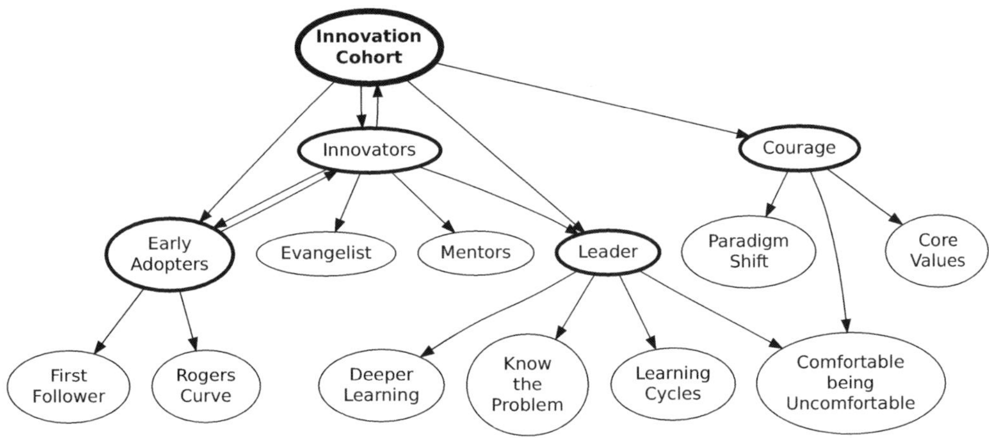

1 Page **162** - **Innovators**

2 Page **141** - **Early Adopters**

3 Page **131** - **Courage**

4 Page **169** - **Leader**

Innovators

In any organization there are members who have the creative courage to try something new, knowing that failure is possible. They are excited and vitalized by this challenge.

Every school has innovators. Often, these teachers are working 'under the radar', independent of each other, hidden away behind the walls of their classroom. There they are experimenting and learning with their students, exploring new ways of teaching, new ways of learning.

The role of the **Evangelist**[1] is to identify those innovators and, with the support of their **Leader**[2], begin to look for a cohort that can be referred to as an **Innovation Cohort**[3].

It is valuable for innovators to have support from **Mentors**[4] to help structure and guide their learning process as they explore new agile-based learning experiences.

The strategic role of Innovators is to inspire **Early Adopters**[5].

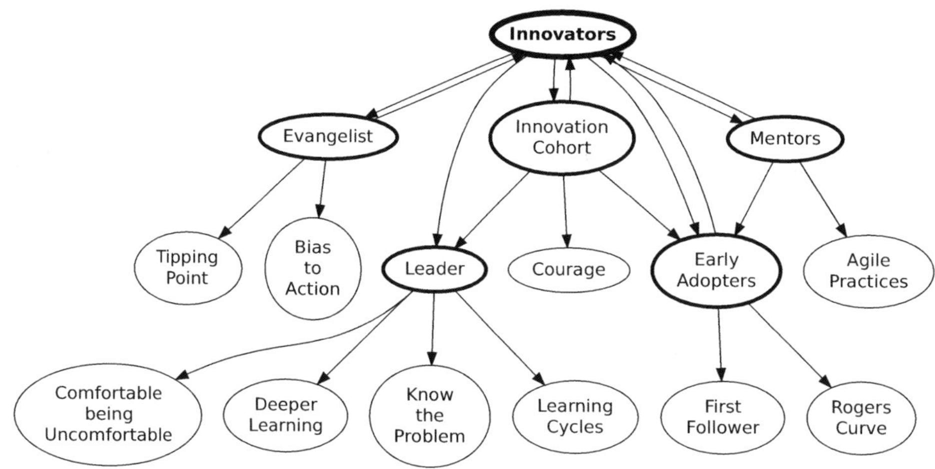

1 Page **146** - **Evangelist**

2 Page **169** - **Leader**

3 Page **161** - **Innovation Cohort**

4 Page **182** - **Mentors**

5 Page **141** - **Early Adopters**

Iteration

The concept of iteration is based on the understanding that large problems can be broken down into pieces and that each of these pieces can be solved incrementally through a process of discovery.

In the language of Agile, we talk about 'rock crushing' a problem – breaking it down to its components – and then developing **Sprints**[1] to incrementally develop a new solution.

One doesn't have to fully understand the true nature of the problem before attempting a solution to solve it.

The solution to each piece is attempted, recognizing that, as only one piece is being focused on, the risk of failure is manageable. Further, in any failure, there will be a deeper understanding of the problem. As the true nature of the problem is revealed, a better solution can be developed.

Important to this process of iteration is **Collaboration**[2] as part of **Learning Cycles**[3].

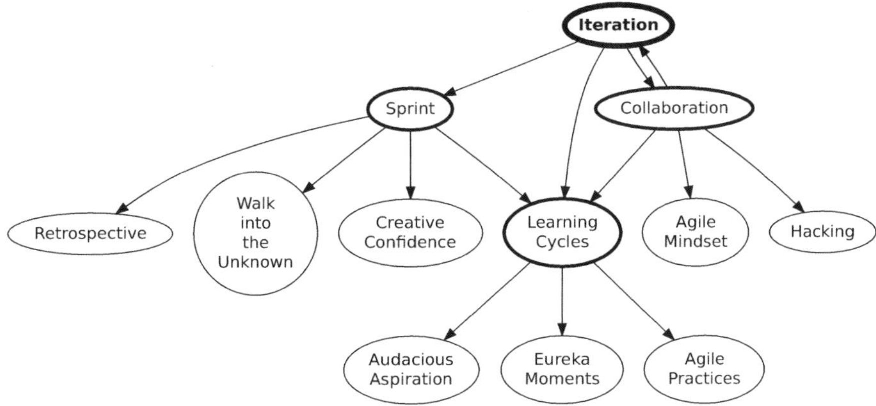

1 Page **205** - **Sprint**

2 Page **126** - **Collaboration**

3 Page **174** - **Learning Cycles**

Jean Piaget

Few people have had more impact on the theory of education that Jean Piaget, whose ideas first became widely known in the 1960s.

His theory of cognitive development created a powerful learning model that challenged traditional concepts focused on rote learning. This work underpins the concepts of **Project Based Learning**[1] and **Deeper Learning**[2].

Arguably, the most powerful concept he articulated was the relationship of learning to an individual's **Schema**[3].

His theory of learning, called Constructivism, deeply influenced the thinking of **Seymour Papert**[4] and **Alan Kay**[5].

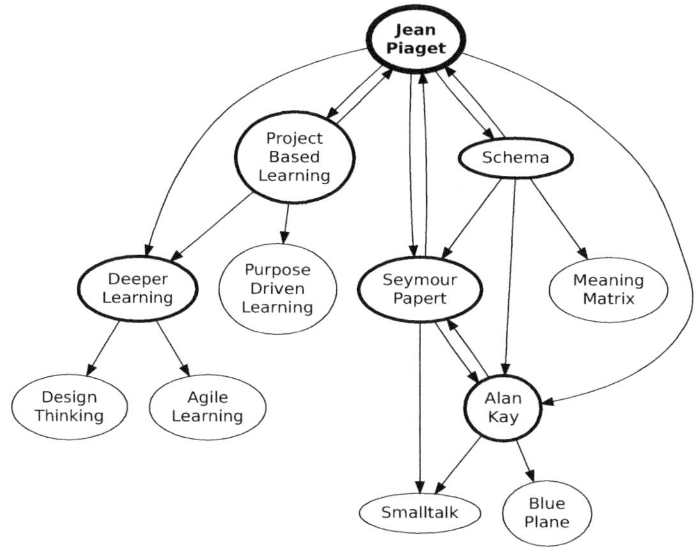

1 Page **192** - **Project Based Learning**

2 Page **138** - **Deeper Learning**

3 Page **198** - **Schema**

4 Page **200** - **Seymour Papert**

5 Page **119** - **Alan Kay**

Joyful Sandboxes

Joyful sandboxes are learning experiences, led by our curiosity, in which we rekindle the innate joy of discovery.

One evening, with beers in our hands, we were reflecting on our journey. At the table with us was Ward Cunningham, one of the original signers of the Agile Manifesto.

We were exploring parallels between the experiences in Dayton with the experiences that he and Kent Beck had when they were working together at Tektronix back in the mid-eighties – experiences that were instrumental in the development of Agile.

What were we to call that shared experience that bound together different communities and different times?

And then Jami named it: 'the joyful sandbox.' I looked over at Ward and his eyes lit up. Yes, that is what he was experiencing with Kent as they experimented with pair programming using a new language called **Smalltalk**[1]. That experience which became the catalyst for a profound transformation in the software industry and beyond.

Our society has foisted on us two great fallacies. One is that we do not have, each and every one of us, genius. Genius, by its original Latin definition, means innate spirit. We all have a unique and beautiful innate spirit. We all have genius. It is the gift that we are bringing to the world that gives our life meaning.

The second fallacy is that we don't deserve joy. For far too many, to become an adult implies that we must discard joy and struggle through a world in a quest simply to survive. For far too many, a joyless journey.

But to thrive and to become whole, we must **Claim the Joy**[2]. For our children, for us. For our co-workers. For our friends. For strangers.

---

1 Page **203** - **Smalltalk**

2 Page **125** - **Claim the Joy**

Educators can understand, within seconds, if there is true learning happening in a classroom. They don't need to look at the test scores, they know it by the eyes. Do they see joy?

When visitors walked into Dayton, they could see that the learning was real. They felt the joy. They sensed the joyful sandbox. **Joy Matters**[1].

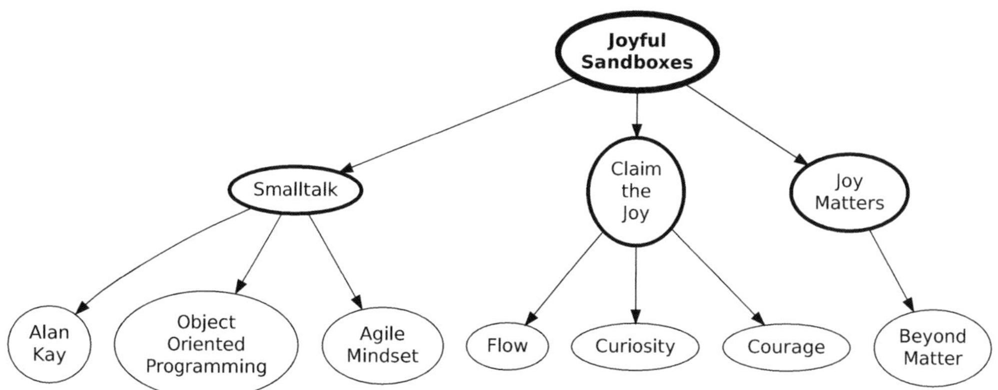

1 Page **91** - **Joy Matters**

Just-In-Time Learner

There are some students who are compliant learners and thrive in traditional learning environments. They do well on tests and are rewarded with good grades. They have mastered the 'game of school'.

Then there are the rest of the students – the vast majority. Many of these are not interested in the game, they are bored and wondering why they are even showing up to school each day.

But these students are certainly capable of learning. They can be thought of as just-in-time learners. Give them a purpose, and they will learn. But without that purpose, they have little interest in being receptacles for what they may feel is irrelevant information.

Why should they, when in their pocket is a smartphone that can access, in a blink of an eye, the vast store of human knowledge? So I set out to **Learn from my Daughter**[1].

As I did, I began to understand that our challenge is to create **Purpose Driven Learning**[2]. To give their learning a new meaning. One that recognizes and, indeed, celebrates that they actually think differently from us, with their **Digital Minds**[3].

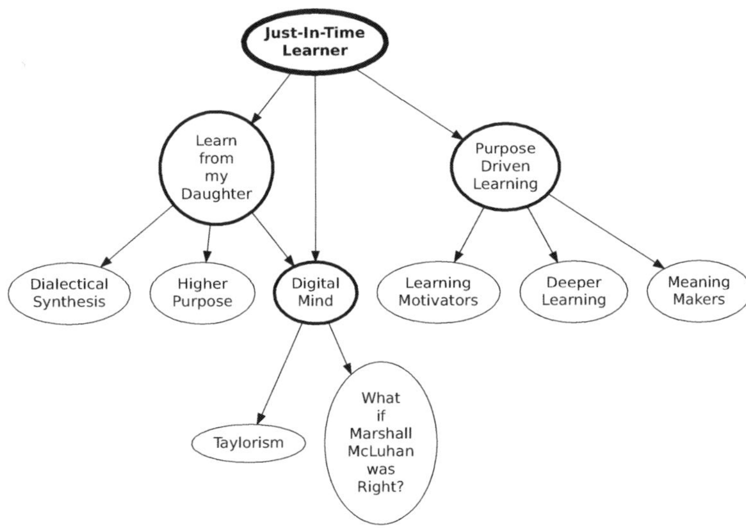

1 Page **172** - **Learn from my Daughter**

2 Page **193** - **Purpose Driven Learning**

3 Page **140** - **Digital Mind**

Know the Problem

The reason that we fail is not because we are a failure – we fail because we don't know the problem deeply enough. When crafting a solution, we are making too many assumptions that are incorrect.

The only way for us to know which of these assumptions are incorrect is by trying a solution that we think might work. When it fails, which it likely will, some of our incorrect assumptions are revealed. We then try again, this time understanding the problem more deeply. So our next solution is incrementally better. But again, perhaps not the right one. So we have to try another time. Each time, we are smarter.

But that is okay, because if we can iterate these **Learning Cycles**[1] quickly, we can know the problem faster, ultimately allowing us to create solutions at a speed never before possible.

But to fail, we must pull back the **Shadow Curtain**[2].

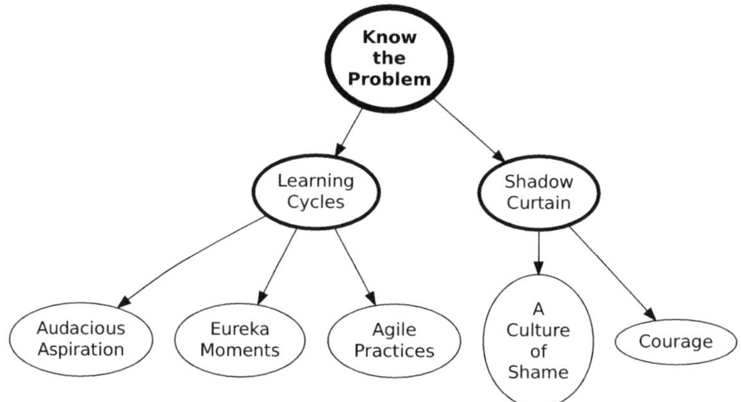

1 Page **174** - **Learning Cycles**

2 Page **201** - **Shadow Curtain**

Leader

Innovation is messy. One must be willing to become **Comfortable being Uncomfortable**[1]. The process involves taking risks and recognizing that failure is an essential part of the process. We call this failing forward to learn.

In order for members of an organization to walk into this uncertainty where transformation can happen, they must be given permission from their leadership. And they must trust that permission.

So for teachers to begin to walk down this path of bringing the vitality of **Deeper Learning**[2] into the classroom, they need to know that they are supported by their principal, their superintendent, and their school board.

They need to know that when they fail, they will not be shamed but encouraged to **Know the Problem**[3] better, and then challenged to embark on the next round of **Learning Cycles**[4]. By so doing, they model for their students authentic, courageous, life-giving learning.

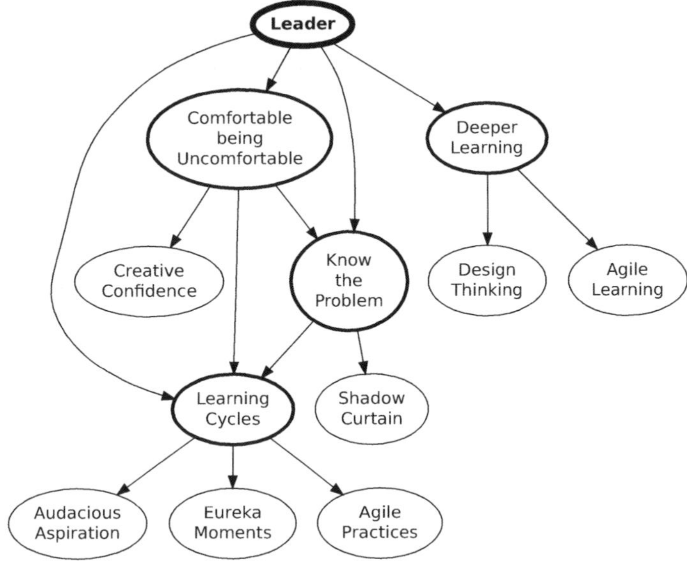

1 Page **128** - **Comfortable being Uncomfortable**

2 Page **138** - **Deeper Learning**

3 Page **168** - **Know the Problem**

4 Page **174** - **Learning Cycles**

Leapfrog

In marketing, it's all about the market share: What percentage of customers are buying your product compared to your competitors.

When you are not the market leader, you have two choices. Make incremental improvements to try to catch the leader, or boldly reimagine your offering to leapfrog beyond the market leader's product.

In 2012, Oregon was 45th in the country in terms of graduation rates. We would joke that Oregon was called the 'Mississippi of the West', except that Mississippi's graduation rates were higher than Oregon's.

There has been a great deal of effort over the last five years to improve the performance of the education system in Oregon. And graduation rates have improved – but not enough.

But, by 2019, Oregon was ranked 49th in terms of graduation rates. Only New Mexico had a lower rate.

The reason for this decline is that Oregon is not alone in its effort to improve its educational system. Every state is doing the same thing. And most are improving faster than Oregon, meaning that, despite all of our efforts, we are falling further and further behind.

Innovation-based companies know one thing. If you are in a dynamic, hyper-competitive market, a catch-up strategy will almost always fail. The reason is that market leaders are also innovating, and if their rate of innovation is faster than yours, you will keep falling behind.

Sometimes, then, you are faced with only one option – one that carries significant risk.

And that is to leapfrog – with **Courage**[1]. To create a bold new model that changes the rules of the game. That is what we were doing with our **Audacious Aspiration**[2].

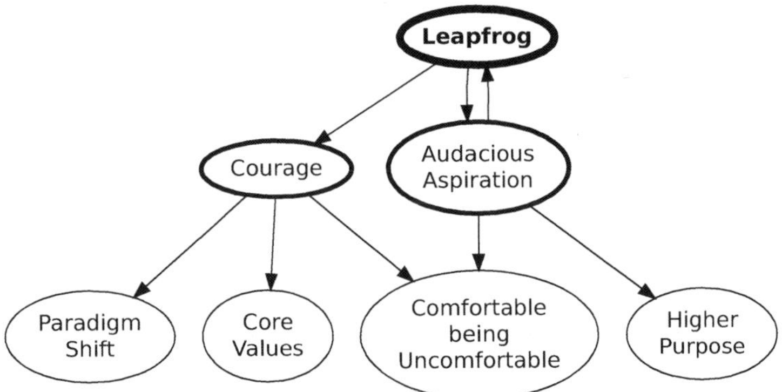

1 Page **131** - **Courage**

2 Page **120** - **Audacious Aspiration**

Learn from my Daughter

I have learned a lot from my daughter. One of the most important things that I've learned is that she doesn't think like me.

When she was in high school, I worried about how she would do academically. You see, my older son was a great 'traditional' student. A teacher would tell him to learn something and he would – a compliant learner.

Caitlin, on the other hand, would ask, "Why?" If she didn't know the reason for learning something, she wouldn't; she would dig in her heels. It drove me crazy.

I knew that by the time she got to high school this behavior would get her into trouble, especially when she started taking more challenging classes.

And then along came AP Chemistry – a class not to be taken lightly. The textbook was heavy, weighing almost three pounds. Each chapter needed to be read slowly multiple times to be understood.

But day after day, I would see her book go unopened. I worried, seeing a train wreck coming. When I asked her how she was preparing for her tests, she would blithely respond that she was just Googling the answers she needed.

Clearly, she lacked conventional academic discipline, but it forced me to ask deeper questions. Why was it so difficult for her to study these chapters? Was she destined, as a child of the digital age, to suffer from some type of learning disability?

I began to watch her closely. Could she learn? If so, how did she learn? And was the way she was learning common for her generation of digital natives?

I noticed that while my mind had been trained to go step by step through a sequential collection of knowledge, such as that found in a textbook, her mind would dart from place to place in a seemingly scattered way.

But then I began to notice something quite remarkable. I would ask her a question, and after a typical deadpan look of a 16 year-old, she would go to her phone and start to poke away on its screen. Then, after a few minutes, she would turn to me and give me an answer that was surprising in its depth of understanding.

What just happened there? How could she go from knowing nothing to knowing so much, so quickly?

I began to watch her finger movements on her phone more carefully and then later, asked her to explain her learning path.

Apparently, after an initial Google search, she would quickly jump through several related sites and then synthesize the information into an understanding, all in a matter of a few minutes.

I could barely keep up with her fingers on the screen.

So while I might have a more disciplined mind for a sequential linear learning path, hers was non-linear – a much faster spatial path of rapid triangulation. Something that might be called **Trialectical Synthesis**[1].

Turns out, my daughter is not that unusual. Many teachers complain that their students don't learn the same way they did, and they are struggling to engage them in the classroom.

These kids are not dumb. But most are not interested in being taught in the same way previous generations were. However, given a **Higher Purpose**[2] to learn, they are astonishingly fast learners.

They think differently from us. They have **Digital Minds**[3].

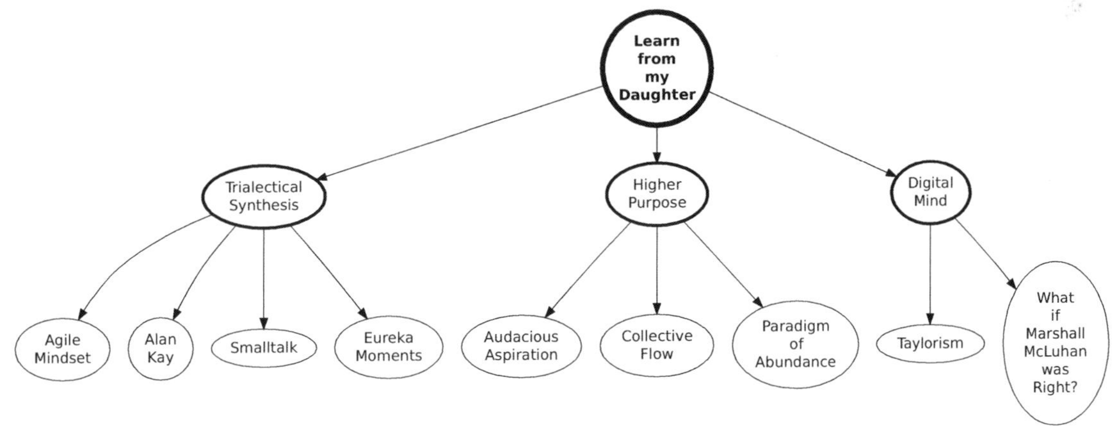

1 Page **214** - **Trialectical Synthesis**

2 Page **154** - **Higher Purpose**

3 Page **140** - **Digital Mind**

Learning Cycles

The key to the transformative power of Agile is fast, iterative learning cycles.

The learning cycle begins with an intention. Then comes a commitment, an action, and a reflection. Then it begins again.

The intention may be a question. Or it may be a desired solution. This intention is best inspired when aligned to an **Audacious Aspiration**[1].

Each of these learning cycles have three primary components:

- Define
- Do
- Decipher

You first have to define what you are going to do and what success will look like. You then have to do what you committed to. And then you have to reflect on that experience to decipher what you learned.

Each learning cycle has an element of experimentation, guided by curiosity. Each time we are called upon to walk fearlessly into the unknown.

Each learning cycle is launched based on how we understand the problem. We accept that often we may not understand the problem well enough to solve it. So we are forced to move forward based on multiple assumptions, not knowing which ones are true and which are not.

Inevitably in this process, things won't work out as we thought they would. And there are elements of failure.

When we reflect on each cycle, we are able to identify the incorrect assumptions that were responsible for these failures. This process allows us to better understand the true nature of the problem and become more empowered to solve it.

But then there are those **Eureka Moments**[2] when all of the pieces come together into a solution.

---

1 Page **120** - **Audacious Aspiration**

2 Page **144** - **Eureka Moments**

These moments of clarity feel magical. They often come when we least expect them, when we are sitting uncomfortably in a void of unknowing. Then, suddenly, understanding manifests.

The faster we can move through these learning cycles, the faster we can understand the problem and develop an elegant solution, something that feels good, feels whole.

This process requires structure and discipline. That is why **Agile Practices**[1] are helpful.

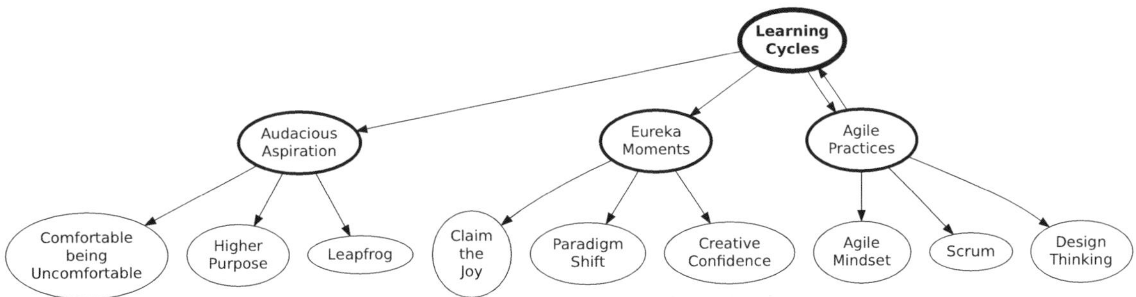

1 Page **115** - **Agile Practices**

Learning Motivators

In order for students to have agency and to be fully engaged as authors of their own learning journey, there must not only be purpose – a reason for the learning – but also the motivation to learn, that emotion which ignites action.

Learning is difficult without motivation. Unfortunately, far too often, fear has been used as the prime motivator. Or should we call it a manipulator?

Fear of failure, fear of rejection. Shame.

In **The Dayton Practice**[1] students were inspired by a different set of motivators that created **Joyful Sandboxes**[2]. The Dayton teachers found that there were three primary types of motivators for their students:

- Curiosity
- Creativity
- Competition

Some students were motivated to do the sprint by their innate curiosity about the topics. But many students, given their past academic experiences, struggled to tap into their curiosity. They often lacked the confidence and courage to walk into the unknown. For them, other learning motivators were needed.

For some students, this motivation might have come from their desire to create something. For other students, motivation would come from a sense of competition.

Students who were motivated by curiosity, tended to enjoy the **Rabbit Hole Research**[3] part of the learning sprint.

Those students who were motivated by their desire to make something, tended to enjoy most the creating phase of the process.

And those who were motivated by competition tended to enjoy the **In & Out Demo**[4], particularly the prospect of winning the da Vinci award, a recognition given to the best

1 Page **210** - **The Dayton Practice**

2 Page **165** - **Joyful Sandboxes**

3 Page **194** - **Rabbit Hole Research**

4 Page **158** - **In & Out Demo**

presentation at the end of each sprint cycle.

While students tended to enjoy one phase more than others, they were willing to do all three as they realized that by doing the other two, they would have the opportunity to do that phase they most enjoyed.

Interestingly, Dayton teachers noticed that students who tended to struggle in traditional classrooms were often most inspired to learn by the creativity phase of the sprint.

They would, for instance, be willing to research, synthesize, write and ultimately share their learning with others if that allowed them to get out to the shop and get their hands dirty making something.

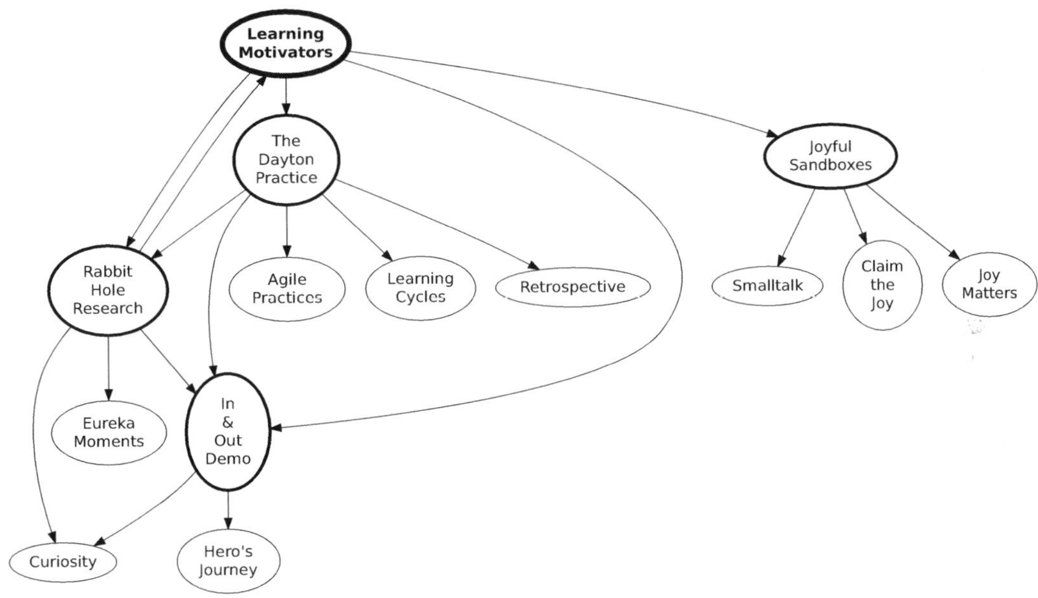

Make-a-thon

The concept of a make-a-thon came out of the challenge we faced when we wanted to share with other schools the experience of **Agile Learning**[1] that we were developing with the Dayton teachers.

Our hope was to use Dayton as a **Positive Deviant**[2] that would become a catalyst for a larger transformation of the education ecosystem in Oregon.

At a meeting with regional leaders, Derek Runberg from SparkFun suggested that we create an event called a make-a-thon that would bring students, educators and community members together to hack solutions using software and electronics – an opportunity to taste the **Agile Experience**[3].

In January of 2016, we held our first make-a-thon at Chemeketa Community College. We brought 60 participants from around the county, most of whom had never written a line of code or ever worked with a circuit board.

We broke the participants into multi-generational teams and launched into a three-hour boot-camp on coding and circuit design. Right before lunch the teams were given three challenges to choose from. They had the afternoon to prototype a solution to one of those challenges.

What happened that day, which has been repeated at every make-a-thon held since, was something magical. Joyful learning led to real, deep learning, learning that manifested in the creation of something that each team could not have imagined before the day began.

1 Page **110** - **Agile Learning**

2 Page **189** - **Positive Deviant**

3 Page **108** - **Agile Experience**

Many of the educators in the room saw a powerful truth: that students can learn faster than they can be taught. Much faster.

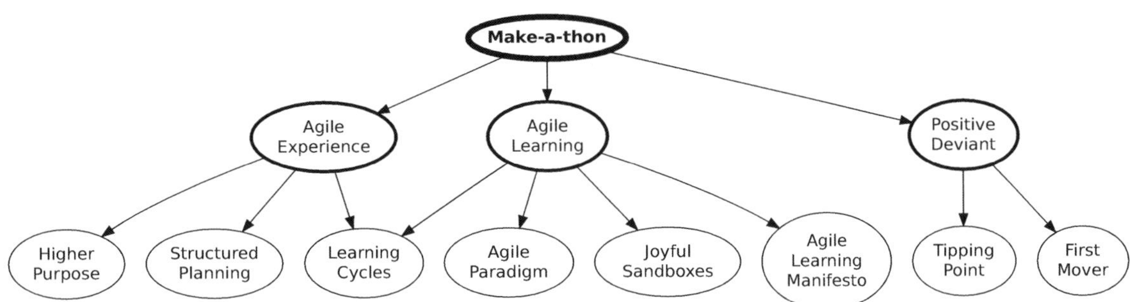

Meaning Makers

Life is a mystery. We walk our solitary path in the hope that our lives will have a meaning for ourselves and, ultimately, for others.

Our spirit rails against the angst of Macbeth's lament:

> *Out, out, brief candle! Life's but a walking shadow, a poor player that struts and frets his hour upon the stage and is heard no more. It is a tale told by an idiot, full of sound and fury, signifying nothing.*

From our earliest days, then, we are trying to make meaning of our experiences, to find a narrative that helps explain our world. To create a **Meaning Matrix**[1].

Our desire to make and share meaning ignites our **Curiosity**[2] and empowers us as creators. It is what gives us our vitality, our passion, our meaning.

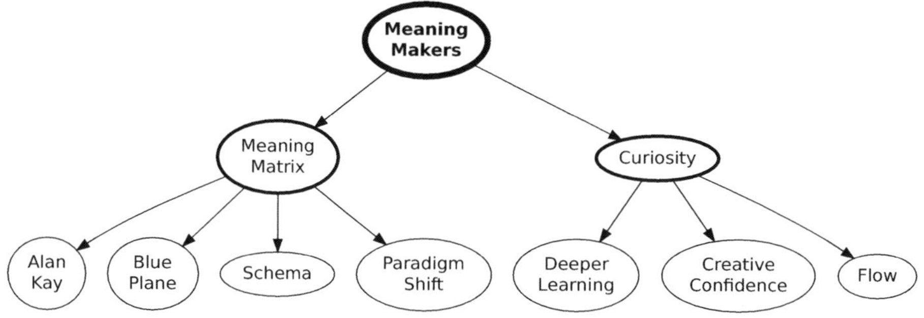

1 Page **181** - **Meaning Matrix**

2 Page **136** - **Curiosity**

Meaning Matrix

We make meaning through increasingly complex patterns of linked ideas. At first a concept sits alone, but then it gets connected to others. And a web of deeper understanding starts to form.

Some neuroscientists refer to these webs as 'inference networks'. Arthur Koestler, in his book *The Act of Creation*, called them 'matrices of thought' – a concept that was instrumental to the development of Alan Kay's idea of the **Blue Plane**[1]

In Latin, matrix means 'womb'. A meaning matrix is a pattern of connected concepts, a matrix, from which meaning is birthed.

Meaning matrices form our **Schema**[2] – our plane of consciousness. As long as that schema operates with others that are similar in form (based on shared culture and experiences) it remains relatively stable.

But when there is an intersecting of alternatively configured schemas, or when there is new learning that doesn't fit the existing schema, there is a disruptive reconfiguration of that meaning matrix – something called a **Paradigm Shift**[3].

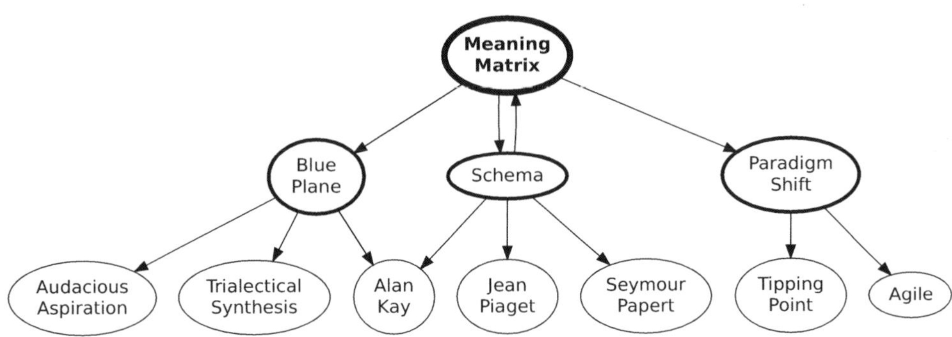

1 Page **122** - **Blue Plane**

2 Page **198** - **Schema**

3 Page **187** - **Paradigm Shift**

Mentors

The process of transformation is accelerated when the walls between educators and industry professionals are torn down.

For this reason, we find it valuable for **Innovators**[1] and **Early Adopters**[2] to be connected with those that have experience with **Agile Practices**[3], but may not, themselves, be educators.

Many educators have never worked outside of education. Most industry professionals have never taught in a classroom. For this reason, it is important that they develop trust and a commitment to learn together.

By so doing, they can begin to develop a co-creative partnership that can be profoundly life-giving for both of them.

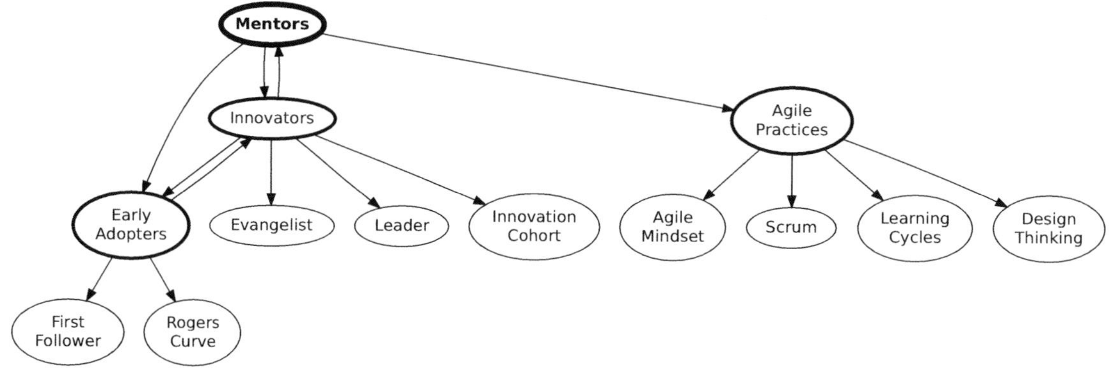

1 Page **162** - **Innovators**

2 Page **141** - **Early Adopters**

3 Page **115** - **Agile Practices**

Object Oriented Programming

Most modern software programs are built on the concept of Object Oriented Programming (OOP).

The concept was first fully introduced in a radically new programming language, **Smalltalk**[1] that was developed by a team lead by **Alan Kay**[2] at Xerox's research lab, PARC.

The idea of OOP was that lines of code and data sets could be defined as self-contained 'objects'. As such, they could be utilized multiple times by multiple programs by simply referring to them by name.

Kay developed this concept based on a software language called Simula.

Ward Cunningham, Kent Beck and others integrated the concept of **Pattern Languages**[3] into OOP and used it as the foundation for the new agile experience they were exploring.

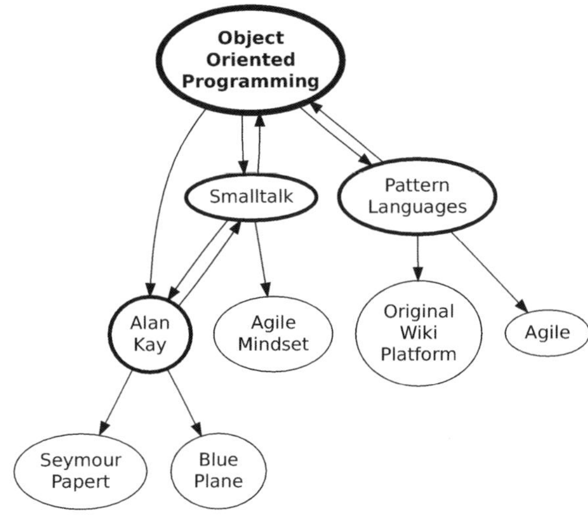

.

1 Page **203** - **Smalltalk**

2 Page **119** - **Alan Kay**

3 Page **188** - **Pattern Languages**

Original Wiki Platform

The wiki has helped fundamentally transform how we think of knowledge.

Ask someone a question, and one of the first things they might do is go to Wikipedia. From there, they will follow links to other pages in what is now the largest repository of human knowledge ever created.

This access to knowledge has had a profound impact on our opportunity to learn. Previously, knowledge was stored away in large libraries, often in distant places, accessible to relatively few.

But even more profoundly important is how this knowledge is created. By being community-sourced, it was no longer dependent on a relatively small group of academic authorities, enabling a much broader collection of knowledge. The original wiki platform, created by Ward Cunningham, allowed this community authoring to happen.

But the original wiki, called WikiWikiWeb, did not set out to be a communal knowledge base. Instead, Ward sought to develop a way for software programmers to share new ideas and programming practices that utilize the concept of **Pattern Languages**[1].

This platform was instrumental in the launch of the movement that was to become **Agile**[2].

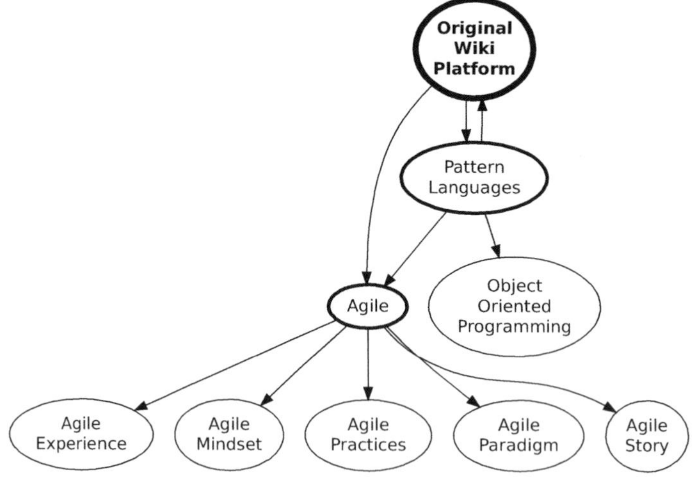

1 Page **188** - **Pattern Languages**

2 Page **103** - **Agile**

Paradigm of Abundance

In the creative economy, there is a sense of abundance of opportunity, due, in large part, to the continued introduction of new technologies. These technologies have allowed people to develop new solutions faster than ever before.

On the other hand, most educators live in a world with ever-decreasing resources, a world defined by scarcity.

We have, then, two distinct paradigms: a paradigm of scarcity and a paradigm of abundance.

Part of the experiment in Dayton's school district was to see if their school could move from one paradigm to the other by living out an **Audacious Aspiration**[1]. And, if it did, to understand the impact of that transformation.

And it worked. Sure, they still had all of the financial pressures of working within an underfunded educational system.

But when Jami, their principal, moved into this new mindset, she helped unleash an abundance of opportunity for her, her staff, and her students.

As they began to **Claim the Joy**[2], partnerships started being formed all over the place. Equipment started showing up at their door that was being gifted. New funding opportunities appeared.

1 Page **120** - **Audacious Aspiration**

2 Page **125** - **Claim the Joy**

New community resources were identified and tapped to open the door to new opportunities for their students.

At times the abundance felt a little overwhelming.

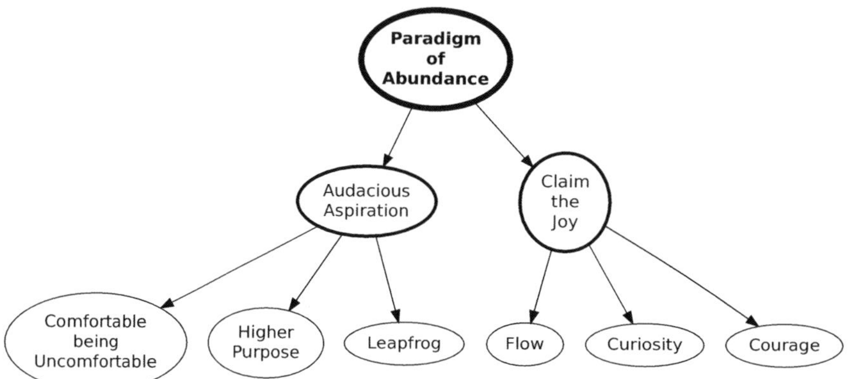

Paradigm Shift

The commonly used term 'paradigm shift' is actually a fairly recent concept, one that dates back to the 1962 publication of Thomas Kuhn's book *The Structure of Scientific Revolutions*.

The book itself represented a paradigm shift.

Kuhn was exploring the evolution of our scientific understanding. He found that there were moments in time when new experiences forced radically new models.

Existing models of understanding would incrementally evolve until new experiences began to emerge that didn't fit. A tension between the old model and new experiences would continue until a radical restructuring of the model appeared that integrated these new experiences.

A struggle between adherents of the old and new models would then erupt, until there was, in a sense, a **Tipping Point**[1], and the new model became the dominant one.

Agile[2] is a paradigm shift that underpins our transition from an industrial economy to a creative economy. It is transforming how we create value, how we run our companies and, potentially, how we might teach.

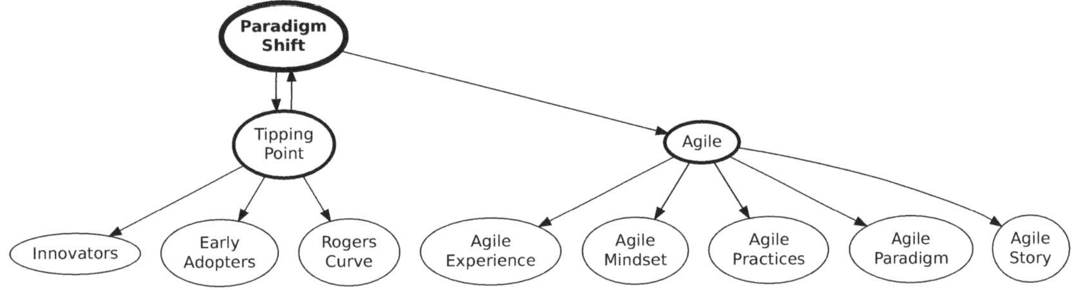

1 Page **212** - **Tipping Point**

2 Page **103** - **Agile**

Pattern Languages

The concept of pattern languages was developed by Christopher Alexander, an architect and urban planner. He sought to define a set of universal architectural elements that created living spaces filled with vital energy.

These elements relate to each other, forming interconnected patterns that could be defined and shared as guidelines, something he called pattern languages. These pattern languages are frameworks that can help others discover creative solutions.

He introduced this concept in a three-volume set. One book, *The Timeless Way of Building*, explored the theory of patterns in architectural design. *A Pattern Language* defined common patterns found in traditional architecture. *The Oregon Experiment* explored how pattern languages were used to develop the design of the University of Oregon's campus.

His concepts were deeply influential in the development of **Object Oriented Programming**[1], the **Original Wiki Platform**[2] and **Agile**[3].

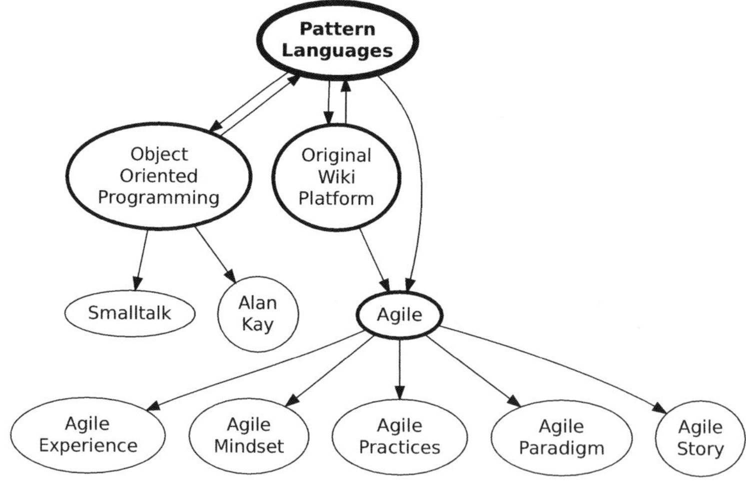

1 Page **183** - **Object Oriented Programming**

2 Page **184** - **Original Wiki Platform**

3 Page **103** - **Agile**

Positive Deviant

Positive deviants are individuals or groups that have adopted new mindsets and skill sets to create value in a way that can be held up as an example for others to follow.

The story goes back to the 1990s. After several years of trying to launch nutrition programs in Vietnam, Save the Children finally found a government official who would let them into the country. But there was a caveat to the invitation. If they could not demonstrate success quickly, the invitation would be withdrawn.

The directors of this program, Jerry and Monique Sternin, knew that if they applied their traditional teaching model, they would fail. In that model, instructors were sent to teach villagers about nutrition. This process would have to be repeated over several years to see a significant change in behavior.

But they had only months to demonstrate a significant impact.

With little to lose, they chose a radical new path, one that had been piloted back in the 70's by a pediatrician at a Boston hospital. This was a model of positive deviance.

They went into the villages not as authorities, but as learners. They asked the villagers what they were feeding their families and observed the relative heights of their children. They then went back to the families with taller children – those with better nutrition – and explored the diet and gardening practices more deeply. They then asked the families if they would be willing to share these practices with the other villagers.

Not only did the other villagers quickly adopt these nutritional practices, they began to share best practices in other areas of their lives, like home construction. Transformational change happened quickly, with a profound impact on their community.

I started using the model of positive deviancy when I was a marketing consultant for Tektronix and then applied it to work I was doing leading innovation initiatives at the Portland Police Bureau. It became a key component in our strategy for reimagining education, using Dayton as a positive deviant for others.

Prime Pattern

A prime pattern is a pattern that has been simplified down to three parts, what could be called a **Trivium**[1].

In software development, the process of simplification is called 'refactoring'. When you refactor code, you're having the code do the same tasks, but simplifying how it does them. In this process, the code becomes more 'elegant' and easier for others to use.

A similar process is possible when working with complex ideas. If ideas remain in a complex form, it is very difficult to share them with others. As a result, their impact, within a larger community, is limited. But if those concepts can be distilled down to a simple form – a pattern – they can be easily shared.

A great example is the Theory of Relativity, an immensely complex concept. By Einstein's 'refactoring' this concept to $E= mc^2$, his theory became well known to an audience far beyond his scientific community.

A prime pattern that can be thought of as a 'three-legged stool' – dynamically balanced as a powerful container of meaning. **Core Values**[2] are best expressed as prime patterns.

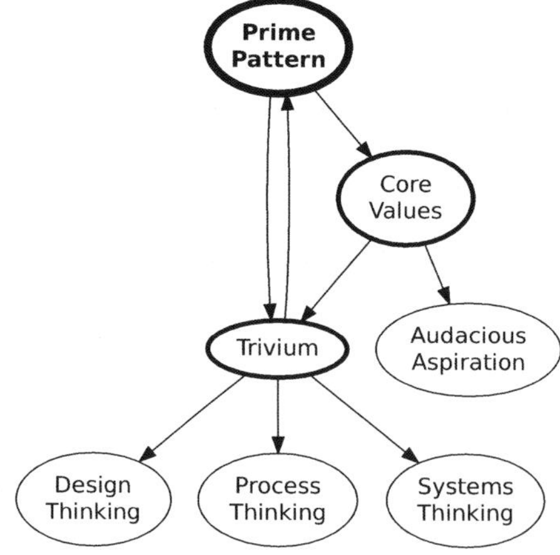

1 Page **216** - **Trivium**

2 Page **130** - **Core Values**

Process Thinking

Process thinking is the ability to design and manage sequential steps in a creation process. By developing these steps, we are not only able to replicate them, but also improve efficiency.

Process thinking allows a team to deliver a project, for engineers to design a production line, for software developers to program a computer, for a student to know how to write a paper.

Computer programming uses complex process thinking, one that uses a specific aspect of process thinking called **Computational Thinking**[1] where one needs to think algorithmically in increasingly complex logic structures.

Process thinking is empowered when it is integrated with **Design Thinking**[2] and **Systems Thinking**[3].

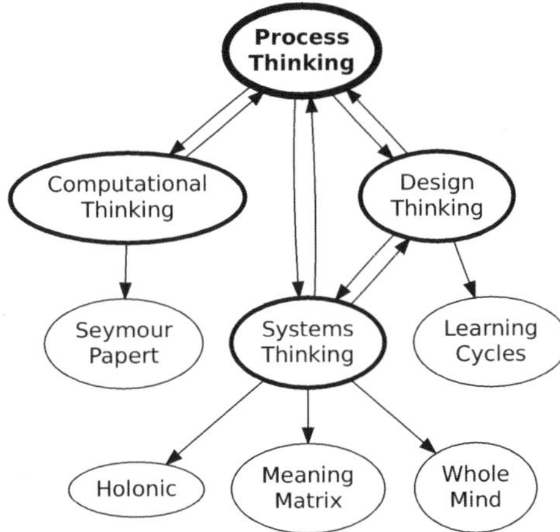

1 Page **129** - **Computational Thinking**

2 Page **139** - **Design Thinking**

3 Page **207** - **Systems Thinking**

Project Based Learning

Project-based learning (PBL) is a student-centered education pedagogy that is based on the belief that students experience **Deeper Learning**[1] when they are acquiring knowledge by exploring real-world challenges and problems.

High Tech High in San Diego was established as a model PBL learning environment. The key to PBL is defining purpose, the 'why' of learning, and then challenging students to learn through a creative process.

Purpose Driven Learning[2] is an amplification of PBL which challenges educators to understand the purpose of the learning from the student's perspective, a purpose that is often beyond the classroom.

This learning approach is based on the learning theories of **Jean Piaget**[3] and others.

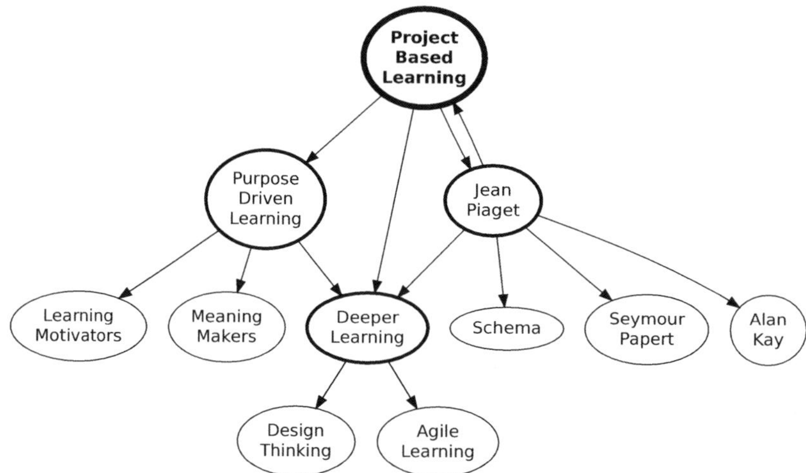

1 Page **138** - **Deeper Learning**

2 Page **193** - **Purpose Driven Learning**

3 Page **164** - **Jean Piaget**

Purpose Driven Learning

There are different types of motivators for learning.

If we are truly being honest, much of traditional education uses fear as the primary motivator; the fear of failure, the fear of rejection.

But purpose driven learning inspires us to learn in new ways using different **Learning Motivators**[1]. For some, it may be curiosity. For others, it is creativity. And then, for others, it is competition. Each student can reveal the motivator that works best for their catalyst.

Deeper Learning[2] happens when we are trying to make meaning in order to solve a problem that is important to us: fulfilling our human commission as **Meaning Makers**[3]. Our best learning is for a purpose that is meaningful for us.

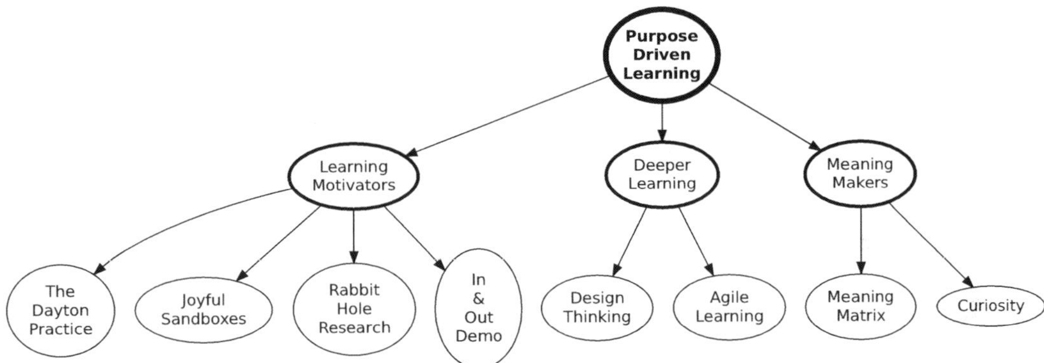

1 Page **180** - **Meaning Makers**

2 Page **176** - **Learning Motivators**

3 Page **138** - **Deeper Learning**

Rabbit Hole Research

Real learning begins with **Curiosity**[1]. But you cannot script someone else's curiosity, certainly not a student's. But in that journey of curiosity, there are moments of discovery where understanding is illuminated – **Eureka Moments**[2]. Moments that turn us into life-long learners.

In **The Dayton Practice**[3], a Genius Hour class was given a shared base topic, for example, 'music'. Each team then drew their scrambler, a randomly selected topic. For example, 'sports'.

Their goal, over the following two to three weeks was to (1) research these two topics, (2) find connections between them, (3) create something that demonstrated what they had learned, (4) share their findings, using their creation, to their fellow students in an **In & Out Demo**[4].

To help spark curiosity, Jenni and her colleagues developed a prompt guide.

The students started their research by identifying aspects of the base topic and the scrambler topic that interested them.

But some students struggled to find areas that they were curious about. To help move them past that barrier, the prompt included two more elements, suggesting the students explore ways that those topics could relate to their passions or to specific projects they wanted to do. Find something that is interesting to research, they were urged. Then explore how it could connect the scrambler to the base.

One student team, for instance, had a student who really wanted to do a baking project. But their topics were art and psychology. So the team agreed to research the relationship between art, psychology, and food. Much to their surprise, they discovered that the artistic flair by which we present food directly affects how we perceive its flavor.

They baked cupcakes, decorated them, and then told their story of discovery to their peers.

---

1 Page **136** - **Curiosity**

2 Page **144** - **Eureka Moments**

3 Page **210** - **The Dayton Practice**

4 Page **158** - **In & Out Demo**

This practice takes advantage of the understanding that students are sparked to action by different **Learning Motivators**[1].

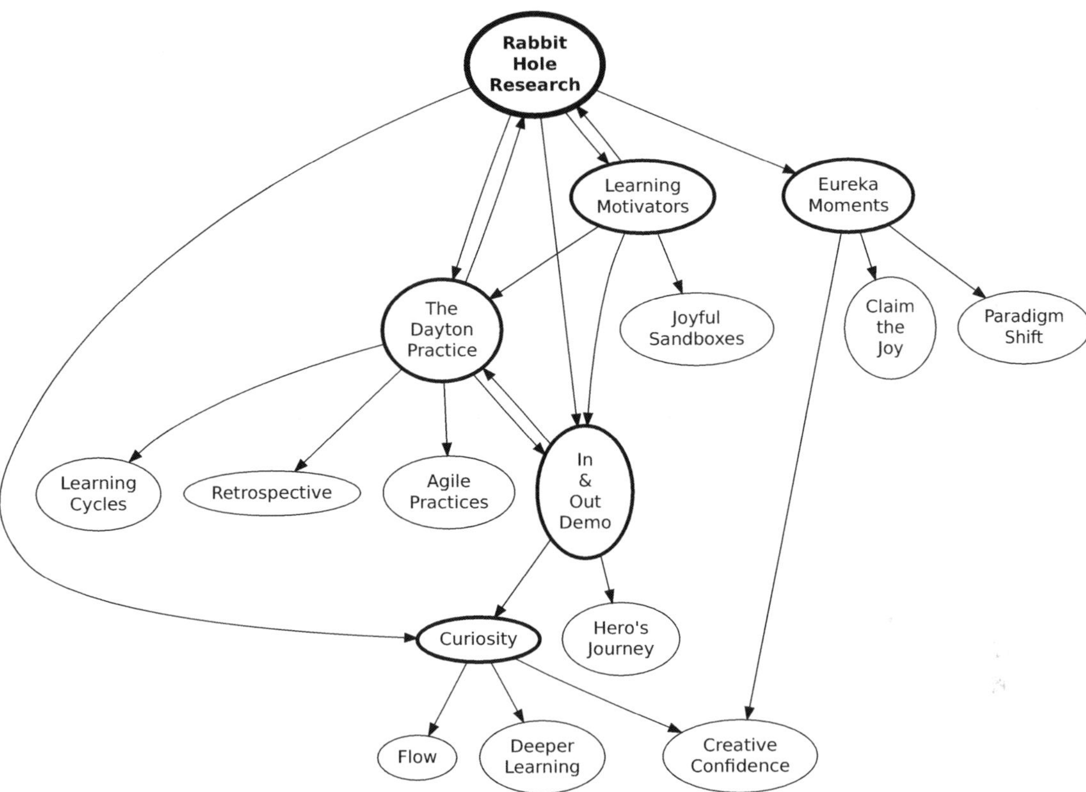

1 Page **176** - **Learning Motivators**

Retrospective

An essential part of a **Sprint**[1] is a retrospective, often just referred to as a 'retro'. This meeting, organized at the end of the sprint, is a time for a team to reflect on their last learning cycle.

There are many ways to structure a retro, but its goal is to reflect on the experience. Typically, the meeting focuses on these four questions:

- What went well?
- What didn't go so well?
- What have we learned?
- What still puzzles us?

This reflection is critical to identify insights that help shape the next sprint.

The retro is a core piece of most agile frameworks, including **Scrum**[2].

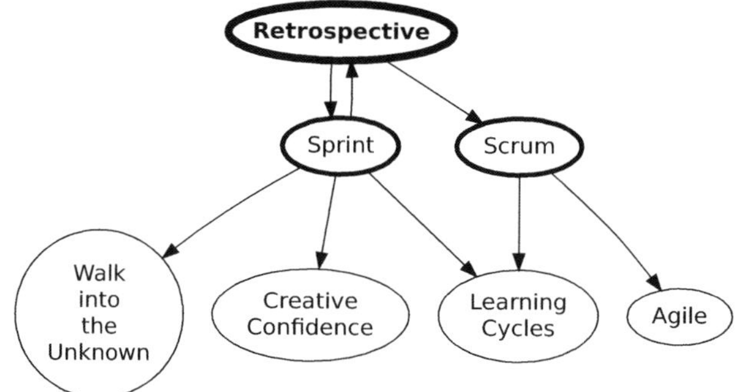

1 Page **205** - **Sprint**

2 Page **199** - **Scrum**

Rogers Curve

Everett Rogers introduced the concept of the **Innovators**[1] in his book *Diffusion of Innovation*, published in 1962.

In his curve, he defined five types of customers: innovators, early adopters, early majority, late majority, and laggards.

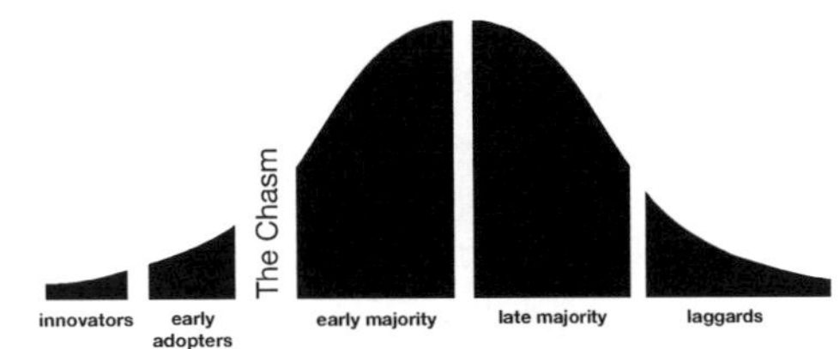

While the number of innovators is small, they play a critical role in influencing **Early Adopters**[2].

Geoffrey Moore modified Rogers' model by introducing one more important element: 'the chasm'. This concept became known as 'Moore's Chasm'. A gap between the early adopters and the rest of the market.

For new technologies or ideas to become adopted by the rest of a community, they must cross this chasm of doubt. While the innovators and early adopters are known for their **Courage**[3], the rest are more risk-averse. They are more fearful of failure.

So they need to have a relatively high level of confidence before they will adopt something new. This confidence is provided by the early adopters, colleagues with whom they can self-identify. It is with the stories of these early adopters that the bridge across the chasm is built.

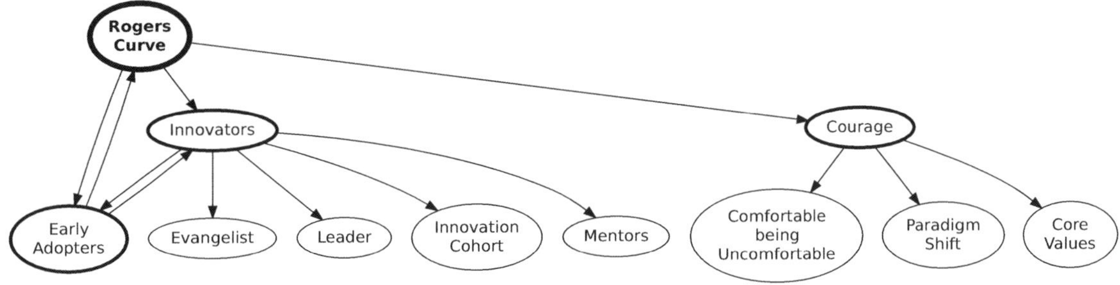

1 Page **162** - **Innovators**

2 Page **141** - **Early Adopters**

3 Page **131** - **Courage**

Schema

Immanuel Kant, the German philosopher, introduced the concept of 'schema'. It is the internal model that we use to interpret the world around us – how we make sense of our perceptions.

We are standing at a street corner, the light turns red and the walk sign ahead is illuminated. We step out into the street although a car coming down the street is still moving. We are, based on a calculation made with our internal schema, deciding that the car will stop and it is safe to cross the street. Every moment we are stepping out into the world based on perceptions interpreted through our internal schema.

One way to think of schema is as our personal pattern language of meaning – a **Meaning Matrix**[1]. It is how we make sense of our personal experiences to shape our understanding of the world.

What the great learning theorist **Jean Piaget**[2] came to understand, is that there are two types of learning: one which deepens the understanding of our current schema and one that actually reconfigures our schema. Piaget's concepts of learning profoundly influenced how both **Seymour Papert**[3] and **Alan Kay**[4] explored the potential of the computer as a tool for learning and creating.

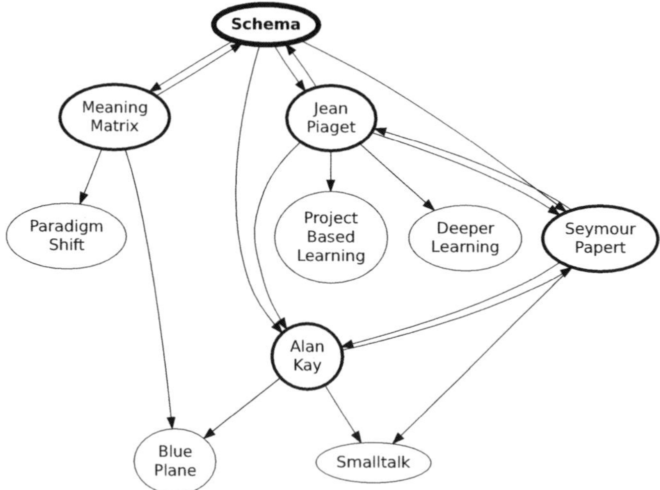

1 Page **181** - **Meaning Matrix**

2 Page **164** - **Jean Piaget**

3 Page **200** - **Seymour Papert**

4 Page **119** - **Alan Kay**

Scrum

Scrum is one of the most popular sets of practices, referred to as 'frameworks', of **Agile**[1].

This framework uses multidisciplinary teams that are commissioned to create something together. This team is called a 'scrum', a rugby reference.

Each team has someone who is responsible for managing it, called a 'scrum master', and someone who represents the needs of the customer, called a 'product owner'.

The teams set about to solve a problem or create a solution through a series of short bursts of very focused development, called a **Sprint**[2]. These sprints, typically two weeks in length, build to a final release of a solution, called an 'epic'.

The key to the success of these types of agile frameworks is that these sprints create **Learning Cycles**[3] that allow the team members to reflect and adjust, based on a deeper understanding of their challenge and changing customer needs.

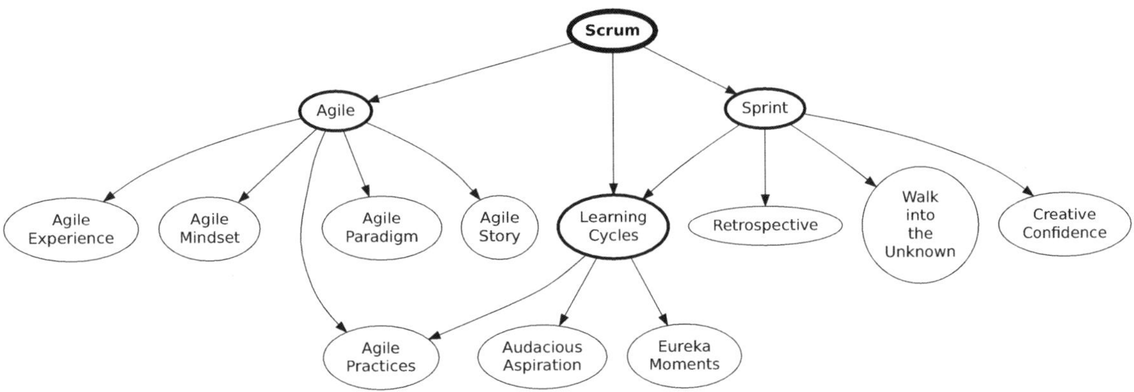

1 Page **103** - **Agile**

2 Page **205** - **Sprint**

3 Page **174** - **Learning Cycles**

Seymour Papert

The theories of **Jean Piaget**[1] inspired Seymour Papert's contributions to the development of the Logo, a programming language. He helped create Logo to explore how children might think and solve problems using computers.

Papert went on to create the MIT Media Lab. There he developed his theory on learning called Constructionism, which was an extension of Piaget's Constructivist learning theories.

His theories and experiences teaching students had a significant impact on **Alan Kay**[2] and the development of **Smalltalk**[3].

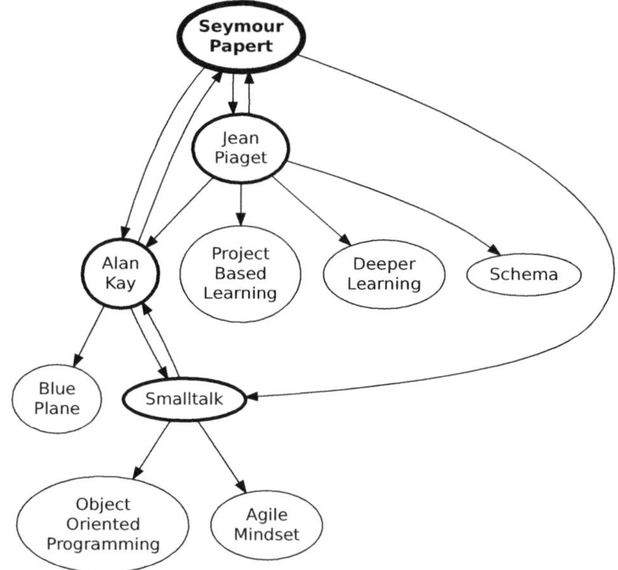

1 Page **164** - **Jean Piaget**

2 Page **119** - **Alan Kay**

3 Page **203** - **Smalltalk**

Shadow Curtain

We all have a curtain of shame. We are human, imperfect beings with imperfect life experiences, some joyful and others painful.

Behind that curtain of shame lies our shadows, our fears. Fears of inadequacy, fears of not belonging. It can feel like we live in **A Culture of Shame**[1].

We don't want to talk about that curtain, we would much prefer to pretend that it doesn't exist.

To keep others from seeing that curtain, we create our bouncer, our ego, that persona designed to shield others from that curtain. The greater the pain behind that curtain, the larger an ego persona we create.

For us to pull back the curtain, and certainly for others to pull back that curtain with us, is an act of excruciating vulnerability. It takes **Courage**[2]. It takes trust.

But behind that curtain, there are not only our fears but also our greatness.

As Joseph Campbell once said, "The cave you fear to enter holds the treasure you seek."

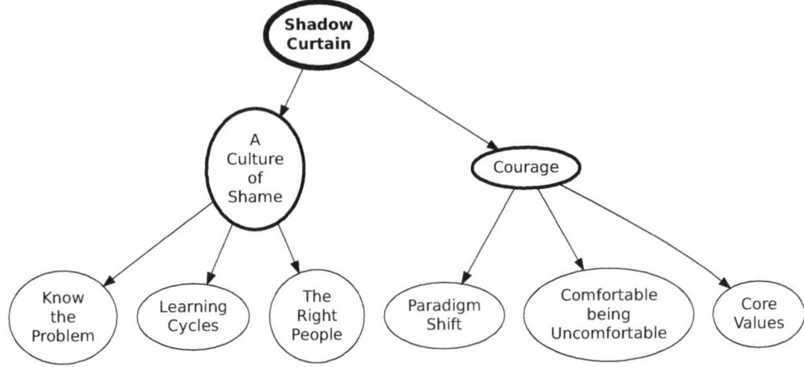

1 Page **67** - **A Culture of Shame**

2 Page **131** - **Courage**

Shu Ha Ri

Shu Ha Ri is a Japanese martial art concept that is used to describe the stages of learning to reach a state of mastery.

It has been used to describe the stages of learning agile practices.

The first stage is 'shu'. In this stage, a student repeats the practices that have been defined by masters. There is no deviation from these practices. They may not be fully understood, but by practicing them, over and over again, they begin to feel familiar, become natural.

In the next stage, 'ha', a student begins to understand the movements and starts to experiment with them. These innovations start to reveal the deeper essence of the movements.

In the 'ri' stage, a student becomes a master, where the creative potential is unleashed and individual expressions reveal the deeper meaning of the practice.

Smalltalk

Smalltalk is a programming language initially developed in the 1970s by a team headed by **Alan Kay**[1] that was designed for experimental learning. It was also the first language to fully utilize the concept of **Object Oriented Programming**[2].

Utilizing the Just-in-Time compiler (JIT) compiler, pieces of code could be written and immediately tested, without having to fully recompile the entire program allowing for programmers to quickly experiment with different ideas.

Kay was intrigued by the challenge of reimagining the computer. Previously, the computer was largely seen as a machine for analytical computation. But, at the dawn of the age of personal computers, he wanted to explore how it could transform into a tool for personal creativity.

Three elements needed to be reimagined to bring this radical idea to life – the hardware, the computer interface, and a software language.

From his lab in the Learning Research Group (LRG) of Xerox PARC, these three elements came together to create the precursor to the Macintosh computer, a machine that would come to revolutionize the computer industry when it was introduced in 1984.

When conceptualizing the language, Kay started with the premise that everything was an object, that all objects contained sets of objects (classes) which shared the same characteristics, and that each object was in relationship with others through the passing of messages.

Here is how Kay talked about this new language:

> *It became the exemplar of the new computing, in part, because we were actually trying for a qualitative shift in belief structures – a new Kuhnian paradigm in the same spirit as the invention of the printing press – and thus took highly extreme positions which almost forced these new styles to be invented.*[3]

---

1 Page **119** - **Alan Kay**

2 Page **183** - **Object Oriented Programming**

3 Kay, Alan. "The Early History of Smalltalk." http://gagne.homedns.org/~tgagne/contrib/EarlyHistoryST.html

Core elements of the **Agile Mindset**[1] grew out the experience of programming with Smalltalk.

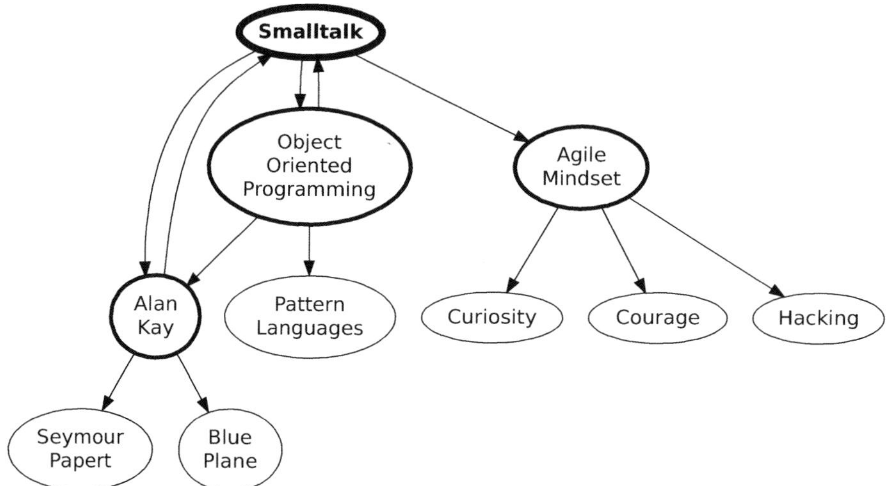

1 Page **112** - **Agile Mindset**

Sprint

A key practice of Agile is a sprint. A sprint is a short, focused commitment to accomplish a definable set of tasks. Often these sprints last one to two weeks.

By making a commitment to achieve something definable, it is possible for an individual or team to then reflect on what was accomplished over that short period of time. In a **Retrospective**[1] of this effort, insights are illuminated that help define the goals of the next sprint. This process creates a tightly defined **Learning Cycle**[2] that exponentially accelerates the speed of learning.

Each learning cycle begins with a set of assumptions. With each sprint, as teams **Walk into the Unknown**[3], some of those assumptions are proven wrong. Deep learning happens when we identify those wrong assumptions. They are redefined and tested until they are no longer assumptions but become new 'knowns'. This process increases our **Creative Confidence**[4] as we plunge into the next sprint.

Failure occurs when our assumptions are wrong. The faster we fail and redefine those assumptions, the faster we learn. Failure, then, is not to be avoided. Indeed, failure is at the very heart of the learning. It is through failure that we better understand the true nature of the problem – an understanding that ultimately leads to a solution.

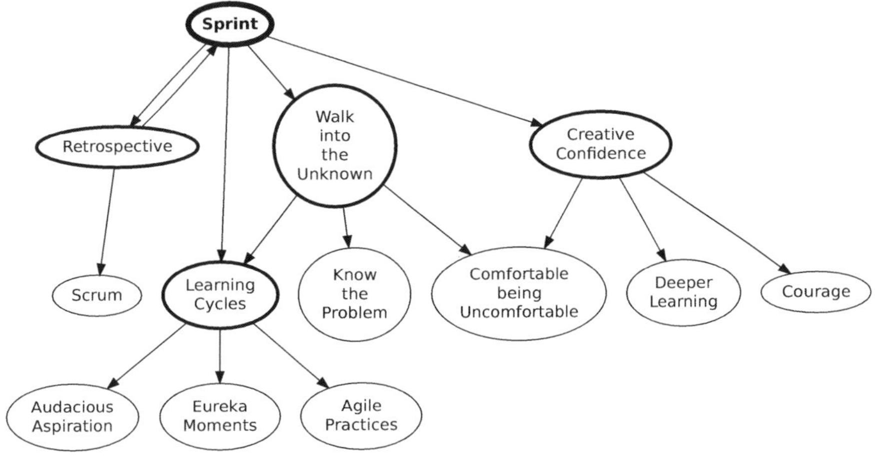

1 Page **196** - **Retrospective**

2 Page **174** - **Learning Cycles**

3 Page **218** - **Walk into the Unknown**

4 Page **133** - **Creative Confidence**

Structured Planning

Structured planning is defined by the concept of the Gantt chart.

This planning model was introduced by Henry Gantt in 1910 as a tool for engineering processes through a series of sequential tasks.
It embodies a core premise of the **Cartesian Mindset**[1], one that believes that complex systems can be broken down into their parts, understood in their entirety, and then reconfigured.

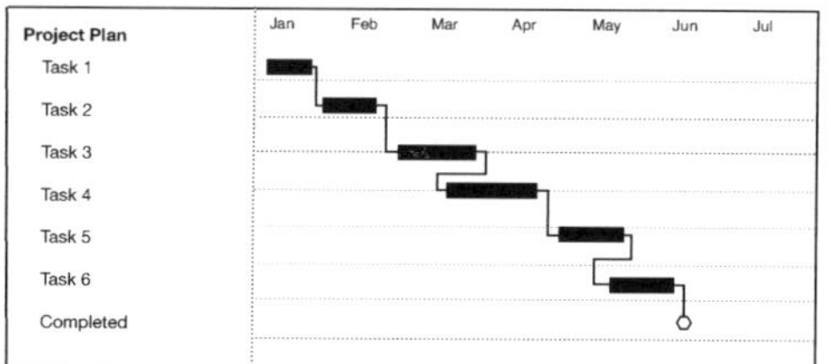

This premise was deterministic and assumed a hierarchical control structure. One that became known as 'command and control' management.

The concept of Gantt charts was a key model of scientific management, called **Taylorism**[2] that developed out of the **Efficiency Movement**[3].

The original architects of our education system used these principles when defining the structure of education – one that has been in place for more than 100 years.

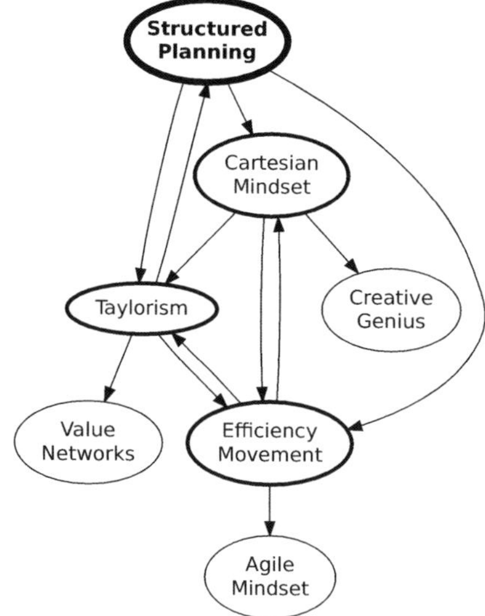

1 Page **124** - **Cartesian Mindset**

2 Page **208** - **Taylorism**

3 Page **142** - **Efficiency Movement**

Systems Thinking

There are three critical types of thinking necessary to be empowered creators in the new economy – three types of thinking we are challenged to develop in our students.

There is **Design Thinking**[1], where we are called upon to listen deeply and empathetically to users in order to develop, through iterative discovery, new *solutions*.

There is **Process Thinking**[2] which calls us to think abstractly in complex logical structures to develop new *processes*.

And then there is Systems Thinking, which challenges us to understand patterns of relationships in order to create self-sustaining *systems*. In the Industrial Age, these systems were thought of as mechanistic. In our new creative economy, at the threshold of what might be called the Imagination Age, complex systems are understood to be more like living organisms, **Holonic**[3] in nature.

Great innovators are system thinkers. Leonardo da Vinci certainly was. At the root of his immense capability was his insatiable curiosity about many diverse areas. He would explore each of these areas deeply, linking his observations to create complex webs of understanding – each a **Meaning Matrix**[4]. Developing all three of these types of thinking allows us to unlock the potential of the **Whole Mind**[5].

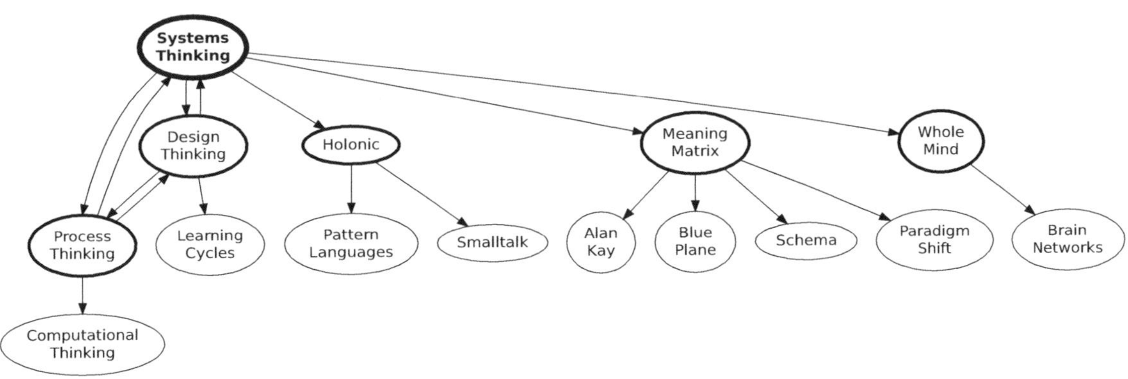

1 Page **139** - **Design Thinking**

2 Page **191** - **Process Thinking**

3 Page **155** - **Holonic**

4 Page **181** - **Meaning Matrix**

5 Page **221** - **Whole Mind**

Taylorism

Frederick Winslow Taylor was his name – a man of the Edwardian Age. He was a significant participant in the **Efficiency Movement**[1] and the founder of Scientific Management. He was, arguably, one of the most important men of the Industrial Age.

His theory of management became known as Taylorism.

At the core of this model was the precise analysis of workflows to improve efficiency and labor productivity.

In this approach, production tasks were broken down, put into a sequential order, and precisely timed – creating production lines. These production lines became the primary production model throughout the industrial economy – managed through **Structured Planning**[2].

These industrial production lines were developed with the premise that those responsible for designing and controlling the process, the engineers and managers, possessed superior intellect. The workers were expected to obediently follow instructions.

Compliant workers were needed who would be malleable to the will of their superiors.

This theory was then applied by the early leaders of public education to deliver workers to this economy.

The goal of this industrial education system was to teach a consistent body of knowledge, sort students by their potential role and, above all, teach them how to follow instructions. The system was to create compliant learners who would become compliant workers.

---

1 Page **142** - **Efficiency Movement**

2 Page **206** - **Structured Planning**

But our new economy needs vastly different skills. We need creative problem solvers who can become nimble architects of complex systems in **Value Networks**[1] that deliver new solutions fast.

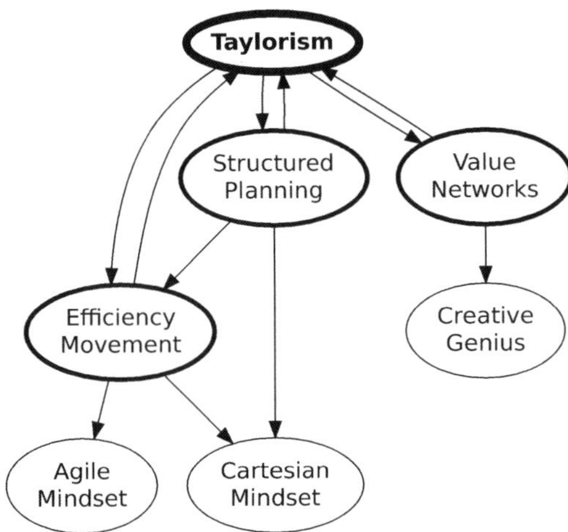

1 Page **217** - **Value Networks**

The Dayton Practice

The Dayton Practice is a framework that adapted **Agile Practices**[1] to the classroom. It was developed by a team of teachers at Dayton working with industry agilists.

This framework uses short, tight **Learning Cycles**[2] that provide a clear purpose for the learning.

This learning model challenges students to find connections between two diverse topics, synthesize meaning from those connections, and then communicate that new understanding to others.

Each sprint challenges students to become more proficient as meaning-makers and storytellers. It is also a practice that helps them to become creative polymaths that are increasingly empowered. A practice that emulates the essence of Leonardo da Vinci's greatness.

The sprints begin with students being given their 'base' topic and randomly choosing a 'scrambler' topic. All teams have the same base, but different scramblers. For instance, a base might be 'art' with one team having a scrambler of 'psychology' while another team has 'sports'.

The students then launch into a two to three-week sprint that has three primary experiences:

- Researching
- Creating
- Sharing

Researching
After the teams are given their topics, they entered the **Rabbit Hole Research**[3] phase. There they research both topics and discover connections between them.

To help assist this process, they could also begin this research journey from a personal perspective that challenges them to connect one of their passions, or a project they would like to make, to these topics.

1 Page **115** - **Agile Practices**

2 Page **174** - **Learning Cycles**

3 Page **194** - **Rabbit Hole Research**

Creating
Once the students have done their research and discovered the connections between their base and scrambler topics, they are challenged to create a project that illustrates this understanding.

Sharing
For students to have true learning agency, they must also become good communicators and teachers. The **In & Out Demo**[1] gives students that opportunity. This fast-paced exercise challenges students to use their creation to convey concisely the meaning of their learning to others.

After every sprint cycle, the class holds a **Retrospective**[2] that allows them to reflect on this experience and helps shape the next sprint.

Through these experiences, trusted learning communities are built, ones that continue to amaze as they unleash the creative genius hidden within each student – and in each teacher.

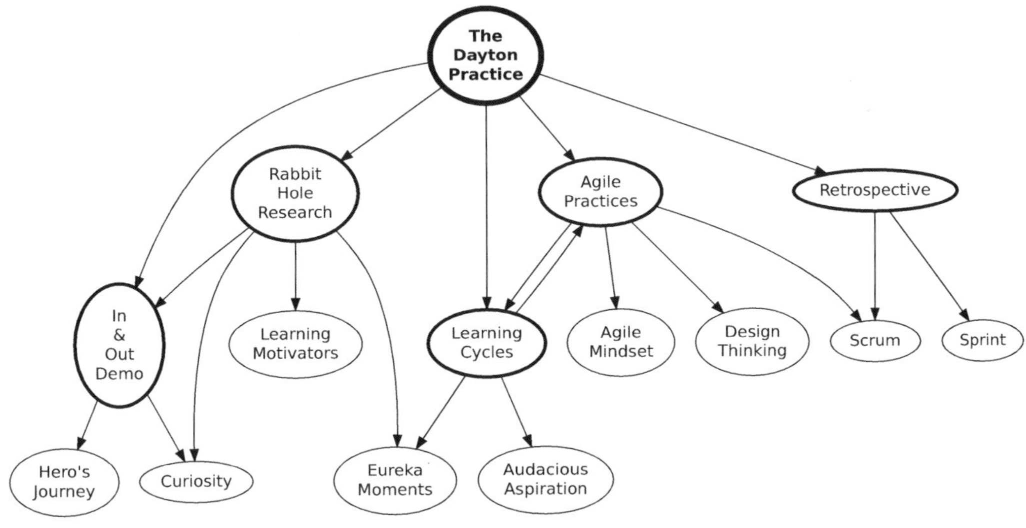

1 Page **158** - **In & Out Demo**

2 Page **196** - **Retrospective**

Tipping Point

In 2000, Malcome Gladwell published the book *The Tipping Point: How Little Things Can Make a Big Difference,* in which he introduced the concept of the tipping point – that moment in time when a new idea or paradigm becomes broadly accepted.

Gladwell explored how new concepts that represented a **Paradigm Shift**[1] could move from a minority to a majority of members in a community. He paid particular attention to the role of connections, surmising that everyone was connected within six relationships. These connections facilitated the dissemination of new ideas.

Then, in 2010, scientists at the Rensselaer Polytechnic Institute published a study[2] that found that when just 10 percent of the population embraced a new paradigm, the paradigm was quickly adopted by the majority of the community.

This understanding of tipping points is critical for developing a strategy for cultural transformation in schools and businesses. It brings into focus the critical role of **Innovators**[3] and **Early Adopters**[4] that are embracing new mindsets. They play a critical role in building a bridge over Moore's Chasm in the **Rogers Curve**[5] – allowing a culture to quickly reach its tipping point.

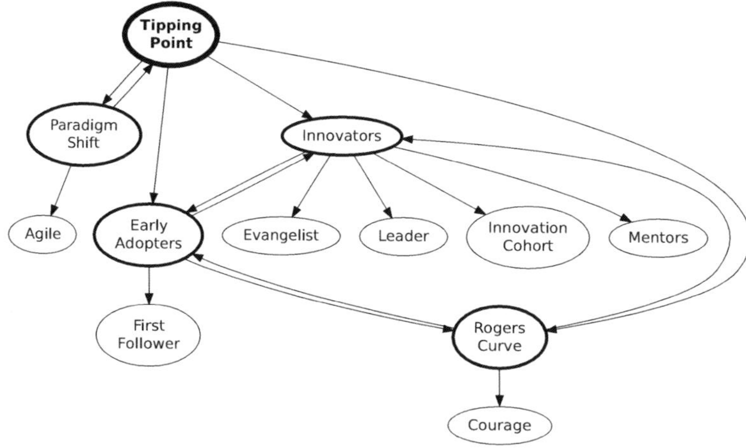

1 Page **187** - **Paradigm Shift**

2 Rensselaer Polytechnic Institute. "Minority Rules: Scientists Discover Tipping Point for the Spread of Ideas." https://news.rpi.edu/luwakkey/2902

3 Page **162** - **Innovators**

4 Page **141** - **Early Adopters**

5 Page **197** - **Rogers Curve**

Transmutational Experience

A transmutational experience is one in which something deep inside of us changes based on an experience that we have had, an internal experience that precedes the manifestations of an external transformation.

At first, externally, our form has not changed. We are still the same person, wearing the same clothes. But, in this shift, we begin to see the world in a different way. We begin to act differently, a process that begins to transform our world.

For many, this shift happens the first time they have an **Agile Learning**[1] experience. We hear this comment all the time from teachers during reflections following a **Make-a-thon**[2]: "How is it that these students could learn faster than they could be taught?" "What was that joy we just experienced?"

These are experiences that cannot be unseen. They cannot be unfelt. They define a new personal truth.

They open the door to a new **Curiosity**[3].

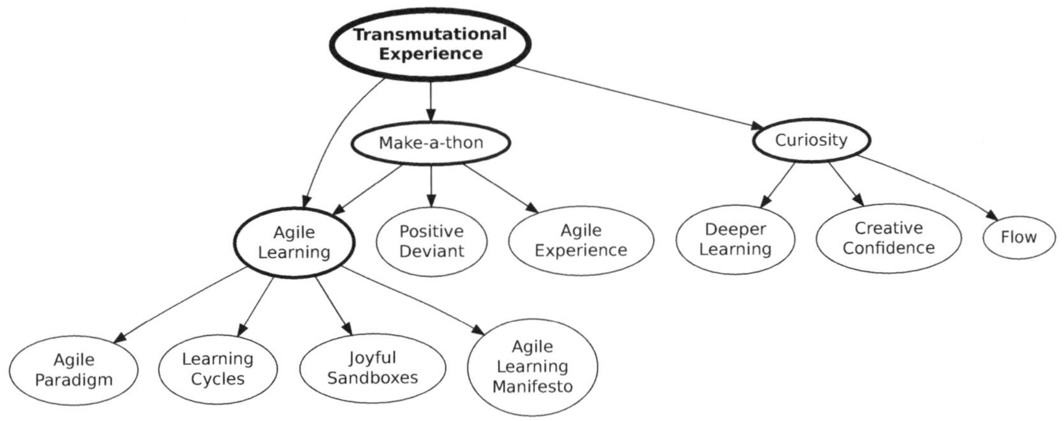

1 Page **110** - **Agile Learning**

2 Page **178** - **Make-a-thon**

3 Page **136** - **Curiosity**

Trialectical Synthesis

Trialectical sythesis is the simultaneous melding of multiple pieces of information, each in a spatial relationship with the others, to gain a new understanding.

In our traditional education, we have been taught to think with a logic that is linear in nature. As a result, we are, for the most part, linear thinkers.

This thinking approach utilizes two fundamental models: the serial logic that A leads to B which leads to C or that A is in conflict with B, which leads to C, a synthesis that is known as the Hegelian Dialect.

It is from these model that we understand our experience in the world, make meaning. But, with discoveries in areas such as quantum mechanics and chaos theory, we now appreciate that linear thinking is inadequate to understand the complexity around us, complexity that is non-linear in nature.

Alan Kay[1] sensed this truth, calling for a new level of thinking, one that was non-linear – where spatial thinking might happen. He developed **Smalltalk**[2] as a new software language that might open the door for software developers to this new level of thinking.

This thinking that lies at the heart of the **Agile Mindset**[3]. One that continually opens new doors to surprise – those **Eureka Moments**[4] that inspire learning.

---

1 Page **119** - **Alan Kay**

2 Page **203** - **Smalltalk**

3 Page **112** - **Agile Mindset**

4 Page **144** - **Eureka Moments**

A type of thinking that is now broadly engendered by the spatially hyperlinked world of the web.

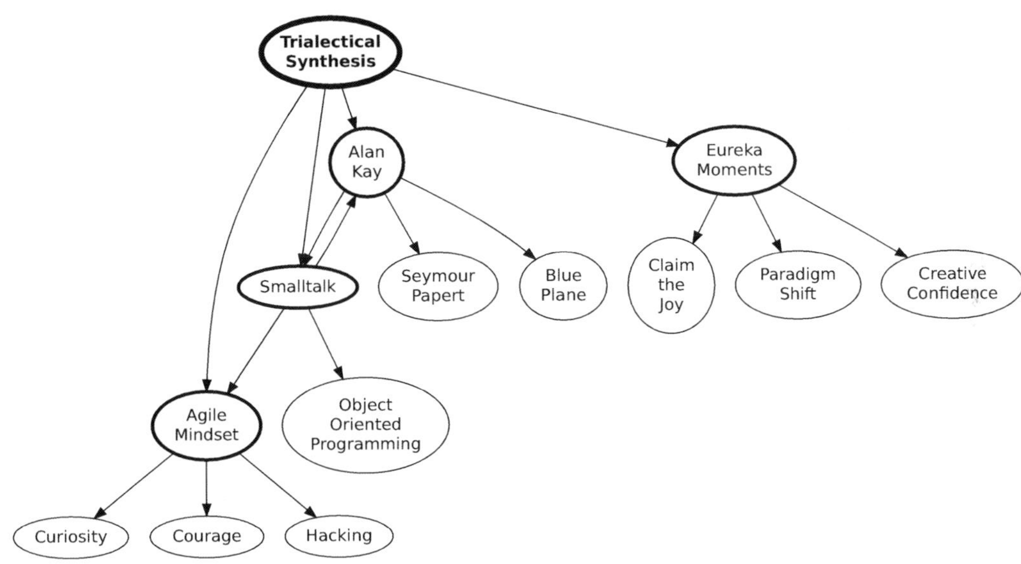

Trivium

A trivium is a 'three-legged stool' to define complex meaning in a way that can be succinctly conveyed to others. The original definition of trivium refers to classical education, which was built on a foundation of three subject areas: grammar, logic and rhetoric.

In developing triviums, we are challenged to define the three core concepts that hold the full meaning of what we are trying to convey in a balance of dynamic tension – one that is a **Prime Pattern**[1].

The early leaders of the Christian church, for instance, distilled the meaning of Christianity down to the Trinity. Each element of the Trinity holds a particular part of the meaning of their religion.

Buddhism is based on the Three Jewels. Einstein's theory of relativity could be seen as a trivium.

We believe that a new trivium to prepare students for a creative economy could be **Design Thinking**[2], **Process Thinking**[3] and **Systems Thinking**[4].

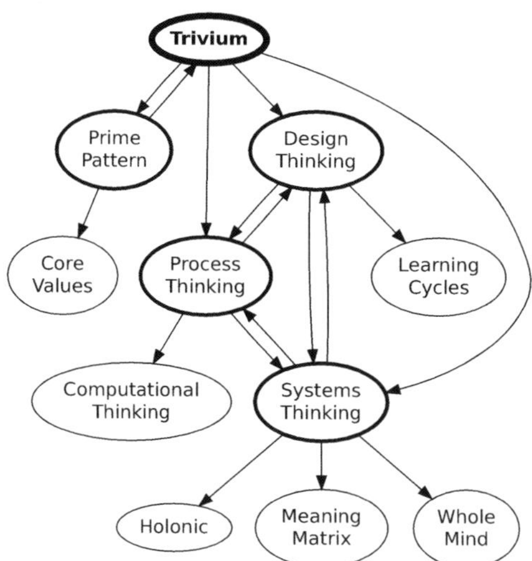

1 Page **190** - **Prime Pattern**

2 Page **139** - **Design Thinking**

3 Page **191** - **Process Thinking**

4 Page **207** - **Systems Thinking**

Value Networks

Industrial organizations structure themselves around the concept of the value chain. This concept, first defined by Michael Porter, extended the ideas of **Taylorism**[1] to explain how organizations create value through a series of progressive steps.

In an industrial economy, competitive advantage was created by managing this value chain to increase production efficiencies. As these chains became international, we created a global economy.

But we are now rapidly evolving into a new creative economy, one that is powered by digital technologies.

This new creative economy has fundamentally new rules. No longer is increased efficiency the prime driver of competitive advantage. Now, it's the *rate of innovation.*

Many companies are reimagining their organizational structures to be more adaptive value networks.

Value networks are complex systems that are inherently organic and evolving – autopoietic by nature. Teams and departments become connected nodes that must all be aligned to a company's core mission.

When we seek to reimagine education, we are challenged to begin to think of schools as value networks, where the system is organic and adaptive. From the outside, these structures can appear to be messy, but their dynamic nature accelerates the rate of learning for both students and teachers. One that unleashes **Creative Genius**[2].

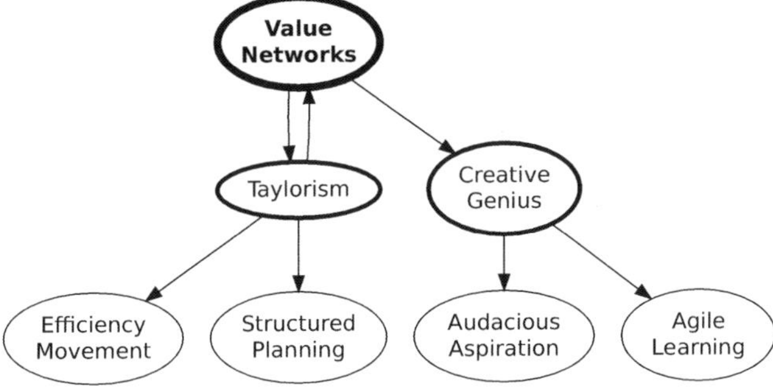

1 Page **208** - **Taylorism**

2 Page **134** - **Creative Genius**

Walk into the Unknown

We love the comfort of the known. It is a place of belonging, of security.

But to innovate, we must have the courage to try new things that carry with them the risk of failure. To risk failure is uncomfortable. To be an innovator, we must become **Comfortable being Uncomfortable**[1].

As we walk this journey into the unknown, we must confront our fear of failure. For many of us, this fear is deeply embedded in our psyche.

If we are honest, most of our entire traditional educational system is defined by this fear. To fail is the worst outcome of the experience. One that, if it becomes a repeating pattern, can lead to failure in life and society – the ultimate rejection, our ultimate shame.

But inherent in the innovation process is the understanding that failure is not only possible, but expected and desired. It is through failing we are able to better **Know the Problem**[2]. By creating short, fast, **Learning Cycles**[3] the learning potential is maximized while the cost of failures is minimized.

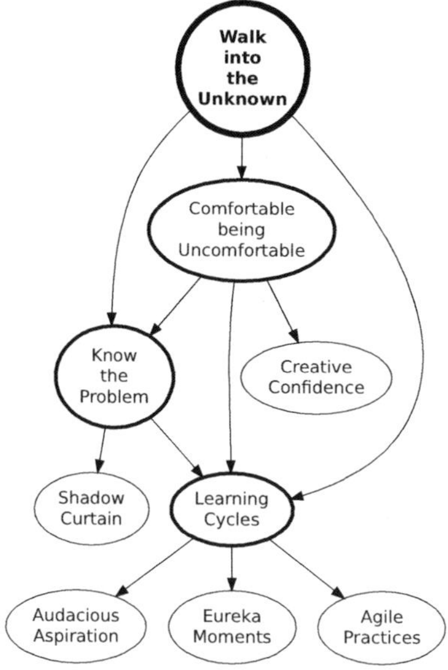

---

1 Page **128** - **Comfortable being Uncomfortable**

2 Page **168** - **Know the Problem**

3 Page **174** - **Learning Cycles**

What if Marshall McLuhan was Right?

Marshall McLuhan was an academic and a writer who coined the term 'global village' to explain our new media-connected world. He predicted the internet well before it was invented.

McLuhan introduced the idea of the global village in his book *The Gutenberg Galaxy* and went on to explore the argument that how we *learn* fundamentally shapes how we *think*.

For those of us who were taught in the pre-digital age, we primarily learned from printed books. In fact, for the last five hundred years, learning has been primarily from printed books.

McLuhan argued that the ability to learn from books was transformative for human society, launching the Age of Reason and ushering in modern nationalism and industrialism.

By its nature this learning is linear, based on sequential logic. There is a beginning, middle, and end for every book. One idea builds on the next, in order, until there is a conclusion.

Perhaps this type of thinking helped develop that part of our brain that is analytical – the Executive Network.

But this we know: how we learn shapes how we are wired to think.

But, take a moment and observe: that is not how digital natives learn. Students today have never known a time where there was not the internet filled with information that is all hyperlinked together. In this interconnected environment, there is no single path of learning. Instead, each person's path is self-defined by their **Curiosity**[1].

As a result, many of these digital natives don't primarily learn and think linearly. Instead, their learning process is far more multi-dimensional – spatial – as they jump from page to page to create meaning through dynamic triangulation. Something that we might call **Trialectical Synthesis**[2].

---

1 Page **136** - **Curiosity**

2 Page **214** - **Trialectical Synthesis**

Perhaps this type of thinking is activating their brain's Salience Network, that network that creates meaning by synthesizing contrasts.

Activated, the **Whole Mind**[1] can be unleashed for new capacity for creative thinking.

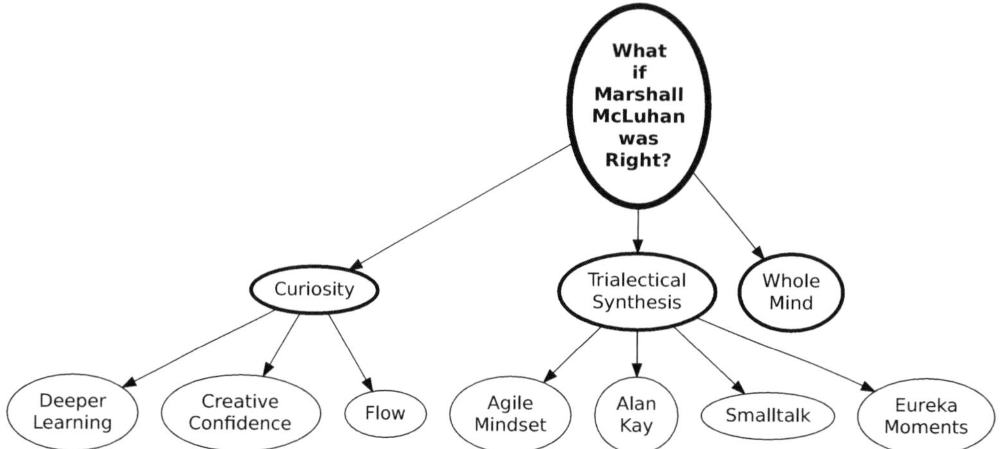

1 Page **221** - **Whole Mind**

Whole Mind

For many years we thought of the brain as having two parts, the left brain and the right brain. The left brain was thought to be our analytical brain, the right brain our creative brain.

The only problem is that this model is wrong.

When neuroscientists could begin to explore the brain activity using a functional MRI (fMRI)], they began to recognize that a more complex dynamic was going on.

They identified that parts of our brain were lit up by different networks that are functioning within a complex neural web called the connectome.

One network is called our *Default Network* – our primal network that has been key to our survival in the wild. Then there is the *Executive Network*, that has been developed to allow us to think analytically.

But then they found another network, called the *Salience Network*, that is activated to find meaning in things that are contrasting. Perhaps the spatial, non-linear thinking that we experience through hypertext utilizes this network.

Researchers from Harvard recently discovered that the more fully we activate all three of these networks, the better we can creatively solve complex problems.[1]

---

1 Beaty, R.E., Kenett, Y.N., Christensen, A.P., Rosenberg, M.D., Benedek, M., Chen, Q., Fink, A., Qiu, J., Kwapil, T.R., Kane, M.J. and Silvia, P.J., 2018. *Robust prediction of individual creative ability from brain functional connectivity.* Proceedings of the National Academy of Sciences, 115(5), pp.1087–92.

Wu Wei

Wu wei lies at the heart of Confucianism. It lies at the heart of Taoism. And it lies at the heart of Zen Buddhism. In each case, the meaning is different.

The literal translation of wu wei is 'no action'.

Coming from a western mindset, it is one of those terms that is difficult to grapple with. In our cultural mindset, we see ourselves defined by our ego, an ego that acts upon the world to achieve goals. Without our ego, we are nothing.

Confucius talked about wu wei as the supreme behavior of an emperor as they lead their nation. Where there is a silent guiding. Where a harmonious balance can be achieved.

Lao Tzu spoke of wu wei as a way of being. Where we live our lives as if floating down the river. Observing, accepting, letting go. But all with a clarity of intention.

In Zen, the meaning of wu wei went further, referring to the nothingness of nirvana, the luminescent emptiness of non-being. That mystery which is said to lie at the center of the ensō.

When wu wei leadership is practiced in a company or a classroom, action is gently guided and learning is actively supported. Motivation is from purpose, not as a response to fear. The dynamics are fluid. The systems are complex. There is a vitality that is palpable. But there is no ego – an embodiment of servant leadership, where leadership seeks not to control, but to empower those who they lead.

3x3 Reflection

background

The idea of the 3x3 Reflection came out of a discussion I had with Ward about practices that companies could use to better learn from valuable insights that arise when complex systems fail.

Our companies have complex systems and, despite best attempts, these systems unpredictably fail.

Unfortunately, far too often, the tendency of management is to "blame and shame" when there is a failure. That is, to try to identify who was responsible for the failure and to shame them for it. Knowing this response, individuals will often attempt to hide themselves and the reasons for the failure.

But this behavior does not allow the organization to learn from these failures. Each failure illuminates assumptions that have now been demonstrated to be false. By identifying these incorrect assumptions and then developing new supporting solutions, systems can become more resilient.

One practice of learning from these failures is to probe the problem by progressively asking about the reasons for failure, a technique called the Five Whys.

When Ward was explaining this concept to me, I wondered if we could use this same approach for the progressive exploration of insights. We developed the 3x3 Reflection and tested it in the follow-up interviews for the pilot of the **Agile Partnership Program**[1].

1 Page **114** - **Agile Partnership Program**

the format

The 3x3 Reflection uses a note-taking template that has three sections.

The first part captures the story of the experience.

The second part captures three insights that came from that experience.

And in the third part we capture the deeper emotions of those insights.

The three whys for each insight make up a 3x3 matrix, the core of the 3x3 Reflection narrative.

the practice

After brief introductions, the person being interviewed is told they will be asked to provide a brief overview of their experience, identify three insights from it, and that those insights will be probed more deeply.

We then jump in, recording notes in our template. This template is a table with multiple cells. At the top is a large cell for the story. Below that are three horizontal cells – one for each insight. Below each of those cells are a set of three smaller cells to capture the deeper understanding for that insight, creating a 3x3 matrix.

While the story is being told, it is written in the story section. Then the three insights are captured in their cells.

We then go back to the first insight and ask why that is an insight. We let the conversation flow, identifying keywords that have a particular emotional resonance. We then take that word or phrase and ask them to explain that feeling further.

As the story continues to unfold, we listen for the emotional keyword, then ask about that feeling. By probing each insight three times, we are able to fill in the nine cells of the matrix.

Once the matrix is complete, we share the document with the person we are interviewing. We review it together, highlighting the emotional keywords or phrases underneath each insight.

In closing, we read those keywords or phrases in reverse order, from the last cell to the first. We then ask the interviewee about this interview experience.

the impact

Each time we used this practice it was a powerful experience, both for us and for the people we were interviewing.

Typically, before we started, the interviewee had only a vague sense that the experience was meaningful. But they didn't know why.

Through this interviewing practice, we were able to quickly identify and clarify the underlying meaning of these experiences. Experiences that were important for them, that had touched them deeply.

By walking together through each of the emotionally rich words and phrases, a connection of meaning became illuminated.

When reading it backward, those connections became more clearly seen as a pattern. A pattern of meaning.

Empowering them as **Meaning Makers**[1].

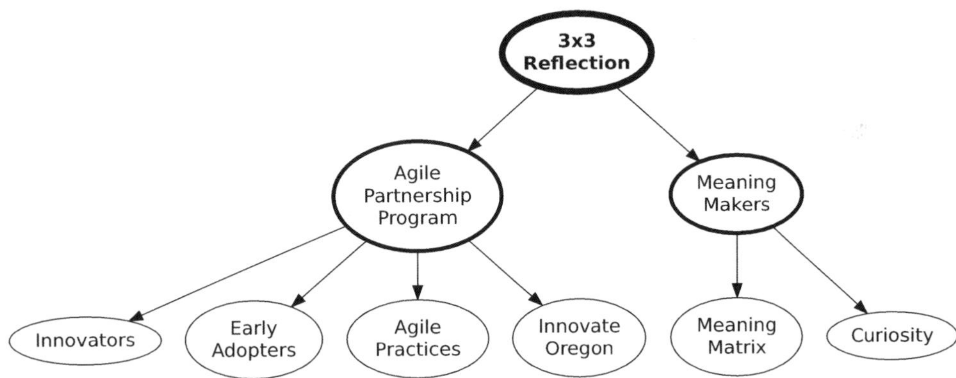

1 Page **180** - **Meaning Makers**

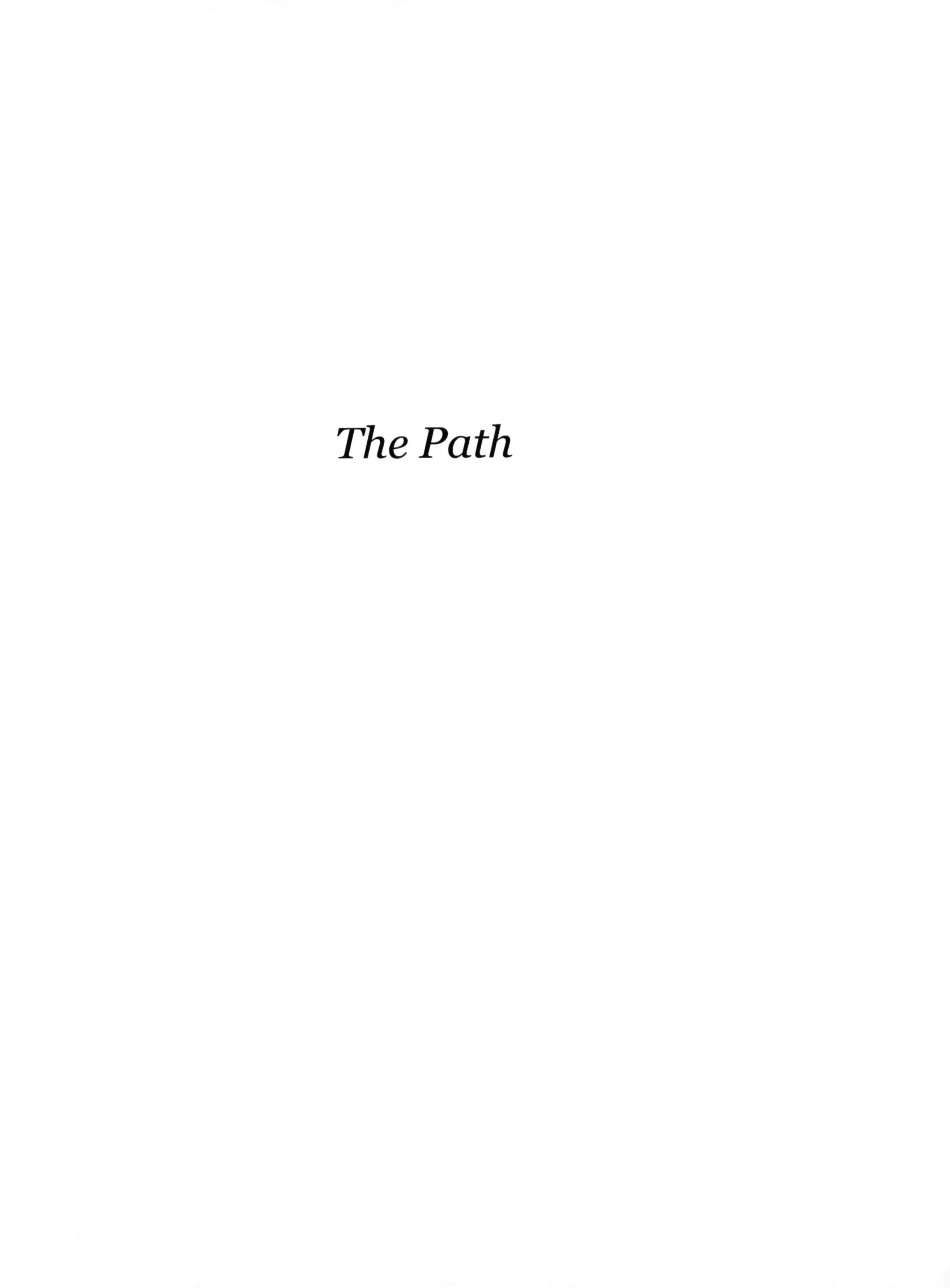

The Path

Path of Transformation

You have read *The Story* and explored *The Garden*. You are now left to wonder, where to from here?

There is no predefined script for the cultural transformation in any organization, much less a school district. It will look different in every school and every community. And know that you are embarking on a wonderful process of emergence that will continually unfold but will, at times, feel quite challenging and messy.

We strongly recommend working with an external coach or guide as you walk into this arena of transformation. You will stumble, you will get bruised – that is the nature of the process. Having someone to regularly talk with to help make sense of what you are learning is essential as you repair and then prepare to enter the arena again. This work is not for the faint-hearted. But is the right work.

There is, however, much wisdom to help guide your journey. Wisdom that is drawn from our experience and that of others.

Here, in *The Path*, we share a collection of activities and practices that can inform your path of discovery, your path of transformation. These activities and practices are patterns of behavior that form a simple pattern language.

Each journey begins anew. Here are three groups of patterns that may help you:

Getting Started: some small steps to help start you on your way.

Building Capacity: developing new skills for this journey.

Assessing Progress: illuminating the journey for yourself and others.

Getting Started

Some small steps to help start you on your way.

Intention

You want to step up as a change agent in your school and community. You sense new possibilities for educational experiences that not only will empower your students but open new doors to joyful learning.

You are wondering how you can help become a catalyst for this change, perhaps as an **Evangelist**[1].

Situation

Being a change agent is challenging, one that carries real professional and personal risk. While many may know change is needed, some around you are cynical and others may feel threatened.

Your courage, however, leads you to explore further so that you might begin to find your path of transformation.

Action

You can start down this path by:

Exploring **Multiple Windows**

Observing **Real Sense**

Experiencing **Joy Felt**

1 Page **146** - **Evangelist**

Getting Started: **Multiple Windows**

Exploring ideas from a wide range of resources.

Intention

You want to explore other types of learning experiences that may be more effective for engaging your students, particularly those who are struggling in a traditional classroom environment.

Situation

As an administrator or as a teacher, you are often reacting to unexpected challenges – leaving you feeling tired and depleted. You may also be feeling frustrated and stuck in a learning environment that isn't empowering students.

When you are feeling depleted, it's difficult to find the energy to explore your curiosity about other ways of learning that might be more effective in releasing students' potential. But you sense that there may be other approaches and want to explore further.

Action

Start by taking small steps to follow your curiosity. Try to find a time each week that you can set aside to explore new ideas through reading books and blogs, watching movies and videos, or listening to podcasts.

Getting Started: **Real Sense**

Observing and listening to students and teachers who are are being empowered.

Intention

You want to see learning environments that are more effectively engaging and inspiring students, particularly those who are not feeling successful in traditional classrooms.

Situation

As a professional educator, you have seen multiple learning pedagogies come and go. Many were defined by promises that were not fulfilled, leaving you apprehensive of new learning practices

Theory on its own is not sufficient. You know in your heart when you witness deep learning that is empowering students.

Action

Ask colleagues and education leaders for recommendations of schools to visit. Look for programs that schools have implemented that are changing the learning experience for their students. You can also organize a trip to visit schools in other states that have been pioneering this effort.

Getting Started: **Joy Felt**

Participating in a learning experience that reignites the joy of learning within you.

Intention

You want to have a learning experience that allows you to see the joy of learning in others and to feel it in yourself. You have many questions: What is this joy that you see in students' eyes when they are surprised by a new discovery? How might you connect what you are seeing and feeling into your own classroom experience? These questions inspire you to continue to move down this path.

Situation

For most of your education, the teacher has been the conduit through which knowledge flows to students. The teacher is the primary authority and fount of knowledge – the *sage on the stage* – in the classroom.

Teachers are often judged on how well the classroom is managed, and how well students perform on assessments. However, you sense that the learning experience could be much more dynamic. You have seen moments of joy in the eyes of students and you remember your own moments of joyful learning. You are curious about those moments and how you might be able to create more of them in your classroom.

Action

Explore innovative professional learning opportunities in your area or around the country that provide immersive experiences in new ways of teaching and learning. Look for opportunities to engage in experiences around design thinking, innovation, maker education, invention, and deeper learning.

Building Capacity

Developing new skills for this journey.

Intention

You are ready to build a new learning culture in your school.

Situation

Schools are incredibly complex social environments and there are many stakeholders – including teachers, administrators, board members, and parents. And last but certainly not least, there are the students, the reason that all the rest have come together.

Given this complexity, it is easy to feel that change, real change, may never be possible. For some of the stakeholders, there is comfort in the safety of the known and venturing out into uncharted territory can be deeply threatening.

However, real change is possible and there are stakeholders that are ready to embark on this courageous journey alongside you. As a matter of fact, they have been waiting for a changemaker like you.

Action

Start to build capacity by:

Defining your **North Star**

Aligning with others to create a **Shared Voice**

Embark on experiments of **Courageous Discovery**

Building Capacity: **North Star**

Finding a North Star to guide your transformation journey.

Intention

You want to define an aspiration for the learning experience in your school or district to guide the process of cultural transformation.

Situation

You find yourself in an institution that is defined by well-established rules. Changing the core culture to allow for new learning experiences feels daunting and risky.

You sense, however, that you are not alone – there are others that know in their hearts that the current way of education is not working for students but they are uncertain how to change it.

It is time for real transformation, something that will inspire educators and empower ALL students to discover their individual brilliance. Perhaps, you wonder, is this just wishful thinking or might true transformation be possible?

Action

Facilitate a conversation with your school leadership that defines your aspiration for graduates. The Portrait of a Graduate model is a good starting framework to use.

Organize a group that includes administrators, teachers, students, board members, and parents to redefine the ideal learning experience in your district. What would success look like? Start by exploring your **Core Values**[1] together. Work toward defining not only the skills you would like all of your students to have, but also define the primary qualities that would empower them to be successful after they graduate.

---

1 Page **130** - **Core Values**

Building Capacity: **Shared Voice**

Aligning with others to an aspiration of transformational change.

Intention

You want to find teachers, students, administrators, school board members and community members who are courageous change agents – those who are committed to come together to guide this journey of transformation.

Situation

Culture change is hard work. You know that it is important to be very strategic in this process and to surround yourself with the courageous who are willing to work together toward a common aspiration and are **Comfortable being Uncomfortable**[1]. You also know that trust is essential – trust that allows you to walk into the unknown with authenticity and vulnerability – and that multiple change agents need to be involved from different parts of an organization. You recognize that you must shed your ego – you are on this journey equally with others around you.

Action

Seek the **Innovators**[2] and **Early Adopters**[3] throughout the school district, recognizing that many of them may have been overlooked in the past. Bring them together to form an **Innovation Cohort**[4] for short learning **Sprints**[5] where new ideas can be tested. There is no clear, single path for the journey. Walk into this uncertainty knowing that it may, at times, feel chaotic and require you to release control. Allow everybody's voice to be heard. Through deep listening, clarity and commitment will emerge that astonishes everyone.

---

1 Page **128** - **Comfortable being Uncomfortable**

2 Page **162** - **Innovators**

3 Page **141** - **Early Adopters**

4 Page **161** - **Innovation Cohorts**

5 Page **205** - **Sprint**

Building Capacity: **Courageous Discovery**

Blazing your path of transformation through creative experimentation.

Intention

You want to do more than talk about reimagining education – you want to be courageous and start making it happen in your school district.

Situation

Experimenting can be scary because there is a good chance that it won't work out the way you are expecting. However, when trying something new, failure is not only expected, it is desired. In failure, we are able to **Know the Problem**[1] better.

Depending on the level of trust in your school and district, failure can pose significant risk if that failure is used by others to criticize you. The courage to move forward in the face of fear is where true discovery and joy will be found.

Action

Remember, you are not alone on this journey. There are others who believe in your North Star. Start by asking: What experiment could we launch quickly and complete in a short period of time – in a day or a few weeks? These sprints should not be more than six weeks in length to instill a sense of urgency to act.

Make sure that the cohort meets frequently and regularly – at least once a week to share findings, reflect on emerging insights and to commit to next steps. Recognize that trust in this cohort is essential as this process exposes each person's vulnerabilities when illuminating failures. But this team also becomes the first place where you begin to **Claim the Joy**[2].

---

1 Page **168** - **Know the Problem**

2 Page **125** - **Claim the Joy**

Assessing Progress

Illuminating the journey for yourself and others.

Intention

You want to be able to deeply understand what you have learned and share it with others. This understanding helps build support for your journey and clarifies your next steps.

Situation

You sense that this journey is having a significant impact on others. But it is difficult to find the time to have a fuller understanding of that impact. Without that understanding, it is difficult to share what you are seeing and feeling with others. Sharing is essential in building the support and gaining the clarity you need to continue the journey.

Action

Assess where you are and clarify where you could go by:

Engaging in **Wholehearted Listening**

Reflecting on the **Essence Revealed**

Share to **Illuminate Forward**

Assessing Progress: **Wholehearted Listening**

Gaining valuable insight for yourself and others.

Intention

You want to deeply understand what you are learning from your experiments.

Situation

The interpersonal dynamics within any classroom or school building are complex. There is often a lot of energy spent just keeping focus so that a learning experience doesn't feel like it is spinning out of control. When you are focused on managing this complexity, it is difficult to listen to the different voices in the room. You sense, however, that there are important insights from a new learning experience, particularly when you are seeking to fulfill your commitment to equity.

Action

Make time during and after the experiment to observe, listen, question and reflect. This is one of the most overlooked, yet valuable steps of experimentation because it is where we gain deeper insights into why something worked or didn't.

As you ask others about their experience, listen for words that describe their feelings and probe further to truly understand the essence of what they are saying. Look for clues from their eyes, expressions and body language that makes you want to know more. A moment of deep listening to those whose voices are often unheard in the classroom is profoundly validating and becomes the gateway to deeper insight. You may find the **3x3 Reflection**[1] valuable.

---

1 Page **223** - **3x3 Reflection**

Assessing Progress: **Essence Revealed**

Finding insights that provide a deeper understanding of what is learned.

Intention

You want to understand the deeper meaning of what you learned in an experience. These insights will empower you and inform the next steps in your journey.

Situation

As educators, our lives are hectic and we are continually being pulled in multiple directions. As soon as you finish one activity, you are plunged into the next, with little, if any, opportunity to reflect on what was learned, making your experiences often feel random and disjointed.

Action

At the end of each **Sprint**[1], create time and space to reflect on and process the learning in order to uncover a richer meaning and reveal intentional next steps.

During the **Retrospective**[2], identify surprises, name them, and explore together the implications of this new understanding. By naming and defining your insights, you will be able to better share their essence with others.

---

1 Page **205** - **Sprint**

2 Page **196** - **Retrospective**

Assessing Progress: **Illuminate Forward**

Sharing your story with others in a way that clarifies the next step in the journey.

Intention

You want to tell the story of how far you have come on this journey and share what you have learned in order to illuminate the path forward.

Situation

We live in a world where competing programs, initiatives and projects claim to be the answer to the challenges we are facing. We are often lured by pre-packaged, scripted solutions that are perceived time savers with seemingly believable results. In reality, deep transformational work takes time and patience. This work is messy, and stakeholders need to see the continuity between the work and how it is all connected to a larger aspiration. To participate in iterative **Learning Cycles**[1] without the certainty of the scripted multi-year plan is uncomfortable. You know that you must become **Comfortable being Uncomfortable**[2], but how might you implement those cycles to illuminate the next steps of a journey?

Action

We are all storytellers and this is an important story to tell others. Continually share the insights that you are learning with your colleagues and to the larger community through social media, blog posts, newsletters and exhibition events that highlight the student learning. By doing so, you begin to **Create a Wake**[3] as others begin to be intrigued. Through their questions, you can share more of your deeper findings. These insights illuminate what your next experiment should be and the momentum and joy created inspires others to join you in this journey.

---

1 Page **174** - **Learning Cycles**

2 Page **128** - **Comfortable being Uncomfortable**

3 Page **132** - **Create a Wake**

The Commission

As Jami pointed out in her foreword, culture change is challenging. Very challenging. But as she demonstrated, it can be done.

Culture change starts with a new paradigm, a new understanding of how we might be together and learn together. This paradigm must be experienced. By experiencing it, theories quickly manifest into reality. They become something that we know, deep inside of us. A sacred truth.

We must then find a new vocabulary for these experiences as our existing vocabulary is limited by our past experiences. New experiences need new words, words that can connect us with others who also have had similar experiences. By finding those words, we are able to weave those experiences together into a new culture.

This book sought to introduce a new paradigm, to tell a story of an experience and then provide a new vocabulary that allows us to share similar experiences with others. We all know education needs a radical reimagining – of that there is no doubt. But this change requires a fundamental culture transformation in each building, in every classroom. One experience at a time.

In every school there is a courageous evangelist, perhaps in hiding. We whisper to this evangelist: you are not alone.

If this book speaks to you, find the innovators in the building – those who have flown under the radar, often with their doors closed. Give this book to them. Ask them to see if there is a truth for them within these pages. And then seek out those who are early adopters. Ask them to read the book together. Gather and begin to discuss. Have fun, geek out. Beer can help.

Be curious with each other. Find out what ideas in the book resonate and why. Listen to the feelings in their words, and dig further. Never stop asking why. Listen deeply to each other for, in that exploration, you will find deeper meaning, a shared truth.

Then find the courage to begin small experiments. Seek out help from those outside of your school – those who have already embarked on this path of transformation. They can become mentors that will help accelerate the learning speed.

But always remember: This is good work. Important work, worthy of love and commitment. Work that has the potential to delight, where joy flows.

Coda

Ward's Afterword

Two decades ago a small group met to share what they felt was new about how they developed software. Their operational observations were expressed as unexpected preferences and collectively dubbed "agile." The word stuck. But we might ask, what lead them to the Agile Manifesto, this unusual agreement?

We now know that their observations were so powerful that positive results have been had even when their specific methods were misunderstood and improperly applied. What then is this secret sauce?

Thompson recognizes a specific shift in mindset, the established set of attitudes held by those engaged in an endeavor, as the root of agile. The "agile mindset" then is the patterns of thought that come engaging in agile-like practices whatever they might be.

We can escape this circular definition by looking more closely into what had changed about software two decades ago.

Computers would become very cheap. And they would be personally owned. And linked together. And they would do nothing new without software, original software that did things yet to be imagined.

A few labs in Boston and Palo Alto put these soon to be cheap computers in front of children to see what they could make of them. They reasoned that young mindsets were still open to new things. What would they want? How would they be empowered by the brute force of technology humanized for their use?

The kids were curious. Not yet brilliant but curious in ways that the brilliant researchers had to struggle to remember. And theirs was a profession that honored curiosity. Imagine their dedication in the face of professional demands.

We are a *curious* species.

Our working life favors curiosity even if we at times forget this. I am reminded of my friend, an engineering manager, who was asked, like all employees, to work in the warehouse during the Christmas rush. Why, he wondered while restocking returns, did so many items go to one particular aisle? He walked behind the shelves where bins were loaded to find the SKU numbers were off by one on that side, making every shipment wrong.

The Agile Manifesto authors, and the researchers they followed, and even my friend in the warehouse, were all given space to be curious. They were privileged in a way that many, then and today, are not.

Thompson reminds us that the agile mindset requires *courage* to work outside of expectation.

Only in a one-dimensional linear environment, like working towards sales quotas, does the shortest path to exceeding expectation pass through meeting expectation.

So why do we shame those who take a chance on something different and punish them if it doesn't work out? Even in sales, we will find that the small increments achieved without creative energy will be overshadowed by those who take unexpected leaps. Adherence to routine provides only a long-term path to failure.

Thompson describes one school system's journey towards a process of creative discovery that involved rapid trial and error with the understanding that even disappointment involves learning. This would be the "*hacking*" component of his agile mindset, using the kindest interpretation of that term, one rooted again in Boston's MIT.

In both the educational and industrial versions, the hack must show creative opportunity within acceptable risk. This judgment comes from those closest to the problems: the students themselves, or the computer programmers that the Manifesto authors advised.

This last point can't be overemphasized. Creativity can most easily be motivated by recognition by one's peers. Peer groups, immersed in the details at hand, borrow from each other's successes in a way that does not easily breakdown into measurable parts.

These small clusters of original thought behave as if they are one, a whole as if it is itself alive, motivated by a higher purpose shared by all within.

In this book you witnessed the essence of agile as it was unleashed to reimagine education. It is a powerful and important story, not only for educators but also for industry agilists who are looking to rekindle their creative flame.

– *Ward Cunningham*

Acknowledgments

We never fully appreciated the importance of an acknowledgments page until writing this book. It was only then that we came to understand all the help that is needed to turn a book idea into a published reality.

To the Dayton staff – For asking "What if?" And then testing their ideas to seek the answer. Their courage, love of teaching and dedication to students continually inspired us.

To Debbie Kearns for being the first great connector between local industry and the Dayton School District to allow this experiment to happen, and to Kathleen Hirons and Michelle McShane for welcoming Thompson into the classroom for the first of many experiments.

To Patrick Verdun, Mitch Coleman, Darcy Hatch, Jenni Shilhanek and Carrie Carden for being courageous innovators, believing in what is possible and inspiring and shaping the movement.

To Kelli Hascall, Sherri Sinicki, Charlie Hascall, Michelle Borst, Tera Solem, Jennifer Spink, Abby deSmet, Jason Mix, Corinne Flake, Lisa Fergus and Beth Wytoski for continuing the movement by taking risks in their classrooms and thinking creatively and differently for their students.

To Roger Lorenzen, Michelle Archibald, Efrain Arredondo, Kathryn Nelson-Davis and Lisa Thomas for believing in the aspiration and providing the support and technical assistance that was often "behind the scenes" yet equally essential in keeping us going and moving us forward.

To the Dayton students who engaged in creating a new future. There are too many students to acknowledge, but the following were critical contributors in launching and growing Innovate Dayton. You are our inspiration. You are our future.

To Keenna West, Cole Katzler, Dylan Blanchard, Katelyn Sutton and Caleb Kozell for being the first students to participate in the Summer Innovations Academy and the first in-class experiments. You showed us it was possible.

To Kylie Spivey for unselfishly spending her senior year contributing to the vision, sharing her creativity and dedicating time and energy to launch Innovate Dayton, knowing that she would be graduating and not directly benefiting from the outcome.

To Cate-Lynn Jacks who, as an 8th grader, showed a courageous and innovative spirit that was beyond anything we had seen. She believed in Dayton's future and was the producer of our first "I am Dayton's Future" video. Her leadership and contribution never wavered, even up to and beyond graduation.

To Grace Adams who, as a 7th grader, had the vision to see the possibilities. A strong leader through and through, Grace provided energy and initiative that was beyond believable for a 12-year-old and continues to share that into her senior year.

To Bevin Schrag, who brought the beautiful stories of Innovate Dayton to life for others through blog writing during her junior and senior year. She continues to provide leadership and inspiration to younger writers as she mentors them as storytellers, while attending college and working.

To Jami's daughters Rachael and Maddie Fluke, who had their mom as their principal. Their willingness to share her with others and sometimes sacrifice their own needs was an act of true love. They continue to be Jami's inspiration and have also been her greatest champions.

To Jami's husband, Dave Fluke, who had his wife as his principal. He accepted the boundaries that had to be created to make the school and home partnership work. When asked, he was willing to listen to new ideas, raise the right questions, and provide creative input. Even when he didn't understand it all, he always believed. His sense of humor kept us grounded and provided joy for all.

Then there are the school leaders in our monthly Innovate meetup including Jamie Richardson, Casey Petrie, Karen Pugsley, Tyler Lalack, Luke Neff, Cassandra Thonstad and many others who gave us support and encouragement. They are the true heroes as this story continues to unfold.

For the many industry volunteers who have joined us along the way, we share our thanks. Particular thanks go to Gage Choat, who was the first to jump in with enthusiasm and commitment that opened the doors of opportunity for others.

To Derek Runberg and Sparkfun who boldly created with us learning experiences that opened the door to new ways of thinking about education.

To Kathy Tate, Eric Yeaple and the team at OnlineNW, we offer up our deepest gratitude for sharing our dream of transforming education and investing in that dream with courage. And for bringing Thompson into their company so that he could continue that work so important to us.

To Erin Dieterich, Brent Miller and the rest of the New Relic team including Jon Guymon, April Leonard, Desiree Barrett and Mich HuffMenne that boldly embraced our story and stepped up to partner with us, not only to help us write the story but also to share the story.

To Skip Newberg and the staff of the TAO for all of their support as we launched this initiative and for providing help to promote our efforts.

To Kris Olson and the team from COSA who courageously embraced our story by creating our Innovate conferences to bring that story to educators throughout the state. Our planning team for these events comprised some of the most inspiring educators we have ever had the opportunity to work with, including John Peplinski, G Bundy, Jennell Ives, Mark Siegel, Laura Foley, Pandy Anderson and Jeremiah Patterson.

To the Construct Foundation for partnering with Dayton to bring design thinking to our staff, though the Breakaway workshop, which helped shift mindsets and shape skill-sets for rethinking teaching and learning. Also, for bringing to Oregon the first cohort of School Retool, Stanford d.school's workshop that builds the skills and confidence in school leaders to increase innovation and equitable, deeper learning in their schools. Dayton was the "inspirational site" for the workshop series and the relationships that were formed through this cohort are still growing.

To the Stanford d.school for hosting Dayton leaders and teachers at Hacktivation Nation. Spending 3 days at the d.school helped us engage in deep transformational work with our Dayton team.

To Anna Higgins and Angie Mason-Smith who helped us to share our story in Central Oregon, where it helped amplify their own amazing efforts to inspire innovation in schools within their region.

To Heidi Sipe, Rachael Mortensen and Kyle Ritchey-Noll who played instrumental roles in the launch event for Innovate Oregon, one that brought together industry leaders with educators to sit, listen, and learn from each other.

To Bill Stoller who provided the original funding to support Thompson's work in Dayton and for Gary Mortenson for his bold vision to launch our initiative there.

To Tom Thompson, Mark Freed and other staff members of the Oregon Department of Education that supported our efforts in Dayton.

To Dwayne Johnson, whose support was invaluable as we launched our initiative, challenging us, in each and every step, to remember what it really means to be inclusive and to strive for equity.

To Don Domes, whose courageous leadership as an educator has lit the path for so many others. His support was invaluable. not only to launch the Innovation class at Dayton but also to promote Dayton's story, leading to their trip to showcase their creative genius at MIT.

To D'Wayne Edwards, who provided not only his time but also his space and most of all, a deep commitment to creating new opportunities for all students, particularly those whose voices and talents have often been overlooked.

To Dave Buswell for his courage to bring the Innovate story to his community in Willamina and to Recca Maze and Susan Richman for introducing Christopher Alexander's pattern languages to Thompson.

We were honored to be guided by Takashi Iba in the development of our pattern language – he is a master of pattern languages who has taken the ideas of Christopher Alexander to new levels of understanding.

There were many who helped us turn words into a book as editors and proofreaders, including Charles Martin, Sondra Kornblatt, Hariana Chilstrom, Dan Hannon, David Bernstein, Ann Devadas, and Cathie Pake. We are so grateful for their support. And a special thanks to Brian Scott for helping with the design concepts for the book.

To Thompson's remarkable children, Jason and Caitlin Morrison, who taught him so much about learning, persistence, and courage and have gone on to launch amazing careers – they were the original source of Thompson's inspiration to embark on this journey.

And then there is Thompson's wife, Mary Beth, who gave him the strength to keep writing this story when times were challenging. It is in her embrace that he has come to understand the deepest meaning of love. That love which is the wellspring of joy.

Thank you for reading this book. We would love to hear from you!

Please visit **daytonexperiment.com** to share your thoughts and to get updates as this story continues to unfold.

As we venture forth, we would be wise to remember Margaret Meade's brave words:

Never doubt that a small group of thoughtful, committed citizens can change the world; indeed, it's the only thing that ever has.

Made in the USA
Columbia, SC
10 February 2020

87677867R00146